W9-ACB-759

The Buddhist World of Southeast Asia

SUNY Series in Religion
Harold Coward, editor

South and Southeast Asia

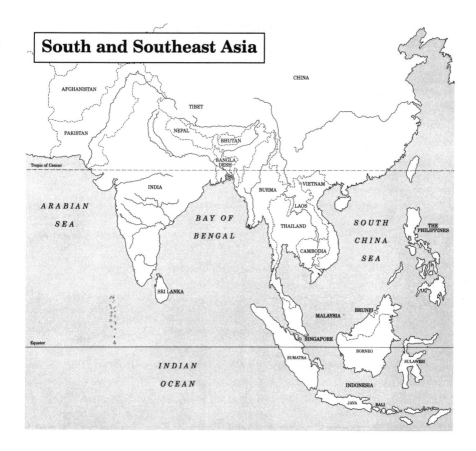

CHINA

AFGHANISTAN

TIBET

PAKISTAN

NEPAL

BHUTAN

BANGLA-
DESH

Tropic of Cancer

INDIA

BURMA

VIETNAM

LAOS

ARABIAN
SEA

BAY OF
BENGAL

THAILAND

SOUTH
CHINA
SEA

THE
PHILIPPINES

CAMBODIA

SRI LANKA

MALAYSIA

BRUNEI

Equator

SINGAPORE

BORNEO

SUMATRA

SULAWESI

INDIAN
OCEAN

INDONESIA

JAVA

BALI

The Buddhist World
of Southeast Asia

DONALD K. SWEARER

BQ
410
.S93
1995

ST. JOSEPH'S UNIVERSITY

3 9353 00300 6184

STATE UNIVERSITY OF NEW YORK PRESS

Published by
State University of New York Press, Albany

© 1995 State University of New York

All rights reserved

Printed in the United States of America

No part of this book may be used or reproduced
in any manner whatsoever without written permission.
No part of this book may be stored in a retrieval system
electronic, electrostatic, magnetic tape, mechanical,
photocopying, recording, or otherwise without the prior
permission in writing of the publisher.

For information, address State University of New York Press,
State University Plaza, Albany, N.Y., 12246

Production by Cathleen Collins
Marketing by Nancy Farrell

Library of Congress Cataloging in Publication Data

Swearer, Donald K.
   The Buddhist World of Southeast Asia / Donald K. Swearer.
      p.   cm. — (SUNY series in religion.)
   Includes bibliographical references and index.
   ISBN 0-7914-2459-6. — ISBN 0-7914-2460-X
      1. Buddhism—Social aspects—Asia, Southeastern. I. Title.
II. Series.
BQ410.S93   1995
294.3'37'0959—dc20   94-29167
                                                        CIP

10 9 8 7 6 5 4 3 2 1

In memory of
Kenneth K. S. Ch'en,
mentor and friend

Contents

Preface

*T*he *Buddhist World of Southeast Asia* is a product of my observation and study of Theravāda Buddhism since 1957. My interest in Buddhism began as a result of personal experience. In the late 1950s I spent two years in Bangkok, Thailand, where I lived in a Buddhist culture and taught at a Buddhist monastic university. Since that time my family and I have spent several sabbatical leaves in Thailand with shorter stays or visits in Sri Lanka, Burma, Cambodia, and Laos. Although my understanding of Buddhism has been influenced by the work of scholars from several different disciplines, this monograph reflects the years of personal experience framed by the liberal arts college classroom, the context in which I have spent my academic career. For these reasons, the book highlights Buddhism in Thailand and seeks to integrate a multidisciplinary approach to Theravāda Buddhism in Southeast Asia with a personal appreciation of its depth of meaning and diversity of expression; furthermore, it is written for readers who wish to study Buddhism not simply as a normative doctrinal system but as a historically and culturally contextualized religious tradition.

This study of Buddhism offers the reader a broad, holistic analysis of the Buddhist tradition as it has been shaped within the historical and cultural milieux of Southeast Asia and Sri Lanka. Diverse forms of Buddhism took root in Southeast Asia, but from the twelfth century C.E. onward the branch of Buddhism known as *Theravāda* ("Teaching of the Elders"), with an extensive and variegated scripture written in the Pali language, gradually assumed a dominating religious and cultural role.[1] Historical evidence ranging from major archaeological sites to contemporary Buddhist rituals demonstrate the influence of Hīnayāna, Mahāyāna, and Tantrayāna forms of Buddhism as well as Brahmanical and Hindu elements. It must be kept in mind, furthermore, that the forms of Buddhism and Hinduism planted

in Sri Lanka, as well as insular and mainland Southeast Asia, grew in diverse
cultural soils enriched by various indigenous belief systems from Sinhalese,
Burmese, Tai,[2] and Lao to Khmer. In short, the notion of a mainland
Southeast Asia Theravāda, Pali "orthodoxy" is an ahistorical projection,
first constructed by monks of the Sinhalese Mahāvihāra monastic lineage
and subsequently perpetuated in the modern period by both Buddhist
adherents and Western scholars. Today, Theravāda Buddhism in Sri Lanka,
Myanmar (Burma), Thailand, Laos, and Cambodia reflects the rich diversity
of its variegated historical and cultural development. In one sense this
monograph provides a demonstration of this claim. My use of the term
Theravāda Buddhism, therefore, presumes this sense of richness and
diversity of the tradition.

A problem also adheres to the term *monk*, which appears throughout
the monograph. Often, Buddhist scholars construct the Buddhist monk as
a rational renouncer who singlemindedly walks the Buddha's path toward
enlightenment (*nibbāna*). They either ignore or are oblivious to the multiple
roles played by the monk not only in the present day but throughout Buddhist
history. The term *monk* is further problematized because it has been
gendered as male, requiring that the female monk be identified as *nun*.[3]

In Theravāda Buddhism the community of Buddhists is divided into four
groups—male and female renunciants or almspersons (*bhikkhu* and
bhikkhunī), and their male and female lay supporters (*upāsaka* and *upāsikā*).
Although it is an oversimplification, it may be said that both men and women
who joined the Buddha's order or *sangha* were fundamentally alike in the
sense that they shared the common designation of "almspersons." I shall
use the term *monk* in this inclusive sense, even though in specific contexts
the reference may be primarily to male almspersons. For purposes of clarity,
however, in some instances I shall refer to monks and nuns and in other
cases simply to nuns. In Chapters 1 and 3 of the monograph specific
historical and contemporary issues of women and Buddhism will be
explored.

In sum, my use of the term *monk* acknowledges both gender distinction
and the historical diversity of roles played by Buddhist almspersons.

The Buddhist World of Southeast Asia is an updated, expanded, and revised
version of my earlier book, *Buddhism and Society in Southeast Asia* (1980).
Although it reflects the basic structure of that volume and incorporates
material from it, the differences between the two monographs were thought
to warrant a change of title. The major revisions, changes and additions
to my earlier work include the following: Chapter 1, "The Popular Tradition:

Inclusive Syncretism," adds a discussion of the ceremonial preaching of the *Vessantara Jātaka*, and the celebration of New Year. It also incorporates wedding and old age rituals into the rites of passage section. Chapter 2, "Buddhism as a Civil Religion: Political Legitimation and National Integration," has been restructured, the section on religion and classical kingship has been significantly revised, and the modern nationalism and Buddhism section has been expanded to account for new developments in Burma (Myanmar) and Thailand. Chapter 3, "Modernization: The Dynamic of Tradition and Change," updates the changing roles of the monk and the changing role of the laity sections incorporating new material from Sri Lanka, Thailand, Burma, Laos, and the development of Theravāda Buddhism in North America. The organization of the material also has been refined and expanded; for example, adding a new section on women and Buddhism, a stronger emphasis on the resurgence of the forest tradition and the widespread practice of meditation in the revival of Buddhism in the twentieth century.

Since 1980 both written and audiovisual resources for the study of Theravāda Buddhism have increased significantly. Dozens of new monographs, translations, and articles by anthropologists, historians of religions, and Pali scholars greatly enrich our understanding of Buddhism in Southeast Asia. The conversion of films to video as well as the ease of producing and projecting video films has expanded the potential range and use of visual media. It is reasonable to assume, furthermore, that in the future computer technology will become a significant factor in visual instructional techniques. Despite the substantial resources now available for the study of Southeast Asian Buddhism and society and the presence of over 300 Thai, Lao, and Cambodian monasteries serving an increasingly large population of Southeast Asians in North America, the American public remains largely uninformed about Southeast Asian religion, culture, and society. The film *Blue Collar and Buddha* (1987),[4] dramatizes the suspicion of average Midwestern Americans to an immigrant Laotian community and their monastery. The tragic 1991 murder of Thai Buddhist monks in Phoenix, Arizona, was headline news in Thailand but received only limited media coverage in the United States.

A 1993 Columbia University study of the twenty-seven major world history textbooks used in public middle schools and high schools revealed that the presentations of Southeast Asia focus primarily on the Philippines and the Vietnam war, that only a few of the textbooks include references to the great high cultures of Southeast Asia, such as Pagan, Sukhothai,

Srivijāya, or Angkor, and that the visual material highlight photos of American soldiers in Vietnam and the seemingly malevolent visage of Ho Chi Minh rather than scenes of Buddhist monks and monasteries. I hope that *The Buddhist World of Southeast Asia* will foster a better understanding of the significance of Southeast Asia and the role of Buddhism in shaping the culture, society, and personal aspirations of its peoples in their traditional homelands as well as in their new Western settings.

Acknowledgments

The first edition of this monograph was published as part of a project funded by the National Endowment for the Humanities to develop bibliography and thematic guides for the identification and use of audiovisual materials in the instruction of Asian religions. The major participants in that project were Robert A. McDermott, John R. Carter, Richard B. Pilgrim, H. Daniel Smith, the late Frederick J. Streng, Robert A. F. Thurman, and myself. I am grateful for the opportunity to have joined with them in this project. I also wish to express my appreciation to Eugene B. Bruns, chair of the Southeast Asian Studies division of the Foreign Service Institute, for the opportunity to lecture regularly at the institute on the major themes of this book.

The completion of this monograph was greatly expedited by sabbatical research support from Swarthmore College and by the Yehan Numata Visiting Professorship in Buddhist Studies at the University of Hawaii, which I held Fall 1993. The final editing took place in 1994 when I was a research fellow at the Social Research Institute of Chiang Mai University (Thailand). I wish to thank its director, Dr. Chayan Vaddhanphuti, the Fulbright Program, and the John Simon Guggenheim Foundation for financial support during the year 1994, and Professor Ratana Tungasvadi for the gracious hospitality of her Chiang Mai home. Thanissaro Bhikkhu (Geoff DeGraff), abbot of the Metta Forest Monastery in Valley Center, California, read and commented on the entire monograph; Dr. Nancy Dowling, professor of Asian art, University of Hawaii, made numerous suggestions regarding Chapter 2; Steven Sowards of the Swarthmore College library provided essential bibliographical help. I am grateful to them, but I am particularly indebted to Nancy Chester Swearer whose critical editorial eye improved every aspect of the monograph and who prepared the index.

I have dedicated this monograph to my graduate studies mentor, the late Dr. Kenneth K. S. Ch'en. A graduate student could not have had a more supportive teacher than Professor Ch'en. He was unfailingly helpful and constructive in his criticisms of my dissertation, and was a true friend (*kalyāṇamitta*) for over thirty years. Professor Ch'en's own work ranges from meticulous studies of Chinese Buddhism to a widely used introduction to the Buddhist tradition. It is with the deepest respect that I dedicate *The Buddhist World of Southeast Asia* to the memory of my friend and teacher.

Introduction

THE STUDY OF RELIGION AND THE VISUAL

Everyone recognizes the saying, "It has to be *seen* to be *believed*." With one rather modest change—"it has to be *seen* to be *understood*"—this familiar quip becomes peculiarly appropriate to the study of religion. A religious system consists of diverse phenomena: sacred texts, myths, symbols, institutions, rites, and rituals for example. A religion encompasses even more than a stipulated set of beliefs and practices; it also embodies and expresses the genius of a particular culture. Because of this diversity and complexity religion cannot be easily comprehended in any holistic sense. The study of a religious system or even of specific aspects of that system calls not only for analytical skills but also the qualities of imagination and empathy. The nature of the phenomena constituting a religious system cannot be adequately understood if one only studies a religious text or analyzes what religious people claim to believe about the nature of the world and of human existence.

Any attempt to study religion that does not take into account the richness and diversity constituting its various contexts runs the risk of reductionism and blatant distortion. The New Testament, for example, should certainly be studied from historical and literary critical perspectives. However, as Wilfred C. Smith suggested over two decades ago,[1] it should also be understood as a sacred scripture that has influenced lives and shaped perceptions throughout a 2,000-year history. From this broad point of view one could argue that a New Testament course using only critical literary methods might be important in the development of exegetical skills, but that it fails as a study of sacred scripture in the sense suggested by W. C. Smith. We might even argue that such a course teaches a particular kind of exegesis but it is really not a course in religion.

1

With this controversial claim, I do not intend to stipulate the best way to study the Christian scriptures, rather, to suggest that a historical-critical methodology by itself is inadequate to understand the nature and role of the New Testament as a sacred scripture within the lives of Christians and the history of the Christian tradition. To understand the New Testament in this latter sense calls for a "seeing," a more complete or total form of awareness, a knowing not limited to analyzing literary forms or conceptual systems of belief.

The difficulty of understanding a religious tradition in its variety and complexity becomes even more acute for non-Western religions. Some of the assumptions operable in a study of Christianity or Judaism may not be as relevant in a study of Hinduism or Buddhism. Some may be entirely irrelevant. And, although our cultural and general educational background have provided us with an introduction to Western religious concepts, history, and institutions, we have little such preparation vis-à-vis non-Western religions. This problem suggests the utility of a variety of instructional resources.

In the first instance, undoubtedly, these resources will be texts and monographs. In the field of Theravāda Buddhism in Southeast Asia such materials range from primary texts in original languages (e.g., Pali, Burmese, Thai, Lao, Khmer) and in translation to historical studies, doctrinal expositions, and an increasing number of excellent anthropological studies. Although the breadth of available written sources makes possible a more holistic presentation of Theravāda Buddhism in Southeast Asia, the cultural and institutional dimensions remain only relatively accessible without firsthand exposure or the use of audiovisual resources. For example, we can verbally describe an ordination ceremony or devotional ritual acts (*pūja*); however, visual depiction compliments ethnographic description and enhances the meaning attributed through the conceptual analysis of such rites.[2] In another context I have taken a similar position in regard to religious practices such as meditation;[3] namely, that actual participation in *vipassanā* meditation or *zazen* illuminates our understanding of this kind of religious practice. The same sort of claim can be made for participation in festivals, rites, and rituals. My argument here rests on epistemological and pedagogical grounds and has nothing to do with the claim made by some religious scholars that to understand Buddhism one must be a practicing Buddhist or to understand Christianity one must be a baptized member of a church. Quite simply, if a religion is most adequately comprehended by accounting for its multiple meanings, our methods of understanding and teaching the phenomena that constitute religion should be appropriate to the nature of the subject matter.

Religions are multiplex, and the phenomena constituting religion embody different levels of meaning. In the light of such multivalency religion has been characterized as a "symbol system."[4] To study and teach religion, therefore, challenges us to go beyond the literal, the obvious, and the purely descriptive, to discern the hidden meanings and deeper levels of human experience embedded in the text, the rite, and the festival. To fail to do so may be to ignore the "essence" of a religious symbol system in the face of its myriad "manifestations."[5]

Audiovisual instructional materials, field trips to the increasing number of Theravāda monasteries throughout North America, and the opportunity to travel or study in Buddhist Asia contribute to a more complete and, hence, more profound understanding of the Theravāda religious tradition that is the focus of this monograph. A student can read descriptions and analyses of funerals or ordinations, but seeing them, even in a film or in a picture, directly involves the perceptual senses in the learning process. To be sure, films, slides, records, and field trips need to be integrated into interpretative frameworks. By themselves their variety of meanings may remain mute; however, without them the study of religion may become overly conceptual and in doing so run the risk of distorting the very nature of the subject matter itself.

AIM OF THE MONOGRAPH

Not so many years ago religion was taught in many universities and colleges as part of the curriculum of philosophy or literature departments. Although historical reasons account for this fact, these departmental loci point to the way religion as an academic discipline was perceived: a system of belief or thought imbedded in particular texts (for the most part Christian). Religion as a cultural institution was taught in anthropology and sociology departments, if it was taught at all. Times, of course, have now changed. Courses dealing centrally with religion as a cultural institution, including non-Western religions, now constitute an important component in religion department offerings.

Furthermore, although religious belief systems may appear to have an atemporal character we readily acknowledge that historical, cultural, social, economic, and political contexts cannot be divorced from religion any more than an individual's profession of faith, be it Christian, Jewish, Buddhist,

Hindu, or Muslim, can be separated from his or her personal, subjective experience.

In the following pages we shall study Theravāda Buddhism within the cultures and historical backdrops of Southeast Asia and Sri Lanka in terms of three differing social and political contexts: the traditional village, the kingdom and nation state, and the modern urbanized environment. Each of these contexts provides a background for examining seminal features of religion, more particularly, Buddhism in Southeast Asia: the integrative and syncretic nature of traditional, popular religion; the role of religion in political legitimation and national integration; and the participation of traditional religion in the forces of rapid change associated with urbanization and modernization.

This monograph, then, serves primarily as an introduction to the study of Theravāda Buddhism and society within the cultural setting of Southeast Asia. In the broadest sense it is an examination of the interaction of a religious worldview and a cultural ethos, or the ways in which the peoples of Southeast Asia have organized and expressed their lives in meaningful patterns.[6] The chapters in this book explore these patterns both in terms of their coherence as well as their rich and fascinating variety.

ONE

The Popular Tradition

Inclusive Syncretism

A ll too often a Western textbook understanding of Buddhism bears little resemblance to the actual practice of Buddhism in Southeast Asia. The popular Theravāda traditions of Sri Lanka, Burma,[1] Thailand, Laos, and Cambodia seem to distort and even subvert the cardinal teachings of enlightenment (*nibbāna*),[2] the Four Noble Truths, or the Noble Eightfold Path familiar to the Western student of Buddhism. The observer enters a Theravāda Buddhist culture to discover that ordination into the monastic order (*sangha*) may be motivated more by a lad's sense of social obligation to his parents rather than the pursuit of transforming wisdom; that the peace and quiet sought by a meditating monk may be overwhelmed by the amplified rock music of a temple festival; that somewhat unkempt village temples outnumber orderly, well-disciplined monasteries; and that the Buddha, austerely imaged in the posture of meditation (*samādhi*) or dispelling Māra's powerful army, is venerated more in the hope of gaining privilege and prestige, material gain, and protection on journeys than in the hope of *nibbāna*.

The seeming contradictions between the highest ideals and goals of Theravāda Buddhism and the living tradition in Southeast Asia has perplexed Western scholars. Decades ago Max Weber made a sharp distinction between what he characterized as the "otherworldly mystical" goal of early Indian Buddhism and the world-affirming, practical goals of popular, institutional Buddhism which flourished in the third century C.E. under King Asoka and later Buddhist monarchs.[3] More recent scholars of Burmese Buddhism have been influenced by Weber's distinction in their studies of Buddhism as a cultural institution[4] and an ethical system.[5]

5

In fact, the Theravāda Buddhism of Southeast Asia, not unlike other great historic religions, defines ideal goals of moral perfection and ultimate self-transformation and the means to attain them; at the same time, however, Southeast Asian Buddhism also provides the means for people to cope with the day-to-day problems of life and to justify worldly pursuits. Both goals are sanctioned in the writings of the Pali canon, the scriptures of Theravāda Buddhism. The way to the transcendence of suffering (The Noble Eightfold Path) found in the first public teaching attributed to the Buddha (the discourse known as Setting the Wheel of the Law in Motion) includes advice appropriate to monks, such as meditation, and also the laity, such as right moral action. The goals of Buddhism, in short, are both ultimate (*nibbāna*) and proximate: a better rebirth, a better social and economic status in this life. The two are necessarily intertwined. For example, the Pali canon uplifts both spiritual poverty and material wealth: the monk or almsperson (*bhikkhu/ bhikkhunī*) eschews all worldy goods and gain, but wealth promotes both individual and social well-being when generously distributed by lay people unattached to their possessions.

Any broad, holistic analysis of Theravāda Buddhism in Southeast Asia must account not only for its highest ideals and its varied practices but also their seeming contradictions. For example, rituals designed specifically for the benefit of the soul of the deceased seem to undercut the central Theravāda doctrine of not-self or not-soul (*anattā*). The student of Theravāda Buddhism should keep in mind, however, that the not-self doctrine may be interpreted as sanctioning monastic pursuits such as meditation, whereas the doctrines of *kamma*, rebirth (*saṃsāra*), and merit (*puñña*) justify a wide range of other kinds of moral and ritual acts.[6] These are distinctive but related domains within the broader context of the Theravāda tradition; they are not contradictory. The Pali texts admit both ultimate and proximate ideals. The tradition affirms that the Buddhist path is a many-sided affair and that different types of people are at different stages along the path.[7] Explanations that seek somewhat arbitrarily and rigidly to differentiate teaching and practice, the ideal and the actual, run the risk of sacrificing the interwoven threads of religion to the logic of consistency.

Keeping this admonition in mind we use the term *popular tradition* with some hesitancy. No value judgment is intended. *Popular* does not mean less serious, less rigorous, or distant from the ideal; rather, it is intended to mean Theravāda Buddhism as commonly perceived, understood, and expressed by the average, traditional Sri Lankan, Burman, Thai, Cambodian, and Laotian. What defines their sense of religious and cultural identity, the contexts in which this identity is most readily investigated, are rites of passage, festival celebrations, ritual occasions, and behavior as exemplified in traditional stories. We go to the temple or the temple-monastery to observe many of these activities and hear the teachings as handed down orally from monk to lay person, to view their depiction in religious art and reenactment in ritual. Institutionally the religious life of the Theravāda Buddhist focuses on this place of public worship, celebration, and discourse. Symbolically the temple-monastery is not only the "monk's place" (*sangha-vāsa*) but also the "Buddha's place" (*buddha-vāsa*) represented by his images and enshrined relics, ceremonies and rituals.

In the following section we shall explore popular Buddhism in Southeast Asia in the contexts just mentioned: rites of passage, festival celebration, ritual occasions, and ideal behavior or life models as embodied in traditional myths and legends. The two underlying themes will be: (1) the syncretic nature of popular Buddhism as part of a total religio-cultural system, and (2) the function of religion to enhance life's meaning through the integration and interpretation of personal, social, and cosmic dimensions of life.

IDEAL ACTION

Doctrinally, ideal action in Theravāda Buddhism can be described as meritorious action (*puñña-kamma*) or action that does not accrue demerit (*pāpa-kamma*). At the highest stage of spiritual self-realization, the state of arahantship, one's actions are totally beyond the power of *kamma* (Sanskrit: *karma*) and rebirth (*saṃsāra*). Terms used to characterize ideal behavior and attitudes are truthfulness (*sacca*), generosity (*dāna*), loving-kindness (*mettā*), compassion (*karuṇā*), equanimity (*upekkhā*), wisdom (*paññā*), morality (*sīla*), to mention only a few. In both Theravāda and Mahāyāna Buddhism these virtues are referred to as *perfections* (*pāramī* or *pāramitā*) of character associated with the person of the *bodhisatta* (Sanskrit: *bodhisattva*). One finds these virtues elaborated in various types of schema and frameworks appropriate to audience and context. Rather than being presented as abstract ethical teachings, the Southeast Asian Theravāda tradition most often embodies these virtues in the narratives of moral exemplars, such as Vessantara and Sāma who appear in the last 10 of the 547 Pali *jātaka* tales,[8] other late canonical texts, such as the *Cariyāpiṭaka*, the fifth century commentaries of Buddhaghosa and Dhammapāla, stories in the vernacular languages of Southeast Asia, and most important, by the life of the Buddha. Such stories are well known and are the principal means through which ideal life models are taught.

It may seem self-evident to emphasize the centrality of the Buddha for Southeast Asian Theravāda Buddhism. Nevertheless, all too often students may focus their study of Buddhism on doctrine, ritual or meditation, to the near exclusion of that singular prince, Siddhattha Gotama, who was to become a universal figure, a Buddha or enlightened one.[9]

Historically the Buddha must be understood as the founder of the tradition (sāsana). Beyond that, however, his life story becomes paradigmatic for every devout follower who seeks the same enlightenment he achieved, especially for the Buddhist monk. Prince Siddhattha sought a deeper meaning to life beyond the inevitable limitations of old age, suffering, and death. He embarked on a quest for a personal knowledge that transcended the inherited traditions of highborn social class. He became a mendicant bhikkhu (almsperson), seeking out learned teachers, engaging in the ascetical regimens of the renunciant, training the mind in contemplative exercises (samādhi). Eventually Siddhattha discovered a higher truth (paramattha-sacca) not limited by the conventional dualistic constructions of self and other, eternalism and annihilationism. His profound apprehension of the noneternal and nonsubstantive (anicca, anattā), interdependent and co-coming-into-being (idappaccayatā, paṭicca-samuppāda) nature of things enabled Siddhattha to overcome the anxiety (dukkha) rooted in the awareness of human finiteness and of the conditional nature of life. In an ideal sense every follower of the Buddha seeks the same enlightenment (nibbāna). Nibbāna is not merely an abstract concept; the Buddha embodies this mode-of-being-in-the-world, pointing to that way of life as a reality to be achieved. Although we cannot always ascertain the intentions that take a young Burman or Thai into the Buddhist sangha (monastic order), symbolically his ordination reenacts the Buddha's story.[10]

The central teachings of Theravāda Buddhism emerge from the narrative of the Buddha's life. Broadly speaking the sutta literature in the form of dialogues of the Buddha represents episodes linked together as segments of the Buddha's life, much as pearls are strung on a single strand. Each pearl can be admired in and of itself but only when connected together by a thread do they make a necklace. Similarly, each sutta episode conveys particular teachings but these teachings are embedded in the larger framework of the Buddha's life. The Buddha's teaching (the dhamma) is inseparable from the prince who sought to see through the apparent contradictions and sufferings of life to a deeper truth and, having succeeded, taught this truth by word, deed, and example.

Figure 1.1. The main Buddha image at Wat Haripuñjaya monastery, Lamphun, Thailand. Photo by Donald K. Swearer.

When Sri Lankan, Burmese, Thai, Laotian, or Cambodian Buddhists enter a temple or approach a pagoda (*cetiya*),[11] they are, among other things, encountering the Buddha. The *cetiya* reliquary may enshrine Buddha relics, artifacts of his physical being. Buddha images of varying postures remind the viewer of the Buddha's struggle with the tempter Māra, his enlightenment, his teaching; murals depict in a narrative form long-remembered, embellished episodes from his life. Among the most frequent in occurrence are his miraculous birth; the four sights or scenes where he encounters old age, suffering, death, and a wandering truth-seeker; his enlightenment experience under the *bodhi* tree; and his first teaching delivered to five ascetics.

Bronze images and mural depictions of the life of the Buddha tell a story, not merely an inspired tale of the past but an everpresent reality. The Buddha represents not only the possibility of overcoming the blinded ignorance caused by sensory attachments and the attainment of the twin ideals of dispassion and compassion, but he also personifies the way whereby others may discover this truth for themselves or by relying on the Buddha's power can at least improve their lot in this life or in future lives.

The Buddha's story, of course, does not stand alone as an ideal life model.[12] In the Theravāda tradition the lives of saints, particularly in the form of *jātaka* tales purporting to be previous lives of the Buddha, embody particular virtues. They provide paradigms to be emulated rather than scholastic discussions of Buddhist doctrine. Of these, the best known is the story of Prince Vessantara,[13] the last life of the Buddha prior to his incarnation as Siddhattha Gotama, and the embodiment of the perfection of generosity (*dāna*).

The story begins with Vessantara, prince of Sivi, offering his kingdom's white elephant with magical rain-making powers to the neighboring territory of Kaliṅga to overcome the drought they are experiencing. The citizens of Sivi, incensed by this generous act, banish Vessantara and his family to the jungle. Before his departure he arranges a *dāna* or gift-giving ceremony, where he gives away most of his possessions. Upon leaving the capital a group of Brahmins request his horse-drawn chariot, which he willingly surrenders, afterward proceeding on foot with his wife and two children into the forest. As we might expect and as the logic of true *dāna* requires, soon after Vessantara and his family are happily settled in their simple jungle hut, the prince is asked to give up his children to serve an old Brahmin, Jūjaka, and his young wife. When Indra appears in disguise and Vessantara accedes to the god's demand that he give up his wife, the prince's trials come to an end. Having successfully met this ultimate test of generosity—the sacrifice of his wife and children—Vessantara's family is restored to him and he succeeds his father as king of Sivi.[14]

As the Buddha story embodies the ideals of *nibbāna* and nonattachment, so the Vessantara story illustrates the *kamma* doctrine, in this case, a reward for the meritorious (*puñña*) action of generosity (*dāna*). Western scholars have made much of the differences between nibbanic or noble-path action and kammic-merit motivated action. When these two types of action are placed within their well-known narrative contexts, however, the inter-relationships become more readily apparent. Both Siddhattha and Vessantara exemplify modes of selflessness symbolized respectively by a quest and

Figure 1.2. Temple mural. Wat Luang monastery. Pakse, Champassak Province, Laos PDR. Vessantara, Maddi, and their two children walking to their forest hermitage. Photo by Donald K. Swearer.

a journey; renunciation marks the beginning of a critical threshold or testing period preceding a return or restoration. In the Buddha's case the threshold state is one of intensive study and ascetical practice from which he emerges transformed as the Buddha. Vessantara's residence in the forest represents a testing stage from which he returns to be rewarded with an enhanced degree of secular power.

To be sure, the stories differ. Prince Siddhattha becomes the Buddha, the awakened one, the *Tathāgata*, one who has realized the perfection of the Truth; nonetheless, the two tales embody a similar structure. In particular, both focus on the virtue of selflessness: in Vessantara's case generosity (*dāna*), and in the Buddha's the total transformation of one's being symbolized by the term, *not-self* (*anattā*); that is, a state of being emptied of any sense of self as independent and self-existent (*svabhava*).[15]

Despite the general tenor of androcentrism in the Pali texts,[16] paradigmatic tales of women, both monastic and lay, also exemplify the interrelationship between generosity, selflessness, and equanimity. Visākhā's selfless generosity in support of the monastic order is as unbounded as that of her male counterpart, Anāthapiṇḍika. She sacrifices her wedding dowry to support the Buddhist religion (*sāsana*).[17] Although institutionally female monks were subject to the authority of their male counterparts, the poetry of the *Songs of the Nuns* (*Therīgāthās*) testifies to the high spiritual attainments of female members of the *sangha* as evidenced in the following poem attributed to Sakulā, a member of a Brahman family, who reached arahanthood and was singled out by the Buddha as the foremost among nuns, having achieved the psychic power of the "eye of heaven," the ability to see all worlds far and near:

When I lived in a house
I heard a monk's words
and saw in those words
nirvāṇa
the unchanging state.

I am the one
who left son and daughter,
money and grain,
cut off my hair,
and set out into homelessness

Under training on the straight way
desire and hatred fell away,
along with the obsessions
of the mind
that combine with them.

After my ordination,
I remembered
I had been born before.
The eye of heaven became clear.

The elements of body and mind
I saw as other,

Figure 1.3. Temple mural. Wat Phrathāt Pha Ngaw, Chiang Rai Province, Thailand. Lay persons presenting alms food to nuns. Photo by Donald K. Swearer.

born from a cause,
subject to decay.
I have given up the obsessions
of the mind.
I am quenched and cool.[18]

Both men and women have the potential to achieve the moral values of selflessness and equanimity, ideals associated with the highest level of spiritual attainment in Buddhism.

The stories of those individuals who have traveled to the highest stages of the Buddhist path appear in canonical Pali texts and commentaries as well as fables written in vernacular Southeast Asian languages. But they are not merely hagiographies from a bygone age. Many are the stories of modern Buddhist "saints"—both monastic and lay—embodied in written narratives, oral legend, and living personal example. The tradition of forest monks, in particular, has contributed significantly to Buddhist hagiographic lore in the modern period as well as the past. In Thailand, for example, the life of the forest monk, Āchān Mun (b. 1870), as told by one of his disciples, Āchān Mahābua, has taken on a normative significance for the lives of other forest monks.[19] As the paradigm of the ideal forest-meditation monk, Āčhān Mun has been elevated to the status of the founder of the modern "forest tradition" in Thai Buddhism.

Exemplary contemporary tales of dedication, perserverance, and realization include women as well as men. One such story appeared in a leading Thai English language newspaper, the *Bangkok Post*. It relates the story of a former prominent scholar, Āčhān Runjuan Indrakamhaeng, who became a nun in 1982 upon her retirement from professional life. As related by Sanitsuda Ekachai, a liberal feature writer for the Post, Āčhān Runjuan's story is one of personal persistence and fortitude in the face of a social bias against women renunciants in Thailand:

> An old woman in white with a shaved head sat on a sleeper train bound for Bangkok, trying her best to hide her anxiety at having to travel alone.
>
> She heaved a sigh of relief when a group of monks occupied the three seats around her. No more fear of sitting with rowdy strangers. It was turning out to be a safe journey with "temple people" after all.
>
> Her relief was short-lived.
>
> The monks stonily told her to go sit somewhere else. "These are monks seats," one of them said. 'Don't sit here.'
>
> Despite her anger and hurt, she reluctantly complied...

Āčhān Runjuan, now a highly respected dhamma teacher, was sharing the anecdote with feminists during a 1994 meeting on "Feminism and Buddhism":

> "Part of me wanted to resist and see how things turned out. But then I reminded myself that I was an old woman with a shaved head, that these people were temple people like me. And that I shouldn't make a scene.
>
> "In my new seat, I was surrounded by drinking men. I was angry. What is this? How could monks think only of their own purity to the extent that they lost consideration of others?
>
> "My mind was burning like fire," says Āčhān [teacher-professor] Runjuan...
>
> She had been studying the eight-fold path which says that the right perspective comes from wisdom.
>
> "From this principle, I told myself these monks only knew about *sīla* [the moral precepts] but zero about wisdom...."[20]

Ǎchān Runjuan exemplifies a new approach to women's spiritual practice in Thai Buddhism. Rather than wearing the white robes typical of the traditional Thai female renunciant (Thai: *mae chī* or *chī phā khāw*), Ǎchān Runjuan wears a white blouse with a black skirt, and refers to herself as a female lay disciple of the Buddha (*upāsikā*) rather than *nun*, a custom followed by a community of religious women in Petchburi province south of Bangkok. She has taught at Wat Suan Mokkhbalārāma (The Garden of Liberating Power), founded by the late Bhikkhu Buddhadāsa, a monk well-known internationally,[21] and she was the driving force behind a major handbook of core concepts in Buddhism. "Women are today," comments Ǎchān Runjuan, "given equal rights. In this era of science and technology, let us hope that women will help lighten the burdens of men [to propagate the Dhamma]. . ."[22]

Many other stories characterize different facets of both spiritually ideal and morally objectionable behavior and their respective reward and punishment. For example, motivated by selfish jealousy, Devadatta, the Buddha's cousin, attempts to cause a schism in the monastic order and even tries to kill the Buddha. He ends up in hell.[23] Other stories illustrate the five moral precepts or training rules fundamental to the normative ethical system of popular Theravāda Buddhism in Southeast Asia: the prohibitions against taking life, stealing, lying, committing adultery, and drinking intoxicants. One such tale relates the experience of the pious monk Phra Malai, who is given the opportunity to visit both the Buddhist hells, populated by those who have broken the precepts, and the heavens, enjoyed by those who have faithfully kept them. He then instructs humankind about future rewards and punishments for present actions. Temple murals also depict episodes from this popular story, not as a model of ideal behavior, as in the case of the Buddha and Vessantara, but as a vivid illustration of the consequences for failure to follow the Buddhist moral code.[24]

Theravāda Buddhism teaches the ideals of selflessness, wisdom, and compassion, which are identified with the person of the Buddha and the goal of *nibbāna*. It also establishes normative moral principles and rules necessary for social harmony. These rules are reinforced by such stories as Phra Malai and are elaborated by commentaries, viz. the commentary on the *Dhammapāda* (the *Dhammapādāṭṭhakathā*), and canonical *suttas* like the *Sigālaka*. In the latter text, the Buddha teaches a Brahman youth, Sigālaka, about the duties and responsibilities that should obtain between parent and child, husband and wife, teacher and student, friends, servants

Figure 1.4. Phra Malai teaching men and women about the punishments of hell and the rewards of heaven. Wat Phra Thāt Haripuñjaya, Lamphun, Thailand. Photo by Donald K. Swearer.

and masters, mendicants and lay supporters (see Appendix 1). Southeast Asian Buddhism, to be sure, encompasses more than the individual and social ideals represented by the Buddha, Sakulā, Vessantara, Visākhā, Phra Malai, and Sigālaka. In particular, it locates human beings within a complex cosmology of various divine, human, and subhuman powers and provides a system for coping with them.[25]

Popular Buddhist moral tales (e.g. *jātaka*, *Cariyāpiṭaka*) assume the inherent interrelationship among these various cosmological levels and states of existence. As the following brief narrative from the *Cariyāpiṭaka* (Basket of Conduct) illustrates, the dramatis personae of these moral fables can be monkeys, deer, buffalo, fish, *yakkhas* (demons), and *nāgas* (serpents) as well as human beings. The story illustrates moral virtue (*sīla*). It is about a buffalo who upholds the precept (*sīla*) against taking the life of a sentient being and who controls anger justified by social humiliation and ritual pollution.

> When I was a buffalo roaming in a forest...strong, large, terrifying to behold....Wandering about in the huge forest I saw a favourable

Figure 1.5. Monk preaching seated on a "preaching chair" (*dhammāsana*). Chiang Mai, Thailand. Photo by Donald K. Swearer.

place. Going to that place I stood and I lay down. Then an evil, foul, nimble monkey came there and urinated and defecated over my shoulder, forehead and eyebrows. And on one day, even on a second, a third and a fourth too, he polluted me. All the time I was distressed by him. A yakkha [demon], seeing my distress, said this to me, "Kill that vile evil one with horns and hoofs." This spoken, I then said to the yakkha, "How is it that you (would) besmear me with a carcass, evil and foul?" If I were to be angry with him, from that I would become more degraded than him; and morality [*sīla*] might be violated by me and wise men might censure me. Better indeed is death through (leading a life of) purity than a life subject to disdain. How will I, even for the sake of life, do an injury to another?[26]

As we can see, this folklike tale has a humorous as well as a moral dimension. In modern society we tend to see religion as a sober-sided enterprise devoid of humor; not so for traditional, orally based religious instruction in Buddhist Southeast Asia. Lay storytellers and even monk-preachers often use humor—occasionally ribald— to keep the attention of their audience.

RITUAL OCCASIONS, MERIT, AND THE
APPROPRIATION OF POWER

Buddhist rituals can be classified in various ways. Melford Spiro, for example, characterizes Theravāda ritual action in Burma in terms of a fourfold typology: commemorative, expressive, instrumental, and expiatory.[27] Commemorative ritual is performed in remembrance of historical, legendary, or mythological events; expressive ritual serves to manifest emotions and sentiments felt toward objects of reverence, such as the Buddha, his teaching (*dhamma*), and the monastic order (*sangha*); instrumental ritual aims to achieve some goal in this life or in future lives; expiatory ritual is performed to atone for misdeeds.[28] Like most religious phenomena, rituals can be interpreted on several levels. Melford Spiro's analysis is useful but should not be taken as exhaustive nor should its categories be construed as mutually exclusive. Furthermore, although rituals vary in nature, function, and intent, Theravāda ritual in Southeast Asia often seems calculated to gain access to a wide spectrum of beneficent and malevolent powers.

Broadly speaking, these powers can be defined as either Buddhist or non-Buddhist. The Buddhist symbols operative in various ritual contexts are most often associated with the Buddha himself and include Buddha images, his relics enshrined in reliquary mounds (*cetiya*), and Buddha amulets. Symbols associated with individual Buddhist monks or nuns reputed to be particularly holy are an important extension of these objects. The charismatic power ascribed to individual monks derive, in part, from the power represented by the Buddha because monks follow his *dhamma* (the Buddha's teaching); even more so, monks' charisma stems from their reputed abilities to foresee the future, to heal psychic and physical maladies, and other extraordinary powers associated with trance states (*jhāna*). Consequently, images, relics, and amulets of famous monks are venerated for their own sake.[29]

At the level of popular cult the nonphysical, nibbanic values and ideals represented by the Buddha, his teachings, and by the Buddhist *sangha* take on specific physical or material characteristics. Even the Buddha's teaching or *dhamma* has a physical representation in the material form of inscribed palm leaf texts. Because of their association with the Buddha's teaching, palm leaf manuscripts become objects of power in their own right. The term *sacred text* in this sense refers not only to its content but to the text as a physical object of sacred power.

Symbols to which special powers are ascribed within ritual contexts which may or may not be overtly Buddhist have been classified as either animistic or Brahmanistic.[30] These include Brahmanical deities such as Indra (Sakka in the Pali canon) and Viṣṇu invoked to guard the place or occasion of a Buddhist ceremony, a pantheon of Hindu gods in Sri Lanka, such as Kataragama,[31] and various indigenous deities and spirits such as the *nats* in Burma,[32] and the *čhao* and *phī* in Thailand and Laos.[33]

A syncretic flavor imbues most popular festivals, ceremonies, and rituals in Theravāda Southeast Asia. With some, such as the festival of the Buddha's birth, enlightenment, and death (Visākhā Pūja), the Buddhist element dominates; however, Buddhist monks will also be invited to chant protective Suttas (*paritta*)[34] at a variety of rituals, ranging from house dedications to weddings, whose underlying significance seems far afield from the Buddhist ideals of self-transforming knowledge (i.e., *nibbāna*). If religious ritual is interpreted primarily as a system for access to a broad range of powers constituted within a cosmology of human, superhuman, and subhuman realms, then the ritual context itself determines its meaning rather than a predetermined definition of what counts as Buddhist or non-Buddhist (e.g., animistic, Brahmanical).

In gaining access to power, Buddhist ritual in Southeast Asia functions in two primary ways: reciprocal exchange and appropriation. Reciprocal exchange emerges from a donor-donee situation typical of merit making (*puñña*) rituals. The lay person-donor offers material gifts for the benefit of the monastic order (*sangha*). In return the virtuous power of the *sangha* engenders a spiritual reward of merit (*puñña*), thereby enhancing the donors' balance of *kamma/karma*, which in turn affects the status of the person's rebirth on the cosmic scale. All ritual situations in which presentations are made to the monastic order function in this way. These include acts as frequent and informal as giving food to monks on their morning alms rounds (*piṇḍapāta*), to the annual and formal presentation of new robes and other gifts to the *sangha* at the end of the monsoon rains retreat (*vassa*) after the October full-moon day. Even though the form of merit making rituals in Theravāda Buddhism in Southeast Asia varies greatly, the structure of reciprocal exchange remains constant.

Merit making links the cosmology of Theravāda Buddhism in graphic and practical terms to peoples' daily lives. We have already referred to the story of the pious monk Phra Malai who taught human beings the heavenly rewards of good deeds and the grim consequences of punishment in hell. Late canonical texts, such as the *Stories of the Heavenly Mansions*

Figure 1.6. Monks on the morning alms rounds (*piṇḍapāta*). Photo by Donald K. Swearer.

(*Vimānavatthu*) and *The Stories of the Departed Ghosts* (*Petavatthu*), commentaries (*aṭṭhakathā*), and many tales in the vernacular literatures of Southeast Asia reenforce the future negative and positive results of behavior in this life. The following brief selections from the *Petavatthu* provide a sample of the graphic horrors of this realm of punishment. The *petas* are departed spirits who occupy one of the levels of Buddhist hell (*niraya*). Contemplating their condition, often depicted in illustrated manuscripts or temple murals, presumptively encourages (or threatens) a person to positive, moral behavior.

"You have a beautiful, heavenly complexion. . . [said the venerable monk, Narada]. . .Yet worms are devouring your mouth which has a putrid odour; what act did you commit of yore?"

The [male] Peta replied: "A monk I was, wicked and of ill speech; though fitted for austerity, I was unrestrained with my mouth; I obtained my complexion with austerity and a putrid mouth on account of my slander."[35]

[The venerable monk, Sāriputta, spoke to a female Petī who appeared to him at night] "Naked and of hideous appearance are you, emaciated and with prominent veins. You thin one, with your ribs standing out, now who are you, you who are here?"

Figure 1.7. A Buddhist hell. Punishment for breaking the precepts. Phra Malai murals, Wat Haripuñjaya, Lamphun, Thailand. Photo by Donald K. Swearer.

The Petī [replied]: "I, venerable sir, am a peti, a wretched denizen of Yama's world; since I had done a wicked deed, I went from here to the world of the petas."

Sāriputta [asked]: "...Because of what act have you gone hence to the world of the petas?"

"Reverend sir [she replied], I did not have compassionate relatives, father and mother, or even other kinsmen who would urge me, saying, 'Give, with devotion in your heart, a gift to recluses and brahmans.'"

"From that time for five hundred years in this form I have been wandering, nude, consumed by hunger and thirst; this is the fruit of my wicked deed."[36]

Other Southeast Asian religious rituals use somewhat different mechanisms for appropriating the power of the religious object. A pilgrimage to a famous *cetiya*-reliquary containing a Buddha relic; paying respects to a Buddha image with holy water lustrations during the April lunar New Year celebration; receiving and wearing an amulet containing the charred hair of a holy monk; "calling" spirits at times of crisis or life junctures; making offerings to the deities of the four directions, the zenith, and nadir—all of these ritual acts aim at appropriating power, whether represented by the Buddha or other kinds of divine or demonic beings. Of course, elements of exchange can be found in these rituals as well. A gift is given, an offering made, a sum of money is donated in the expectation of some kind of return varying from an immediate and practical benefit to a general sense of well-being or even spiritual attainment.[37] The structure of these rituals, however, mirrors less clearly the reciprocal nature basic to all merit making exchanges.

In the remainder of this analysis of Buddhist ritual in Southeast Asia we shall examine three different ceremonies that exemplify and justify this interpretation of ritual reciprocal exchange and appropriation of power.[38] The first of these ceremonies is the presentation of new robes at the end of the monsoon rains retreat (*vassa*); the second is the consecration of a new Buddha image; and the third is the annual preaching of the *Vessantara Jātaka*.

Kaṭhina Ceremony
(Presentation of Robes at the End of the Rains Retreat)

The presentation of new robes and other gifts at the end of the monastic rains retreat in mid-October takes its name from the robes offered at that occasion, namely, the *kaṭhina*.[39] This ceremony takes place during the month immediately following the full moon sabbath (*uposatha*) day in October. According to the *Mahāvagga* of the Theravāda Book of Discipline (*Vinaya Piṭaka*), during a three-month period from mid-July to mid-October monks were required to adopt a settled residence and were allowed to leave this encampment only under special conditions. In this environment the mendicant nature of the Buddhist monkhood began to change. In particular, customs and practices of a collective life gradually emerged including the recitation of a set of disciplinary rules (*paṭimokkha*) and the distribution of robes (*kaṭhina*).[40] These ceremonies have continued to this day and have evolved from culture to culture as the Theravāda form of Buddhism taught by the Sinhalese Mahāvihāra monastic lineage became dominant not only in Sri Lanka but won the favor of ruling monarchs in Burma, Thailand, Laos, and Cambodia from the eleventh and twelfth centuries onward. Today in Buddhist Southeast Asia the *kaṭhina* ceremony provides one of the most popular occasions for merit making. In village society this event usually involves the entire community, and in towns the monastery "parish" participates as a communal group.

The *kaṭhina* ceremony may last from one to three days. Although nearly every family in the community or parish will be involved in the preparation of food and other material gifts offered to the monks at a particular monastery, the principal donor may come from another village, town, or region. This custom stems from the traditional view that greater merit accrues when the identity of the donor is unknown to the *sangha*. In Thailand today this practice may also result from the fact that upcountry monasteries are considered to be closer to the monastic ideal than urban ones. For this reason, affluent patrons from cities often sponsor *kaṭhinas* in rural areas. Most of the *kaṭhina* ceremonies I have witnessed followed this pattern. In one of the most memorable of these occasions, a set of robes completely spun and woven at the monastery within a twenty-four hour period was presented to the abbot of a rural northern Thai monastery noted for his austerity and skill in meditation. Dozens of women were paid to card, spin, and weave in temporary quarters built for the occasion. In this case the sponsor was a wealthy business woman from Chiang Mai, the largest city in northern Thailand.

The actual presentation of robes, money, and other offerings for the livelihood of the monks highlights the *kaṭhina*. It frequently involves a procession varying in size and constituency according to the nature of the community. Included might be musical groups with traditional instruments—drums, cymbals, and horns—or school bands playing Western musical instruments. Traditional dancers may be part of the processional entertainment and the marchers often wear traditional costume. In addition to the *kaṭhina* robes, symbolically the most important gift presented to the monastic order at this time, is a "wishing tree" with money and other offerings attached occupies a place of honor in the procession. The wishing tree, often in the shape of a palace, represents the hope of the villagers that the merit they accrue in this celebration will enable them to live in a heavenly abode in some future lifetime.[41]

The procession wends its way through the streets of the town or village until it comes to the monastery proper. The participants file into the main assembly hall (*vihāra*) bearing robes, the wishing tree, and other palanquins filled with offerings of soap, towels, writing pads, canned food, cigarettes, and other material goods used by the monks. The ceremony itself begins as do most meetings of monks and lay persons with the congregation taking refuge in the Buddha, the teaching (*dhamma*), and the renunciant order (*sangha*) and repeating in Pali after the monks the five basic precepts of Buddhist lay life: not to kill, steal, lie, engage in illicit sexual acts, or drink

Figure 1.8. Rains retreat (*kaṭhina*) procession. Chiang Tung, Shan States, Myanmar. Photo by Donald K. Swearer.

intoxicating beverages. Afterward the lay leader of the congregation conducts the ritual of the presentation of gifts to the entire monastic community which are received on their behalf by the abbot. The chief donor then has the privilege of offering the first set of robes to the gathered monks after he/she first symbolically offers them to a large Buddha image that dominates all such assembly rooms. The ceremony concludes after the monks and novices receive their new robes and chant an appropriate blessing:

> May all blessings be yours; may all the gods (*deva*) protect you.
> By the power of all the Buddhas, may all happiness be yours forever.
> May all blessings be yours; may all the gods protect you.
> By the power of all the Dhammas; may all happiness be yours forever.
> May all blessings be yours; may all the gods protect you.
> By the power of all the Sanghas; may all happiness be yours forever.[42]

A reciprocal transaction has taken place. In return for the offerings presented to the monastic order (*sangha*) the laity receive a spiritual blessing. In the calculus of merit making (*puñña*) the participants hope for a reward in a future life brought about by the power of this good act.

Figure 1.9. Monks chanting. Chiang Mai, Thailand. Photo by Donald K. Swearer.

But why is this particular ritual of exchange so important? All merit making rituals are rooted in the symbolic role of the monastic order as mediator of the power represented by the Buddha, a power not only of supreme enlightenment but of supernatural attainments. On this occasion the *sangha* has a special potency because for three months the monks have followed a somewhat more rigorous regime; for example, restricted travel, intensive study, meditation. In a sense the *kathina* ceremony becomes the means by which the laity gains access to this enhanced potency and power. For this reason the ceremony is especially meritorious and, furthermore, may be one of the explanations why possession of the *kathina* robe itself confers on Burmese monks such privileges as being able to leave the monastery without the abbot's consent.[43] In short, the *kathina* robe may be said to represent not only a particular period of tenure and training in the monastic order but also the spiritual power inherent in "wearing the robe."

Consecration of a Buddha Image

A second ceremony[44] that helps us understand the significance of the transactional nature of Theravāda Buddhist ritual in Southeast Asia is the consecration of a Buddha image.[45] Nearly all Theravāda rituals that take place at the monastery occur in an assembly hall containing a Buddha image. The image resides on a dias or altar, making it higher in elevation than either the monks who may sit on a raised platform or the laity who sit on the floor. In Thailand, Laos, and Cambodia during most ceremonies, which consist primarily of the chanting of Pali texts and ritual chants composed in Pali or vernacular languages of the area, the monks will hold a sacred thread attached to the Buddha image that functions as a conduit of the power residing in the image and magically released by the chant. In addition to being the visual focus of attention for any congregation performing a ritual act in the hall, the image is also the recipient of offerings of incense, candles, and flowers. When asked about the meaning of the offerings placed before a Buddha image, most informants reply that these objects are given out of respect to the memory of the Buddha of which the image is a reminder; that is, that the offerings are not given to the image itself. Such an interpretation coincides with the orthodox Theravāda view discouraging superhuman or magical interpretations of the Buddha's power. The ceremony in which a Buddha image is consecrated, however, appears to qualify if not to contradict such an interpretation.

In Theravāda Buddhist cultures the Buddha images installed in assembly halls (*vihāra*) must be formally consecrated. Until that act takes place, the statue can be considered merely decorative, that is, of no special sacred consequence. The consecration ceremony figuratively brings the image to life or empowers it, thereby transforming the image from its decorative and inconsequential status to one of spiritual and religious significance. After consecration, an image is worthy of veneration, an object to which offerings are made not simply out of respect to the memory of a religious founder but with the expectation that an efficacious consequence will follow. Although one might theorize on psychological grounds that making an offering before a representation of a divine being or a saint entails the hope of some sort of reward or benefit, firsthand knowledge of an image consecration ritual provides us with specific cultural information regarding the nature of this expectation and its fulfillment.[46]

An image consecration involves two primary elements, training the image and charging it with power. In Thailand and Laos the ceremony proper, which may be part of a larger celebration, generally lasts one full night, beginning at dusk and ending at dawn of the following day with the opening of the eyes of the Buddha image. Because the details of image consecrations differ rather significantly among Theravāda cultures, the following description comes primarily from a ceremony I witnessed in northern Thailand in 1977 supplemented by others I observed in 1989.

The ceremony was held at a small rural monastery near the town of Lamphun and was the occasion of several days of festivities that served the dual purposes of community celebration and raising money to pay for a new monastery building. The ceremony took place in the assembly hall, where the image was to be installed. At dusk the monks and novices from the monastery and distinguished monks and ecclesiastical leaders from the district and province began chanting before a congregation of lay men and women who had filled the hall. After taking refuge (*saraṇaṁ*) in the Three Gems (Buddha, Dhamma, Sangha) and taking the precepts (*pañca sīla*), the evening chanting began with selections from the *paritta* or "protection" *suttas*. These were collected as the core body of ritual texts in the Sinhalese Mahāvihāra monastic tradition of Theravāda Buddhism and have been widely used as the basis of most chanting ceremonies in Southeast Asian Theravāda Buddhism since the fourteenth century.

The noted Sinhalese monk Piyadassi Thera suggests that the twenty-four standard *paritta* discourses from the five collections of Pali *sutta* texts constitutes a *dhamma* handbook for newly ordained novice monks.[47] A practical argument for their prominence as ritual texts, therefore, would be that in the tradition of Theravāda Buddhism in Sri Lanka and Southeast Asia this group of texts was the most widely memorized. Beyond this practical point, however, Piyadassi offers four doctrinal explanations for the efficacy of *paritta* texts based on the principle that, "paritta recital produces mental well-being in those who listen to them with intelligence, and have confidence in the truth of the Buddha's words."[48] He asserts that the texts establish the hearer in the power of the truth (*dhamma*) of the Buddha; that because many of the discourses describe the virtuous life they establish the hearer in a virtuous state of mind; that the monks who chant *paritta* do so reflecting the compassion of the Buddha for all sentient beings, thereby establishing the hearers in the power of love; and, finally, that the power of the sound of the chant helps to create both mental and physical harmony.[49]

Piyadassi's modern explanation of the meaning of *paritta* recital contrasts with the widely held belief among lay people in the efficacy of *paritta* chant to bring about particular ends, such as curing physical illness. Even in the Pali texts themselves the Buddha is said to have approved chanting the *Karaṇīya Mettā Sutta* to ward off evil spirits and the *Aṅgulimāla Paritta* was specifically sanctioned for a difficult childbirth.

Figure 1.10. Buddha
Image Consecration
Ritual, Wat San Pa
Yang Luang, Lamphun,
Thailand. Photo by
Donald K. Swearer.

With the exception of the two hours between three and five a.m. when those in attendance rested or slept, the entire ceremony at the village monastery was devoted to continuous chanting, sermons on the life of the Buddha, and meditation. During the night both monks and laity wandered in and out of the hall, an air of relaxed informality characterizing this otherwise serious affair. In addition to the *paritta* the canonical and noncanonical texts chanted and preached for this occasion rehearsed the life of the Prince Siddhattha leading up to his enlightenment with a special emphasis on the supernatural attributes and powers the future Buddha (*bodhisatta*) acquired during the course of his religious quest. The chanting concluded at dawn with the recitation of the Buddha's first teaching (*Dhammacakkappavattana Sutta*), performed while the head and eyes of the image were being uncovered by a senior monk.

During the entire night the image resided on a raised platform, its head covered with a white cloth and eyes sealed with beeswax. The act of covering the head and closing the eyes and sometimes the nose, mouth, and ears symbolizes the incomplete or unenlightened condition of the image; that is, it had yet to be taught its personal history, imbued with supernatural powers, and taught the *dhamma* ("truth"). The chanting of the monks and the sermons preached both instruct and empower the image even while the life history of the Buddha is being recited. Prior to the ceremony various gifts for the image were placed before it, including the five royal insignia (fan, crown, bowl, staff, sandals), the eight requisites of a monk highlighted by a begging bowl and monastic robes, a small Bodhi tree, and a grass seat. These elements function as visual representations of the story being told by the chanting monks: the tale of the royal prince who renounced the householder's life, gained special powers through his training and ascetic practice, and finally attained enlightenment seated beneath the Bodhi tree.

Two additional aspects of the ceremony deserve special mention. While the Buddha Image Consecration text (*Buddha Abhiseka*) was being chanted, a group of nine monks sat in rapt meditation around the image. Before them were placed monks' alms bowls from which sacred cords extended to the Buddha image. It is believed that while the monks meditate they project their own charismatic powers into the image, thereby further enhancing the image's potency.

The second noteworthy element was a ritual reenactment of an event in the legend of the Buddha's spiritual quest that occurred just before his enlightenment. In the early morning hours a sweetened rice gruel was prepared by a group of female renunciants (Thai: *mae chī*) within a specially consecrated area outside the assembly hall. After being divided into forty-nine small bowls, monks, nuns, and lay people offer the mixture to the image. This offering recalls an episode from the legend of the future Buddha's spiritual quest: just before Prince Siddhattha reached enlightenment, Sujātā, a wealthy young married woman, presented to him a special mixture of honey sweetened milk-rice in a golden bowl. The future Buddha consumed the rice after dividing it into forty-nine small balls: "Now that was the only food he had for forty-nine days, during the seven times seven days he spent, after he became a Buddha, at the foot of the Tree of Enlightenment."[50] In Burma, Sujātā's offering is commemorated in an annual sumptuous merit making feast held on the first full-moon day after the end of the rains retreat. Sir James Scott (Shway Yoe) provides us with an account of the fete as celebrated in the late nineteenth century: "Mountains of cooked rice send out spurs of beef and pork, with flat lands of dried fish and outlying peaks of roasted ducks and fowls. . . .Chinese patties of sugar and fat pork, plates full of fried silkworms. . .salt-pickled ginger and fried garlic, and a variety of other dishes beyond the ken of occidental cookery, abound. . ."[51]

As the first rays of dawn reach out from the eastern horizon, a monk removed the white hood and beeswax covering the head and eyes of the image. This act symbolizes the Buddha's enlightenment and also indicates the completion of the training and empowerment of the image itself. Coincident with these acts three small mirrors which had faced the image during the ceremony were turned outward. The mirrors represent the three superordinate knowledges achieved by the Buddha: knowledge of his former lives, knowledge of the passing away and rebirth of all beings, and knowledge of the destruction of the cause of suffering (i.e., the moral intoxicants or *āsava*).[52] Meanwhile, the monks intoned three chants: the Buddha's victory over suffering, his comprehension of the interdependent and coarising nature of reality (*paṭicca-samuppāda*), and his first teaching, Turning the Wheel of the Law Sutta (*Dhammacakkappavattana Sutta*). This final sequence of chants begins with the Auspicious Verses of the Buddha Image Consecration (*Buddha-abhiseka Maṅgala Udāna Kathā*):

> Through many a birth I wandered in *saṃsāra*,
>> Seeing, but not finding, the builder of the house.
> Sorrowful is birth again and again.
>> O house-builder! Thou art seen.
> Thou shalt build no house again. All thy rafters are broken,
>> thy ridge-pole is shattered.
> My mind has attained the unconditioned,
>> achieved is the end of craving.[53]

The image consecration ceremony not only dramatizes one of the fundamental polarities in Theravāda Buddhism but also provides insight into the meaning of the syncretic reciprocity that characterizes Theravāda merit making rituals. The polarity is between virtuous wisdom and power. The Buddha embodies wisdom and virtuous perfections (*pāramī*), but he is also endowed with supernatural powers such as the divine eye and divine ear. This polarity manifests itself in a variety of ways throughout the Buddhist tradition. For example, the Theravāda chronicles of Sri Lanka, Burma, Thailand, Laos, and Cambodia tell of numerous miraculous feats of the Buddha, among the most important being his supernatural travel to these countries, an event that prepares the way for the suzerainty of subsequent Buddhist monarchs. Yet, in seeming contrast to such miraculous stories, in other texts the Buddha cautions his followers against displays of supernatural power even as he triumphs over yogic miracle workers with his *dhamma* or teaching. In Theravāda countries such as Thailand these paradoxical qualities applied to the Buddha are embodied in the couplet, the Buddha's "power and virtue." The consecration of a Buddha image provides a particularly rich context for understanding the nature of the interrelationship between these two qualities, especially within the context of Buddhist ritual.

Let us return to the question of the intentionality behind the offerings of incense, flowers, and candles made to a Buddha image on ritual occasions. Although we do an injustice to the tradition to minimize the claim that such offerings honor the memory of the teacher-founder, the expectation of receiving some sort of boon or benefit reflects the belief that the image itself has a special power to grant the wishes of the devotee. A similar dynamic lies behind all merit making rituals. By making an offering, especially a lavish and costly one, the donor hopes to effect a reciprocal response from the power infused into the Buddha image. Knowledge of the consecration ritual gives us insight into the contextual meaning of a Buddha image and, hence, helps us to understand that virtually all Theravāda Buddhist rituals conducted in front of a Buddha image, such as the *kaṭhina* ceremony, are mechanisms of reciprocity and appropriation of power.

We now have a much better comprehension of the richly textured, multivalent nature of Theravāda Buddhist ritual. For example, the *kaṭhina* ceremony can be understood for what it literally appears to be—an annual renewal and replenishment of the clothing and other material requisites of the monastic order. Such an interpretation, however, ignores other levels of meaning that include the *sangha*'s mediatorial role between the Buddha and the laity, the special sanctity ascribed to the monastic order following the rains retreat period, and as we have seen in our analysis of the Buddha image consecration ceremony, the place of Buddha images in the reciprocal transfer and appropriation of power constitutive of merit making rituals.

Our discussion thus far has not focused on the syncretic nature of Theravāda Buddhist ritual in Southeast Asia, as such. Some rituals, like the presentation of *kaṭhina* robes may be relatively free of specific non-Buddhist elements. Others such as the image consecration ceremony traditionally include offerings to the guardians of the four quarters, the zenith, and nadir. A. K. Coomaraswamy has argued, moreover, that the ritual associated with opening the eyes of a Buddha image in Sri Lanka is fundamentally Hindu in character.[54] Other rites like those performed at such auspicious occasions as a career change, fifth cycle birthday celebration (sixty years), or a wedding (see the Rites of Passage section in this chapter) appear fundamentally animistic in nature despite the role Buddhist monks may play in the ceremony.[55] These rituals are designed to appeal to and appease protective spirits or deities (*deva*) that constitute part of an animistic or Brahmanical religious subculture rather than Theravāda Buddhism per se. The presence of Buddhist monks at these passage rites, often to chant *paritta* texts, adds to but does not negate the varied cultural meanings of the event.

Preaching the Vessantara Jātaka (*Desanā Mahājāti*)

Throughout Theravāda Southeast Asian cultures the story of Prince Vessantara (see Ideal Action) rivals in popularity that of Prince Siddhattha's journey to Buddhahood. It has been translated into the major Southeast Asian vernacular languages with minor changes in the text; virtually all monastery libraries contain one or more copies in their palm leaf manuscript collection. How can we account for the enduring popularity of this legend? Explanations might include the following: Vessantara culminates the collection of 547 canonical *jātaka* stories, the penultimate appearance of the *bodhisatta* as Prince Siddhattha; the generous prince embodies the virtue of *dāna* (giving, charity) that completes the list of ten *bodhisatta* virtues (*pāramī*) represented in the last ten *jātaka* stories; Vessantara represents not only a positive moral virtue central to the Theravāda ethical tradition but is also the paradigm of the meritorious consequence of giving, especially when generosity is directed toward the *bhikkhu sangha*. These explanations omit the possibility that the story's popularity developed, at least in part, because in many Theravāda cultures Vessantara's life came to be honored in an elaborate, ritualized preaching of the *jātaka* tale (*desanā mahājāti*). Indeed, in Northeast Thailand the *Desanā Mahājāti* has traditionally been the "grandest merit-making ceremony in the village."[56] The ceremony commemorating Prince Vessantara, not unlike the Buddha image conse-cration ritual, synthesizes the highest moral-spiritual ideals of Theravāda Buddhism with the practical theory of merit making and the consequentialist view of the efficacy of ritual action.[57]

Because we have already reviewed the general outline of the legend of Prince Vessantara's journey from the capital city of Sivi to a forest hermitage

Figure 1.11.   Lay devotees listening to the preaching of the Vessantara Jātaka. Wat Luang monastery. Pakse, Champassak Province, Laos PDR. Photo by Donald K. Swearer.

and his subsequent return and reward for his selfless generosity, we shall now look briefly at the ceremony itself. Although favorite chapters or sections of the *Vessantara Jātaka* might be preached for special occasions throughout the year, the *Desanā Mahājāti* usually occurs sometime after the end of the monastic rains retreat, a relatively slack time in the traditional village agricultural cycle between rice planting and harvest.

In northern Thailand the occasion customarily encompasses two or three days during the twelfth lunar month (early November).[58] The first day focuses on merit making on behalf of deceased teachers, parents, and other relatives. The story of Phra Malai's visit to the hells and heavens and his subsequent moral admonitions to lay devotees is traditionally preached on this day. The throngs of people crowding the monasteries to hear the sermons mill about the monastery compound, circumambulating the assembly hall (*vihāra*) and reliquary (*cetiya*). They may carry small "boats" made of banana leaves containing incense, flowers, small candles, grains of sticky rice, and a coin or two. After spending some time at the monastery they then find their way to a nearby river or pond. There, lighting the incense and candles, young and old, men and women, set their small boats afloat as an offering to the spirits of deceased relatives and friends (see the section "Festival of the Floating Boats").

The second day of the celebration focuses on preaching the *Vessantara Jātaka*. At the entrance to the monastery lay devotees construct a forest gateway from banana tree stalks. They may also demarcate a path to the assembly hall with a "royal fence" named for the mountain where Prince Vessantara had his hermitage. The pathway may be constructed in the form of a maze or labyrinth, suggesting that (1) Vessantara's selfless generosity confounds ordinary sensibilities or (2) concentration and effort are required to attain such moral perfection (*pāramī*). The pillars of the assembly hall itself will be decorated with the stalks of banana trees and sugar cane in an attempt to create the atmosphere of a forest. Thirteen scenes from the *jātaka* tale identifying each chapter are painted on the walls or will be hung as cloth banners especially for this occasion.

Beginning with the recitation of a 1,000-verse summary of the tale in Pali, monks expressly trained to chant one of the thirteen chapters of the Thai version of the *Jātaka* continue the ritual preaching of the story. Each chapter may end with a musical interlude or the preacher may punctuate his recitation with a distinctive ornamented vocalization at the beginning, middle, and end followed by a summary of that part of the text and words of homage to his teachers and the Triple Gem. This section varies according to each monk's preaching ability and is the part where he can display his own creative distinctive style. If the listeners are impressed, they may pass around a silver bowl to collect an additional offering for the monk.[59] The audience may request encores, particularly when a skilled, charismatic preacher recites the fifth chapter with its ribald description of the aged Brahman Jūjaka and his young, shrewish wife.

Each chapter of the *Jātaka* has one or more lay sponsors. They invite one of their favorite monks to preach and are responsible for preparing an appropriate donatory honorarium at the end of his chapter. These will be carried on decorated offering trays in procession through the forest gate and labyrinth pathway up to the assembly hall, sometimes to the accompaniment of drum, horn, and cymbal. The lay sponsors place their gifts before the monk while he chants a blessing. This sequence repeats itself until all thirteen chapters have been completed, a process beginning early in the morning and ending late at night. Because the story of Prince Vessantara prefigures the birth of Siddhattha Gotama, the Buddha, the third day of the *Desanā Mahājāti* ceremony may include the preaching of a Thai version of the legendary life of the Buddha (the *Pathamasambodhi*) and the Buddha's first discourse. The latter contains the most familiar doctrinal formulae of the Theravāda tradition, the Four Noble Truths and the Noble Eightfold Path.

The ritual preaching of the *Vessantara Jātaka* in northern Thailand does more than merely celebrate a popular story. It links the living and the dead, laity and monk, merit making and nibbanic ideals. Although doctrinally the rituals of Theravāda Buddhism are appropriately interpreted in terms of the metaphysics of action (*kamma*), rebirth (*saṃsāra*), and merit (*puñña*), they can also be interpreted as ways to access power in terms of reciprocal exchange and appropriation. Furthermore, in the case of the ritual consecration of Buddha images, the end of the monastic rains retreat, and in the celebration of Prince Vessantara, we encounter a curious paradox: within these ritual contexts, the surrender of worldly power by Siddhattha Gotama, Buddhist ordinands, and Prince Vessantara becomes the basis for the appropriation of power by the lay ritual participants. The operational agency of Theravāda rituals in Southeast Asia should be understood from these varying and sometimes seemingly contradictory perspectives.

FESTIVALS

The festival cycle of Theravāda Buddhism in Southeast Asia features two closely connected patterns, one seasonal, the other Buddhist. The former reflects the rhythm of the agricultural year that moves from the rainy season and the planting of paddy rice through the cool harvest season to the hot and dry fallow season. The second pattern is fashioned around a Buddhist calendar calculated in terms of seminal events in the tradition. Of particular significance are the birth, enlightenment, and death of the Buddha (*Visākhā Pūja*); the occasion of the Buddha's First Discourse (*Āsāḷahā Pūja*); and *Māgha Pūja*, the gathering of 1,250 *arahant* disciples at the Veluvana monastery where the Buddha preached the summary of his teaching. This summary concludes the *paṭimokkha* (i.e., the 227 rules of the monk's discipline): "The non-doing of evil / the full performance of what is wholesome / the total purification of the mind." These three celebrations represent the triple gem of Theravāda Buddhism; that is, the Buddha, the Dhamma, and the Sangha. Other important occasions in the religious year include the beginning and end of the monastic rains retreat period (*vassa*), and the Buddha's appearance as Prince Vessantara, the perfect exemplification of the moral perfection of charity or generosity (*dāna pāramī*). Rituals relevant to these two occasions—the giving of *kaṭhina* robes and the *Desanā Majājāti*—were discussed in the previous section.

Figure 1.12. Māgha Pūjā pilgrims. Wat Phra Thāt Doi Tung monastery. Chiang Rai Province, Thailand. Photo by Donald K. Swearer.

Scholars have observed that the religious festival calendar bears a striking articulation with the phases of nature that define the agricultural cycle.[60] We note, for example, that *Visākhā Pūja* occurs in May at the beginning of the Southeast Asian rice planting season; *Asāḷahā Pūja*, in July during the growing season; and *Māgha Pūja*, after the harvest in February. To be sure, the intertwining of the defining events of a religious tradition with the natural cyclical pattern of a community is not unique to Southeast Asian Buddhism. A similar integration is found in both Christianity and Judaism, as well as other religious traditions. For example, Christmas anticipates the dawn of a new year with longer and brighter days, and Easter signals the renewal of spring.

The New Year Festival

In the Buddhist Era lunar calendar of Theravāda Southeast Asia, the end of the hot, dry season and the onset of the monsoon rains marks the beginning of a new year. It is celebrated during the month of April (in Burma the month of Tagu) for a period of three to four days. In Thailand the New Year festival is referred to as *songkrān* (Sanskrit: *sankrānta*), signaling the change from one season to another or, in astrological terms, when the sun leaves the sign of Pisces in the zodiac and enters Aries. The celebration was probably adapted from South Indian Brahmanism to Buddhism in Sri Lanka and brought from there to mainland Southeast Asia by Buddhist monks.

It is to be expected that all New Year festivals focus on the transition from the old year to the new. Certain aspects of the celebration are based in the home. They include a special house cleaning and the purification of furnishings and clothing. Traditionally the New Year is a time to settle debts and seek forgiveness, especially from respected elders in the family and community. Water-cleansing rites and ceremonies occupy the center stage of New Year festivals. These include various activities ranging from the lustrating of Buddha images, Buddha relics, and Bodhi trees at monasteries, to paying respects to elders with a water blessing, to unrestrained water fights with buckets and hoses. A late nineteenth century observer in Mandalay provides the following description: "There is water everywhere. . . . Some zealous people go down to the river or creek, wade into the water knee-deep, and splash water at one another till they are tired. . . . No one escapes. . . . A clerk comes up to his master, [pays respects] to him, and gravely pours the contents of a silver cup down the back of his neck, saying ye-kadaw mi, 'I will do homage to you with water.' "[61]

A contemporary anthropologist suggests that water throwing during the Burmese New Year provides a socially approved mechanism to flaunt moral conventions and social distinctions: "An integral part of the frivolity is the. . .insulting remarks leveled by the water-throwers. . .at public figures: politicians, officials, businessmen, and so on. Both sexes seize this opportunity to douse each other, and the physical and verbal encounters that accompany the dousing border. . .on the obscene. In general, the clowning, the disrespect for authority, the aggression, the transvestism, the sexual banter. . .mark the urban celebration of the Water Festival. . ."[62] In the 1950s Laotian provincial governors were even occasionally pitched into the Mekong River as part of the New Year festival.

A folk legend of the Tai Lue of Yunnan, China, offers an engaging etiology of the New Year custom of throwing or sprinkling water.[63] Once upon a time, goes the tale, the region of Balanaxi in Yunnan was plagued by a ferocious devil with an enormous mouth and tongue who created fires whenever he breathed. He captured seven beautiful girls from the village and made them his wives. Yidanhan, the youngest, cleverest, and most beautiful devised a plot to avenge the catastrophes caused by the devil. After preparing a sumptuous feast for him with an abundance of whiskey she praised the now inebriated devil, "You are really great, my master. . . .You can be the conqueror of the world."[64] Drunk and flattered, the devil confided to Yidanhan that, in fact, he had a fatal weakness; if someone took a hair from his head and tightened it around his neck his head would come off and he would die. After the devil fell fast asleep, Yidanhan pulled out a hair from his head and wound it around his neck until the devil's head fell to the ground like a huge pumpkin. Unfortunately, wherever the head rolled it set everything ablaze, burning houses and crops, and killing cattle and people. Undaunted, Yidanhan grabbed the huge head while the six other women sprinkled her and the devil's head with water brought from the river. The fire was extinguished and, thereafter, the people led happy and peaceful lives: "To commemorate the seven girls who eliminated the terrible scourge from the region, the Dai people celebrate the Water-Sprinkling Festival every New Year. . . .They sprinkle water over one another, hoping thus to get rid of the sufferings and calamities of the past and to ensure favourable weather, abundant harvests and good health in the coming year."[65]

New Year's celebrations in Theravāda Buddhist Southeast Asia are particularly syncretic. In Burma the New Year marks the descent to earth of the Brahmanical god Indra (the Buddhist Sakka; Burmese: Thagya Min). He takes up residence during the last two days of the old year where he records the names of the doers of good and evil deeds. On the third day he returns to his abode in Tāvatiṃsa Heaven. Similarly, in other Theravāda countries the mythology surrounding the New Year is Brahmanical, not Buddhistic. The first two days of the celebration, furthermore, have very little to do with Buddhism. Water blessings, settling debts, paying respects to elders and so on represent the variety of ways in which the demerits or wrongdoings of the past year are eliminated.

The monastery becomes the focus of New Year activities on the third and fourth days of the celebration. In Burma, Thailand, Laos, and Cambodia lay devotees bring special food offerings to the monks early in the morning of the third day, that is, the first day of the New Year. They will observe the precepts, listen to sermons, lustrate Buddha images, and perform other meritorious acts such as freeing birds and fish often sold at the entrance to the monastery. Because of the day's auspicious character, ordinations and house dedications also may be performed. In northern Thailand men and women, young and old devote part of the day to building a sand "mountain" (*cetiya*) in the monastery compound.[66]

Figure 1.13. Celebrating Thai New Year. Lustrating Buddha images and relics. Wat Chetuphon monastery, Chiang Mai, Thailand. Photo by Donald K. Swearer.

The sand mound serves both practical and symbolic purposes. Practically, the sand can be used to level and clean the monastery compound; symbolically, the mountain represents new beginnings, reconnecting the sacred and mundane levels of existence. Northern Thai legend offers the following Buddhist interpretation of the origin of the sand mountain: In a previous existence the Buddha was a poor man who made his living gathering firewood. Even though he was poor he was very virtuous. One day while walking in the forest in search of dead tree limbs he came across a place covered with clean sand. There he built a sand mountain, put a small flag made from a torn piece of cloth on top of it, and then prayed that he might be reborn a Buddha for the benefit of all sentient beings.[67]

The New Year festival in Chiang Mai, Thailand, climaxes with the procession of the Phra Singha Buddha image through the city streets. According to legendary account, the image was made 700 years after the death of the Buddha in Sri Lanka by a *nāga* king who had seen the Buddha when the Blessed One had visited the island.[68] Perhaps because of its watery origin, devout Buddhists ascribe rain-making powers to the image; hence, in an act of sympathetic magic, the Phra Singha Buddha image is removed from the temple and processed around the city as a herald of the monsoon

Figure 1.14. Sand *cetiya* (Thai: *cedi*). Wat Wǫ Kut monastery. Chiang Tung, Shan States, Myanmar. Photo by Donald K. Swearer.

rains. In the weeks following this event, offerings are also made to the god Indra whose power is enshrined in the city pillar located on the compound of a historically prominent monastery, and a buffalo is sacrificed to the autochthonous guardian spirits of the city. In short, Buddhist celebrations associated with the beginning of the new year anticipate subsequent Brahmanical and animistic rites honoring the founding of the city.

Buddha's Day (*Visākhā Pūja*)

Within the yearly rhythm of Theravāda Buddhism as a historical tradition, *Visākhā Pūja* stands as the most sacred of all anniversary occasions for the obvious reason that it honors the life of the Buddha.[69] From the perspective of the tradition, the day itself is miraculous for on the full-moon day of the month of Visākhā (April–May) in separate years the Buddha was born, attained enlightenment, and died. In short, *Visākhā Pūja* celebrates the entire story of the Buddha from its beginning to its final conclusion. Although in countries like Thailand this triple anniversary was once celebrated for three days, at the present time only one day is set aside as a national holiday.

The manner of its observance varies among different Theravāda cultures. In Sri Lanka night processions with Vesak (i.e., *Visākhā*) lanterns mark the occasion. In Thailand and Burma evening activities also predominate. Instead of festive processions crowds of people holding lighted candles and glowing incense gather in monastery compounds to circumambulate three times around the sacred precincts and to place elaborate flower arrangements in the shape of lotus buds before the Buddha altar. The faithful then enter the assembly hall to hear a discourse on the life of the Buddha which may last most of the night. In Thailand one of the scriptures that might be preached on this night is the *Pathamasambodhi* written in twenty-nine chapters or sections. This text fills in the details of the Buddha's life story highlighted by the three events Viskāhā Pūja incorporates. Because the sights and sounds of the festival itself may divert us from the doctrinal significance of this event, we enter the assembly hall for an all-night reading of the story of Prince Siddhattha's life from his birth and enlightenment to his death and the distribution of his relics, a story in which myth, legend, and history intermingle. The following is an outline of the story:

(1) the wedding of Suddhodana and Mahāmāyā, the Buddha's parents; (2) the Buddha in Tusita heaven, beseeched by the gods to help human-kind, enters the womb of Mahāmāyā, (3) the birth of the Buddha and the miraculous appearance on the same day of his future wife, Yasodharā, his beloved disciple, Ānanda, his horse, Kanthaka, and his charioteer, Channa, and the Bodhi tree; (4) two predictions by Brahmans, one that he will become either a world ruler or a Buddha and secondly that he is destined to become fully enlightened because he possesses the thirty-two marks of the great man (*mahāpurisa*); (5) the Buddha is given the name, Siddhattha, his mother dies after seven days, Siddhattha marries Yasodharā at age sixteen; (6) the four encounters—an aged person, sick person, corpse, and mendicant—prompt the Buddha to follow the mendicant path, (7) Siddhattha follows an ascetic way for six years, e.g., abstaining from food, restraining his breath, then adopts a middle path as more appropriate to mind development; his five followers desert him; (8) Sujātā makes a food offering to the Buddha, mistaking him for a tree spirit; the offering bowl miraculously floats upstream as a sign he will become enlight-ened; the Buddha determines not to move from his seat under the Bodhi tree until he realizes his highest goal; (9) Māra and his forces attack the Buddha; he successfully wards them off by calling the Goddess

of Earth (Thai, Nang Thoraṇī) to witness on his behalf; the Goddess of Earth drowns the forces of Māra by wringing the water from her hair that she had collected every time the Buddha performed an act of virtuous generosity (*dāna*); (10) attainments immediately prior to the Buddha's enlightenment—the eight trance states, knowledge of his previous births, clairvoyance (seeing all beings as they are reborn in accordance with their *kamma*); perceiving the cycle of interdependent coarising (*paṭicca-samuppāda*); the Buddha's enlightenment; (11) the Buddha spends seven days each at seven places after his enlightenment, e.g., the Bodhi tree; the location where he reviews the Abhidhamma; the place where Mucalinda, the serpent king, protects him from the rain; the spot where Indra and the Buddha's first two lay followers make offerings to him; (12) the Buddha worries whether or not people will be able to comprehend his teaching; the gods of *brahmaloka* perceive his concern and send messengers to assure him that there are persons capable of grasping his message; (13) the Buddha teaches the First Discourse (*Dhammacakkappavattana Sutta*); (14) the five former followers of the Buddha to whom his first teaching was given become saints (*arahants*); more people become disciples; (15) the Buddha's activities in Uruvela where he converts 1,000 fire-worshipping ascetics; the Buddha impresses King Bimbisāra of Rājagaha; (16) Sāriputta and Moggallāna become followers of the Buddha; (17) Suddhodana requests that the Buddha come to Kapilavatthu; his people become the Buddha's disciples; (18) Yasodharā's sorrow over her husband's rejection of the princely role; (19) Devadatta, the Buddha's cousin, attempts to kill the Buddha and then create dissension in the Sangha; he is punished by the earth swallowing him up; (20) the Buddha predicts the coming of the future Buddha, Metteyya, and tells Ānanda that the monk with the lowest seniority will be reborn as Metteyya; (21) the Buddha visits his ill father who becomes an *arahant* before his death; an order of nuns is established on Ānanda's request but with a lower social status than the *bhikkhu sangha*; (22) the Buddha performs several miracles but forbids his disciples to do so without seeking permission; (23) the Buddha travels to Tāvatiṃsa heaven and preaches the *Abhidhamma* to his mother; (24) the Buddha descends from Tāvatiṃsa heaven on a crystal ladder provided by Indra; the Buddha ascends to the top of Mount Sineru (Meru) where he performs a miracle witnessed by everyone from the hells (*petaloka*) to the heavens (*brahmaloka*); (25) the death of Sāriputta and Moggallāna, (26) the

Figure 1.15. The Buddha's *parinibbāna*. Wat Thāt Čhǫm Doi, Chiang Tung, Shan States, Myanmar. Photo by Donald K. Swearer.

Buddha's death (*parinibbāna*); (27) the Buddha's funeral; collecting the Buddha relics; the rulers of the major petty kingdoms of northern India come to request relics; (28) Mahākassapa buries the remainder of the relics which are not unearthed until the time of Asoka who divides them among various cities in India; (29) reasons for the decline of Buddhism in India.[70]

In northern Thailand the celebration of *Visākhā* may coincide with the annual anniversary of the founding of a major temple. When this occurs, the length and extent of the festivities will be significantly increased. I witnessed one such occasion that included traditional northern Thai long drum and hot air balloon competitions as well as numerous temple processions and a lustration of the monastery's Buddha relics.[71] Such festivals become a blending of the normative events of Theravāda Buddhism, namely, the birth, enlightenment, and death of the Buddha, with non-Buddhist, culturally relative customs; hence, they celebrate both a particular Buddhist community within a given cultural and social context, and also that community's identity as part of a universal tradition stretching back over 2,500 years.

Our study of *Visākhā Pūja*, the Buddha image consecration ritual, and the *kaṭhina* ceremony complement one another. The transactional nature of the *kaṭhina* as a merit making ritual depends for its meaning on an understanding of the Buddha as a person of special power, a power embodied by the image itself. *Visākhā Pūja* demonstrates the significance of the Buddha's life story as a historical paradigm from which the Buddhist tradition takes its definition. The Buddha story is a constant referent for the tradition. Neither the Buddha's teaching (*dhamma*) nor his power can be abstracted from his person. For Theravāda Buddhism, his person is revealed in the episodic history of a text like the *Pathamasambodhi* rather than in metaphysical claims about the Buddha's absolute and universal nature.

Festival of the Floating Boats (*Loi Krathong*)

Religious festivals serve many functions, some more central than others to the so-called great religious tradition within a given culture. Whereas *Visākhā Pūja* provides an example of a celebration close to the core of Theravāda Buddhism in Southeast Asia, the Festival of Lights or the Festival of the Floating Boats[72] (Thai: *loi krathong*) has little to do with Buddhism as a doctrinal system. Although the Festival of Lights seems animistic or Brahmanical in nature, it has become at least partially assimilated into the Theravāda Buddhist cultural traditions of countries in Southeast Asia.

Loi Krathong is celebrated on the full moon day of November, one month after the end of the monastic rains retreat (*vassa*). As we have seen, in many parts of Thailand the celebration traditionally coincides with a specifically Buddhist ceremony, the preaching of the *Vessantara Jātaka*, the Buddha's last existence before his rebirth as Siddhattha Gotama. By this time the rainy season has come to an end, the rice crops have been planted, and the temperature turns pleasantly cool in the evenings. The farmers have more than a month before the rice is harvested. During this season of maturing crops and moderate climate, people traditionally take time to enjoy themselves at the Festival of the Floating Boats. The celebration is a very simple one with no apparent connection to either Buddhistic or Brahmanical ritual. Small boats are made either from natural materials like banana stalks and leaves or, in recent years, from polystyrene foam and crepe paper, and are floated on rivers or ponds. Lighted candles, incense, and coins of small denominations will be placed on the boats. Everyone participates, elders watching the bobbing lights on the water and the children often swimming out to retrieve the most beautiful *krathongs* (leaf cup) or the coins that might be found on them. Couples picnic nearby and young and old alike enjoy fireworks. In northern Thailand houses may be decorated and in the provincial capital city of Chiang Mai the *Loi Krathong* festival has become a major tourist event including a parade of large floats through the city.

The historical roots and meaning of *Loi Krathong* are ambiguous. It may derive from the Indian festival of lights, *dīpavali*, or from a traditional Chinese custom of floating lotus flower lamps to guide the spirits of people drowned in rivers and lakes. The earliest evidence of the celebration in Thailand comes from the Sukhothai period when the second queen of King Phra Ru'ang (circa 1300 C.E), the daughter of a Brahman family attached to the court, began the custom to please the king. Such an explanation suggests an Indian Brahmanical origin for *Loi Krathong*. Two Buddhist explanations of a mythological nature have been advanced: that the *krathongs* carry offerings to the Buddha's footprint on the sandy shore of the Nammada River in the Deccan by the king of the *nāga* (serpents) who wanted to worship the Lord after his death;[73] or that the river festival is an expression of gratitude to Phra Upagutta who as a *nāga* foiled Māra's attempt to destroy the 84,000 *cetiyas* built by King Asoka.[74] Although these two etiologies differ, they both point to the popular devotionalism that characterizes much of lay Theravāda Buddhist practice in Southeast Asia.

In northern Thailand a historical explanation for the origin of *Loi Krathong* prevails. During the reign of King Kamala of Haripuñjaya in the tenth century C.E. (modern day Lamphun, twenty-six kilometers to the south of Chiang Mai), a severe cholera epidemic forced the populace to evacuate the city. Eventually they found their way to present day Pegu in Burma, where they stayed for six years until the epidemic subsided. After the majority of the people returned to Haripuñjaya they sent gifts of food and clothing down the river to their relatives who remained in Pegu.[75] The festival of *Loi Krathong* celebrates this event, or we might say that it becomes an annual offering to the spirits of departed ancestors. Another explanation is that the *krathongs* are offerings to the Goddess of the *Mae Khongkhā* (i.e., Ganges), the Mother of Waters.[76]

Whatever the historical explanation of the festival of *Loi Krathong*, it remains one of the most picturesque celebrations in Thailand. To be sure, its connections with doctrinal Theravāda Buddhism in Southeast Asia are tenuous. Buddhist rationalizations have been provided for it, and where Buddhist temples are located near rivers, people take their leaf boats into the temple compound to be blessed or to circumambulate the sacred precincts before placing the *krathong* in the water; however, *Loi Krathong* represents one of those festivals that defies ready identification as "Buddhist." Perhaps for this reason both in the past and at the present time some Thai Buddhist monasteries choose this night to preach the *Vessantara Jātaka*, thereby appropriating this celebratory occasion for their own purposes.

RITES OF PASSAGE

Buddhism in Southeast Asia has not only integrated into its own sacred history a community's seasonal, agricultural rhythm, but has marked and celebrated important junctures in the life cycle of the individual as well. These life passage rituals integrate various cultural elements. Birth rites have traditionally had little or no connection with Theravāda Buddhism[77] but adolescent, early adulthood, old age, and death rites have been assimilated into a Buddhist scheme of life passage or transition rituals. Male adolescent or puberty initiatory rites take the form of temporary ordination into the monastic order (*sangha*); in some Theravāda societies, such as Burma, ear boring rituals may be held for girls at the same time; marriage constitutes a major young adult passage rite in which Buddhist monks may play a minor role, primarily to chant *suttas* for the protection and well-being of the couple or to preach a sermon and act as recipients of merit making gifts. Buddhism has been especially associated with death rites or funeral observances throughout greater Asia.

Life passage rites are open to several interpretations: to ensure safe transition to another stage of life; to integrate the life cycle of the individual into the ongoing life pattern of the community; to place the individual within a cosmological structure governed by various unseen and relatively unpredictable powers (e.g., *kamma, čhao, phī, nat*); or to relate the life of the individual and the community to the ethical and spiritual teachings of Buddhism. The remainder of this section will examine the rituals associated with four life passage periods: adolescence, young adulthood, aging, and death. We shall focus on the first and the last of these two rites, novitiate ordination and the funeral ceremony. Regarding the latter S. J. Tambiah observed, "In no other rites of passage. . . is Buddhism so directly concerned with a human event."[78]

Joining the *Sangha*

Ordination into the Theravāda Buddhist monkhood can be interpreted on a variety of levels. From a doctrinal perspective, the monk is a "religious virtuoso"; that is, in seeking ordination monks commit themselves to a lifetime pursuit of the highest goal in Buddhism, *nibbāna*, within the context of the monastic order. The Pali term *bhikkhu/bhikkhunī*[79] means one who gives up ordinary pursuits of livelihood for a higher goal to become a mendicant or "almsperson." Monks' alms seeking "is not just a means of subsistence, but an outward token that. . .[they] have renounced the world and all its goods and have thrown. . .[themselves] for bare living on the chances of public charity."[80] The *Dhammapāda*, probably the best known of all the Theravāda texts characterizes the doctrinal ideal of the monk as follows: "the true monk is one whose senses are restrained and who is controlled in body and speech; he is contented with what he receives, is not envious of others and has no thought of himself. Such selflessness is rooted in the Buddha's truth (*dhamma*), and the monk who dwells in and meditates on the *dhamma* is firmly established in the Truth (*saddhamma*). Such a being is suffused with loving kindness (*mettā*), possesses the cardinal virtues, is refined in conduct, and is filled with a transcendental joy. Confident in the Buddha's teachings, having attained peace and supreme bliss, the monk 'illumines this world like the moon from a cloud.' "[81]

In short, ideal monks are those who seek and attain the truth. Having reached this goal they become morally and spiritually transformed, irradiating the Buddha's *dhamma* for the benefit of humankind.

In all Theravāda countries meditation monasteries maintain an environment of peaceful tranquility where men and women pursue the Buddhist ideal of *nibbāna*: the overcoming of suffering, the attainment of equanimity, and insight into the true nature of reality. Although some enter the monastery to seek *nibbāna*, others fall short of this ideal. Melford Spiro analyzed Burmese men's reasons for entering the monkhood into three conscious types—religious motives, the desire to escape the difficulties and miseries of human life, the wish to obtain an easier living[82]—and three unconscious motives—dependency, narcissism, and emotional timidity.[83] Other, somewhat more socially descriptive reasons for entering the monastery include acquiring an education, achieving a higher social status, a response to social custom and pressure, and repayment of a filial debt, especially to one's mother. Before analyzing the ordination ceremony itself, we shall briefly examine some of these motives.

In Burma, Thailand, Laos, and Cambodia monastic tenure varies greatly in length, depending upon the motivation for ordination. Unlike the norm in Western Christianity, becoming a monk may not involve a lifetime commitment, although many noted meditation teachers and scholar-monks may spend their adult life in robes.

In Thailand one of the principal reasons for being ordained is to acquire an education.[84] Among poorer families often children cannot afford to attend school. Ordination as a novice provides for their material needs as well as a basic education. Indeed, if a boy is bright and highly motivated he may complete secondary school as a novice or a monk, graduate from a monastic college, and then earn an advanced degree from a university in another country, such as India. After teaching in a monastery school for several years or serving as an administrator in a larger provincial monastery he will probably disrobe and take a responsible and respected secular job. Although such exploitation of the monastic educational structure siphons off able leadership, it has become standard practice and bears little or no social stigma.

Undoubtedly this pattern of being educated in monastic schools only to leave the order reflects an earlier practice where a young man would be ordained as a novice near the age of puberty, remain in the monastery for one or more years, and then return to lay society.[85] During this period he would receive a rudimentary education, learn the fundamentals of Buddhism, and prepare to lead a responsible life as a lay Buddhist supporter of the monastic order. This particular pattern, still followed in some areas of Southeast Asia, resembles a rite of passage into adulthood. In this sense, the Western parallel to ordination as a Buddhist novice, customarily between the ages of twelve and nineteen, is the rite of confirmation in the Christian tradition and bar and bas mitzvah in the Jewish. Traditionally these ceremonies symbolize full participation in their respective religio-social communities, just as having been ordained a Buddhist monk is considered an essential stage in the passage to mature male adulthood in Thai, Lao, Burmese, or Cambodian society and culture.

The monk takes a vow of celibacy and is expected to minimize material attachments, however, ordinarily monastic tenure does not involve excessive ascetic practice. Theravāda Buddhism in Southeast Asia consistently upholds the time-honored tradition of the Middle Way. In practice, the monk lives a reasonably comfortable life and occupies a respected status in the community. For children of poorer families, in particular, becoming a monk represents a definite improvement in social, and often economic status. For this reason it is not surprising to find that the majority of Theravāda monks in Southeast Asia do, in fact, come from backgrounds of modest means. For instance, at the two monastic colleges in Bangkok, a high percentage of the students were born in northeastern Thailand, the most economically disadvantaged region of the country.

Finally, it should be noted that ordination is perceived as a way of repaying a debt to one's parents, especially one's mother.[86] That one has come into the world, survived infancy, and become a youth results primarily from her care. Within the calculus of meritorious action (*puñña*), one's ordination gains a spiritual benefit for one's parents. The mutual reciprocity characterizing merit making rituals thus becomes part of ordination into the monastic order. A young man survives infancy due to the material benefits provided by his mother and father, by being ordained he returns to them a spiritual boon.

A village ordination in northern Thailand will customarily be held for one or two days and consists of two parts. The first is an animistic ceremony called propitiating the spirits or calling the spirits; the second is ordination into the novitiate (*pabbajjā*) or, if the candidate is twenty or older, "higher" ordination (*upasampadā*). The first part of the ceremony may be held in the ordinand's home and will be the occasion for villagewide festivities with as much feasting, drinking, and general merrymaking as the young man's family can afford. The spirit-calling ceremony is conducted by a layman who performs similar roles at weddings, house dedications, and other auspicious or crisis occasions. His earlier life as an ordained monk has prepared him for learning the protocols for these rituals as well as the methods of chanting and preaching. His ritual role differs from that of the monk but rivals it in importance. He often functions as a ritual mediator between the *sangha* and the laity.[87]

During the ceremony the lay leader performs a ritual in which he "calls" the ordinand's thirty-two spirits (Thai: *khwan*) away from all previous attachment to the pleasures of lay life so the youth will be unswayed and undivided in his pursuit of the monastic life, especially the trials of celibacy. To attract the *khwan* a special offering bowl is prepared. It may be a relatively simple food offering in a lacquer bowl or a much more elaborate symbolic reconstruction of a cosmic tree symbolizing an axial connection between the human and spirit realms. At the conclusion of the ritual, a sacred thread is then tied around the wrists of the ordinand representing the tying of the *khwan* into his body after they have been "called."

Before the spirit-calling ritual begins, the ordinand will be properly prepared for his ordination. His monastic instructor will shave his head and clothe him in a white robe. These acts symbolize the liminality of this life passage ritual, a transition from householder to monk, a neutering of

Figure 1.16. Novitiate ordination. Young boy dressed as Prince Siddhattha. Wat Yang Khuang monastery, Chiang Tung, Shan States, Myanmar. Photo by Donald K. Swearer.

one's previous identity prior to beginning a new life with a new monastic name. They also represent the monk's disregard for the things of this world, including the vanities of personal appearance. At the conclusion of the spirit-calling ritual, the ordinand, his family, friends, and well-wishers form a procession to the monastery compound. In some instances, the young man will be dressed as Prince Siddhattha and will ride a horse to the monastery reenacting the great renunciation of the Lord Buddha. The procession circles the ordination hall (*uposatha*) three times. Before entering it the ordinand bows before the boundary stone (*sīmā*) at the front entrance, invoking the Buddha to forgive his sins and to grant him blessings. The sacrality of the ordination hall and, hence, the significance of the ordination ceremony, is indicated by the nine boundary stones buried in the ground marking its center and the eight directional points around its perimeter.

Entering the hall, one of the ordinand's friends may play the role of the tempter Māra, pretending to prevent his entrance, or the ordinand may fling a last handful of coins to the well-wishers who have followed him. He approaches the chapter of ten monks seated on the floor in a semicircle in front of a large Buddha image resting on a raised altar at the far end. Bowing to the floor three times before his preceptor (*upajjhāya*), a senior monk who will conduct the ordination ceremony, the ordinand presents to him gifts of candles, incense, and robes. Professing the Buddha, his teaching (*dhamma*), and the monastic order (*sangha*) to be his refuge, he requests permission three times to enter "the priesthood in the Vinaya-Dhamma of the Blessed One."[88] The preceptor receives the robes, instructs the ordinand in the Three Gems (i.e., Buddha, *dhamma*, and *sangha*), and meditates on the impermanence of the five aggregates of bodily existence until another monk designated as the young man's instructor (*ācariya*), formally instructs him in the Ten Precepts upheld by all monastic novices: to refrain from taking life, stealing, sexual intercourse, lying, intoxicants, eating at forbidden times, entertainments, bodily adornments, sleeping on comfortable beds, and receiving money. Having taken the precepts, once again the ordinand approaches the preceptor. Now he is assigned to a senior monk as an instructor and given a Pali name. The instructor hangs his begging bowl over his left shoulder, has the young man identify his bowl and three monastic robes, and then questions him on behalf of the entire chapter. His formal queries include "Do you have leprosy?" "Are you a human?" "Are you free of debt?" "Do you have permission from your parents?" Finding him free of impediments, the instructor then presents the ordinand to the *sangha*, requesting that they admit him into the monastic order. Acknowledging their consent by a collective silence, the assembled monks receive the young man into the order as a novice. The ceremony concludes with the preceptor instructing him in the responsibilites of being a monk.[89]

Among the Southeast Asian Theravāda Buddhist countries, only Burma affords a parallel adolescent life passage ritual for women. The *shinbyu* ceremony includes not only young boys being ordained into the monastic novitiate for a temporary period, but adolescent girls as well. An all day *shinbyu* I witnessed in Mandalay in 1990 included a morning devoted to entertainment. Men, women, and children crowd into a pavillion constructed to resemble a palace. Over a dozen boys and girls dressed in costumes of princes and princesses sit on a center stage watching several storytellers and mimes entertain the audience. At the conclusion of the entertainment the girls' ears are pierced and the boys' heads are shaved. Afterwards the boys take the vows of a novice monk. Pierced ears symbolize entrance into adult female roles; temporary novitiate ordination represents a similar preparation for a young boy to assume an adult male role in society. Only in Burma do these adolescent life passage rites include both sexes.

Can women in Theravāda Buddhist cultures enter the monastic order and pursue the same spiritual quest as men? The answer is complex.[90] As texts such as the *Therīgathā* (*Songs of the Nuns*) indicate, from a doctrinal perspective both women and men may attain the goal of *nibbāna*. Historically, however, the rules of discipline make clear that the order of women monks is subordinate to that of men. Furthermore, the order of nuns (*bhikkhunī*) endured in India only until circa 456 C.E. and the order may never have reached mainland Southeast Asia.[91] Today orders of renunciant women flourish in Southeast Asia, although technically they are not *bhikkhunī*.[92] In comparison to Thailand, Laos, and Cambodia, women renunciants in Burma enjoy a higher social and spiritual status. Referred to in Burmese as *thilashin*, ("one who bears the burden of *sīla* or virtue"), they manage their own monasteries and pursue higher Buddhist studies including Pali. Like male monks, the *thilashin* may collect morning alms donations (*piṇḍapāta*) and may also undergo temporary novitiate ordination similar to their male counterparts. These two practices indicate that in Burma female as well as male renunciants are perceived to represent a religious field of merit. That *thilashin* enjoy a relatively high social and spiritual status is reflected in the participation of girls in the Burmese *shinbyu*. That is, women in Burma have more opportunities to participate in religio-cultural institutions and practices from which they are virtually excluded in Thailand, Laos, and Cambodia.

The ordination ceremony provides an extraordinary opportunity to understand the richness of Theravāda Buddhism as a cultural institution in its Southeast Asian context. Doctrinally, it represents the highest ideals of the tradition; symbolically, it offers a reenactment of the most dramatic event of the Buddha's life narrative; structurally, it illustrates the threshold transition fundamental to the meaning of rites of passage; anthropologically, it provides evidence for the syncretic nature of Southeast Asian Buddhism even in its most essential expressions.

Weddings and Aging Ceremonies

Whereas adolescent life passage rituals mark a youth's entrance into adulthood, marriage signals the beginning of a new adult stage of life, one in which young men and women assume responsibility for a family and broader social obligations within their community. In all cultures weddings mark a crucial transitional stage in the lives of individuals, families, and communities. A decline in religiously based wedding rituals raises questions not only about the waning role of religion in defining cultural identity but also suggests profound changes in the way individuals perceive themselves in relationship to communities. One of the challenges of our own day is the creation of rites of passage symbolizing the assumption of adult responsibilities for the maintenance of communities that reflect social realities.

From a doctrinal or normative perspective, the Buddhist *sangha* has little to do with weddings and aging rites, the latter being a ritual marking the sixtieth birthday or end of the fifth astrological cycle (one cycle equals twelve years). As Sir James Scott observed in regard to nineteenth century Burmese wedding customs, "The ritual is very simple and has nothing whatever of a religious character about it; in fact the celibate *pongyis* [monks] would be grossly scandalised if they were asked to take any part in it."[93] Scott's observation fails to take into account the animistic religious dimensions of marriage rites and the fact that today Theravāda monks may be invited to participate in wedding ceremonies. From a historical perspective one can justifiably argue that the presence of monks at a marriage rite reflects the influence of Western Christian custom; however, as we shall see, the Theravāda tradition legitimates such a practice on its own terms. The following descriptions of a wedding and an "entering old age" rite rely on observations of ceremonies in Lamphun Province, northern Thailand, in the 1970s and 1980s. Customs in other regions of Theravāda Southeast Asia may differ.

As a religious ritual, a traditional Thai wedding reflects both animistic and Brahmanical influences. Traditionally village weddings are usually held in the home of the bride. The day is one of celebration and feasting, often straining the financial means of the couple's families. The main ritual officiant is a layman called a "spirit doctor" (Thai, *mǫ riak khwan*) or one who calls the spirits. In addition, monks may also be invited to participate.

The wedding is usually held in the morning, especially when monks are invited. The day begins early in the morning with the preparation of the wedding feast. Gradually relatives, friends and guests arrive filling the central room of the house. About 10 A.M. a group of five, seven, or nine monks arrive and take their place along the outside wall next to a carved, gilded altar on which a single, crystal Buddha image has been enshrined. A white cord extends from the image to a silver bowl in which are placed offerings for the spirits of the bride and groom: two eggs, two balls of sticky rice, two bananas, two small glasses of rice wine. The lay officiant leads those assembled in paying respects to the Buddha, Dhamma, and Sangha and taking the five precepts. He then requests the monks to chant the *paritta*. For a wedding, monks often chant the *Maṅgala Sutta* and the *Mettā Sutta*, two of the most widely used *paritta*. The following selections from the *Maṅgala Sutta* illustrate its appropriateness for such an occasion in a traditional Buddhist culture. In the text some of the responses to the question what constitutes the highest "blessings" (*maṅgala*) are:

> Not to associate with the foolish, but to associate with the wise.
> To reside in a suitable locality. . .and to set oneself in the right direction.
> Vast learning, skill in handicraft, well-grounded in discipline, pleasant speech.
> To support one's father and mother, to cherish one's wife and children, and to be engaged in peaceful occupations.
> Liberality, righteous conduct, rendering assistance to relatives.
> To cease and abstain from evil, to abstain from intoxicating drinks, being diligent in performing righteous acts.
> Reverence, humility, contentment, gratitude, and the timely hearing of the teaching of the Buddha.
> Patience, obedience, meeting with holy monks for discussions.
> Self-control, chastity, comprehension of the Noble Truths, and the realization of Nibbāna.[94]

Following the *paritta* the lay officiant then offers a lengthy sermon, speaking in a colorful, charismatic style, his vocal cadence moving between high falsetto and low resonant pitches. His speech incorporates many different elements: calling the spirits, a lesson in Buddhist morality, humor. He cajoles the spirits away from previous romantic attachments, enticing them by his artful vocal skills and by the offerings prepared for them. At the conclusion of the sermon the officiant takes a piece of the string extending from the Buddha altar to the offering bowl and ties it around the wrists of the bride and the groom. Relatives and honored guests follow suit. Whereas we might interpret this act as an unusual cultural expression of "tying the knot," within the animistic context of his northern Thai ritual it represents emplanting the spiritual elements of the wedded couple into their bodies. That is, calling the spirits represents the union of the bride and groom on both spiritual and physical planes. The participation of relatives and friends in this act of "tying the spirits" emphasizes the communal significance of marriage.

The ceremony ends with the presentation of food offerings and other appropriate gifts to the monks, who then depart. In the case of a wedding, the meritorious transaction represented by this offering supplements and thereby reinforces the spirit calling rite as a means to ensure the success and well-being of the new family. With the formal portion of the ceremony completed, the wedding festivities begin. After an elaborate lunch, guests spend the remainder of the afternoon meeting old friends who returned for the wedding, gossiping, and wandering in and out of the compound of the bride's parents' house where the ceremony took place. Evening festivities might include another elaborate meal, music played by a local northern Thai orchestra, and general merrymaking. About 9:00 P.M. the couple are led by grandparents, aunts and uncles to the bedroom where they will spend the night. Along their path from the outside of the house up the stairs to the bedroom young boys and girls attempt to obstruct their progress. Only by distributing gifts of small coins and sweets are the bride and groom allowed to proceed on their way. Because the festivities may continue for several hours, the newly married couple has virtually none of the romantic privacy we associate with a honeymoon.

Like a wedding ceremony, an aging ritual or sixtieth birthday celebration incorporates both Buddhist and animistic elements to ensure blessings in this life, in this instance, a long and healthy old age. In the northern Thai cultural context, the ritual marking old age is called a life-extension or life-enhancement (Thai: *su'bchatā*) ritual.[95] *Su'bchatā* rites may be held on behalf of an individual, a family, or a community for the general purposes of warding off evil and engendering good luck, prosperity, and a long life. In addition to being a ritual marking the end of the fifth life cycle, the *su'bchatā* may be performed to cure an illness, to escape from bad luck predicted by a fortune teller, to bless a new home, to celebrate a monk's elevation in rank, or to protect a village from natural disaster.

At the fifth cycle birthday ritual the celebrant sits beneath a tripod constructed of stalks of bamboo placed in front of a Buddha altar. A white cord extending from a Buddha image is tied to the bamboo tripod and wrapped three times around the head of the celebrant. A candle the height of the celebrant stands to one side of the altar. At the base of each leg of the tripod are placed sugar cane, coconuts, bananas, clay pots filled with water, and trays heaped with various food offerings each numbering 108. These include sticky rice, betel nuts, husked and unhusked rice. Behind the celebrant stands a treelike structure made out of a bamboo stalk adorned with sixty small flags.

Together these objects create a sacred space, an axial locus of power uniting the celebrant with various levels of divine and cosmic powers. The sacred number 108 symbolizes the sum of the power valencies of the basic constituents of the cosmos—earth, water, fire, air—and also the numerical sum of the equally potent spiritual power of the Buddha, his teaching (*dhamma*), and the monastic order (*sangha*).[96] The celebrant begins the ceremony by first lighting small candles on the Buddha altar and then a large candle the height of the celebrant. In doing so he or she not only announces the beginning of the ceremony but activates all the divine and spiritual powers in the universe. As the celebrant sits in the middle of this ritually constructed center of the world, the monks chant *paritta* or protection *suttas*, thereby empowering the celebrant with the power of the Buddha and his teachings as well as the potency of all the *devatā* (divine beings). After the monks have chanted for approximately an hour, they are presented food for their noon meal. The blessing they chant after their meal concludes the formal part of the ceremony. A generous luncheon for all of the guests concludes the festivities.

Funeral Rites

Entrance into the monastic order represents a passage into an altered mode of being, ideally one dedicated to the pursuit of a goal that will free the monk from the power of determinative actions (*kamma*) and subsequent rebirth (*saṃsāra*) and the generally unsatisfactory condition (*dukkha*) of mundane (*lokiya*) existence. Marriage and old age rituals reaffirm individuals within the life of a community at times of major personal and social transition.

Death signals another kind of passage, one fraught with ambiguity for the deceased as well as for the living. Consequently, death is marked by rites that assure the survivors of their own well-being as well as for the benefit of the departed.[97] To modern Western eyes a traditional funeral rite in Southeast Asia may appear unusually festive. One must keep in mind, however, that the funeral not only honors the deceased and mourns his or her loss but also affirms the continued existence of the family and the community and of the deceased in a new life. Funerals then not only acknowledge the fact of death; they also celebrate life.

Figure 1.17. Monks chanting before a funeral casket. Lamphun Province, Thailand. Photo by Donald K. Swearer.

Funerary rites in Theravāda Buddhist Southeast Asia may be held in the home or at the temple and will vary in many details depending on the type and circumstances of death (from old age or accident), the status of the deceased (rich or poor, lay or ordained), and the local customs of a particular area. The main ritual officiants will be Buddhist monks; the ritual chants will be from such highly revered Buddhist texts as the *Abhidhamma* ("higher teaching"); and the traditional funeral sermon will deal with the themes of punishment and reward, the impermanence of life (*anicca*), and the ultimate goal (*nibbāna*) beyond the duality of life and death. The rites themselves, however, incorporate many animistic elements designed to dispel the threatening powers of evil associated with death and are even more thoroughly syncretic than the ordination ceremony.

Several good descriptions of Buddhist funerals in Southeast Asia are available.[98] The following account is based on my own observations of funerals in central and northern Thailand as well as several ethnographies.[99] Near the moment of death Buddhist *mantras* may be whispered into the ear of the dying, possibly *"Buddho"* or the four syllables symbolizing the structure of the *Abhidhamma—ci, ce, ru,* and *ni* (mind, mental concepts, body, and *nibbāna*)—or written on a piece of paper and put into the deceased's mouth.[100] At death there may be an extended period of loud wailing, in part to announce to the village community that a death has occurred. After removing the deceased's clothes the body will be washed. This can be interpreted as cleansing the soul in preparation for its passage to heaven. The hands will be clasped together over the chest and a thread will be passed three times around the hands, toes, and neck symbolizing the bonds of passion, anger, and ignorance. Before cremation these will be removed representing the release from these bonds by the power of charity, kindheartedness, and meditation.[101]

Several items are placed at the head of the corpse. These may include food and water for the person's spirit to eat and drink, a kerosene lamp to light its way to the other world, and a three-tailed white flag representing the Three Gems. Flowers and incense are put in the deceased's hands. Traditionally offered before Buddha images they represent the Buddha's teachings. Finally, a coin may be put in the corpse's mouth or a small set of silver and golden flags placed near the body to pay the demons who demand payment for not obstructing the soul's journey to heaven.

After the body is put in a coffin the cremation may take place immediately or be deferred a week or even longer depending on such circumstances as the availability of time, return of relatives from long distances, and so on. In the case of distinguished monks the period between death and cremation may extend up to a year. The coffin, itself, will be made from plain wood planks. The three forming the bottom are said to represent the three levels of the Buddhist cosmology: the realm of desire, form, and the formless realm. When the coffin is taken from the house, the head will be pointed to the west, the direction of death, symbolizing the reversal of life by death.[102] Often a new set of temporary stairs will be set up at a different part of the house. The coffin will then be taken down these stairs, and spun around several times on the way to the pyre to disorient the spirit. Customarily the temporary stairs will have only three steps representing the tripartite cosmological structure of Theravāda Buddhism.[103] When the temporary stairs have been removed and the body cremated, it is hoped that the now freed spirit will reach *nibbāna*.

The days between the actual death and the funeral and cremation are ones of busy activity. In the case of a normal death of a moderately well-to-do villager, the family of the deceased is joined by relatives and friends to prepare for evening festivities. Local orchestras entertain guests, and there will be extraordinary feasting, drinking, and even gambling. During the day monks are invited to the home for funeral chants, and gifts will be presented to them to earn merit for the deceased. Although the noisy evening activities may be interpreted as a means of encouragement against the dead person's ghost, their primary function appears to be a reenforcement of community solidarity and integration in the face of the threat of death.

On the day of the funeral, selected for its auspicious signs for the deceased, the coffin is taken in procession from the home to the temple or to the cremation grounds. The size and extent of the procession varies according to the wealth and status of the deceased. I witnessed a funeral procession in Chiang Mai, northern Thailand, of a distinguished abbot whose coffin was borne on an elaborate funeral car in the form of a mythological elephant-bird in a procession in which thousands of people wound their way through the streets of the city. For this event distinguished monks from various regions of the country were invited and 108 young men were ordained as novices as an act of merit making.

Prior to a cremation a final preaching service will be held, the monks will chant, and a sermon will be delivered. A typical rural northern Thai sermon might include remarks such as the following recorded by Konrad Kingshill at the village of Ku Daeng near the city of Chiang Mai:

Dear friends, I was invited to deliver a speech to you who are attending this merit-making for the dead Mr. Khiow. A good Buddhist presents his guests with two things, good food and accommodations and a sermon by a priest to take back home with them. Today I will preach to you about death.

Death is a common event that will come to everyone without exception. Nobody can live forever, but everybody must die sooner or later. Some people say that a dead person is only trouble to his relatives and friends who stay behind. Dead animals are more useful to us than dead people because we can use their hide, bones, and meat. The only things left by a dead person are his good deeds, which we can remember.

We go to the funeral of a dead person just as if we were going to see off a good friend when he is leaving for another country. Now we have come to see Mr. Khiow off to another world. We do not like to see him go, but when his time came he had to leave. Nobody could stop him, all we are able to do is to make merit and transfer merit to him. . . .

Everybody must remember that we all have to die, not only the person whose funeral we are attending today. Before death comes we must prepare ourselves for it. The Lord Buddha did not cry when death was approaching because he knew the meaning of death. We cry when we see death because we do not have the knowledge of a Buddha.

The Lord Buddha said, "Death is the change of the name and the body of a spirit from one form to another." Nothing in the world, even life or matter, can vanish; it only changes.

To the question where the spirit of a dead person goes, we can say that it is reborn. In Buddhism we say that a person with an unclean spirit of covetousness, anger, and ill temper will be reborn again, but he who has a clean spirit will go straight to Nibbana. The Lord Buddha had a clean spirit; so after his death, his spirit went straight to Nibbana without being reborn again. . . .

I cannot speak any longer because I have already taken a long time. Before ending, I shall suggest again that death is not a strange event; it does not belong to any particular person, but to all of us. We will die when our time comes, the time being scheduled by. . . [Mara], who is the chief of death.

If I should receive any merit for this preaching, I beg to dedicate it to Mr. Khiow. I ask that this merit may help and support him in the right place, or give him a chance to be reborn in a good place. If his spirit should still be wandering around some place, because of his attachment to his family or his property, I beg that this merit lead him from these earthly attachments to some other place.

Finally, I beg for the blessings of the Lord Buddha to come upon you and bring you long life, a light complexion, happiness, and good health.[104]

The cremation itself may take several forms: the wooden coffin may be burned on a pyre of wood; the coffin and funeral car may be burned through an elaborate process of igniting rockets and firecrackers; or the coffin may be burned in a crematorium. Prior to the cremation, the monks attending the funeral approach the coffin and remove sets of robes that lay donors have placed on it to earn special merit for the deceased. While picking up the robes the monks chant the following Pali stanza:

All conditioned things are impermanent;
Their nature is to arise and decay.
Having arisen they cease;
In their stilling is happiness. (*Dīgha Nikāya. Sutta* 16)

Numerous elements comprise the funeral rite in Southeast Asian cultures. Although the ceremony is conducted by Buddhist monks, much that takes place and the interpretations given vary considerably from such fundamental Theravāda doctrines as not-self (*anattā*). In particular, the spirit or soul (*viññāṇa*) of the deceased is perceived as a powerful agent that must be treated properly in a ritual sense to ensure its future well-being and avoid retribution on the surviving family and friends. In Buddhist terms this orientation makes the funeral a significant merit making event for both the deceased and the living. Merit making and protective magic complement one another in mortuary rites. Death rites, futhermore, celebrate the continuance of a social group—family, community, village—thereby mitigating the threat of death to social cohesion and solidarity.

In this chapter we have examined selected facets of Buddhism and society in Southeast Asia on the level of popular belief and practice. We explored the centrality of paradigmatic tales as the medium for conveying the normative values of the tradition. We also studied rituals, festivals and rites of passage from three varied perspectives: as examples of the syncretic nature of popular Buddhism, as contexts for merit making and the appropriation of sacred power, and as expressions of the way in which the people of Theravāda Southeast Asian cultures ascribe meaning to their lives through the ritualization of Buddhist history, the natural cycles of an agricultural community, and the life transitions of individuals. Theravāda Buddhism in Southeast Asia is truly complex, defying simple definitions and characterizations. It uplifts a nibbanically defined master narrative pursued by monk meditators living in tranquil, forested retreats; but, as we have seen, the story of Theravāda Buddhism in Sri Lanka and Southeast Asia is a richly nuanced epic tale with many subplots.

TWO

Buddhism as Civil Religion

Political Legitimation and
National Integration

In this chapter we turn our attention to a different context: the classical Southeast Asian monarchy and the modern Southeast Asian nation-state. We shift from the themes of ritual, festival, and rites of passage to the arena of myth and history: King Asoka as the paradigmatic Buddhist ruler, the symbiotic relationship between Southeast Asian kingship and sacred cosmology, and the Buddha as cosmocrator (i.e., one who establishes the order of the world, who empowers it or makes it sacred). We conclude the chapter with an examination of the rise of charismatic Buddhist political leaders in the postcolonial period. Resources for this subject include the traditional Theravāda Buddhist chronicles of Sri Lanka, Burma, and Thailand, archaeological evidence from the great classical sites of Angkor (Cambodia), Pagan (Burma) and Sukhothai (Thailand) under the influence of Hinduism and Buddhism, and modern historical sources including the work of historians of religion and anthropologists.[1]

Although Max Weber, acknowledged as the founder of the sociology of religion, described early Buddhism as an otherworldly mysticism, the Pali texts of Theravāda Buddhism portray a close relationship between the Buddha and the reigning monarchs of his day in northern India. To be sure, such a depiction was in the material self-interest of a growing Buddhist monastic order (*sangha*) and might, therefore, reflect the actual conditions of a subsequent era. Nevertheless, it is reasonable to assume that early in its existence the Buddhist *sangha* was supported by social, economic, and political elites for social and political as well as religious reasons. It is noteworthy, in passing, that Prince Siddhattha came from the ruling (*khattiya*) class, and legend has it that his own father, the king of the Sakya clan, as well as other monarchs of his day, became ardent supporters of this new religion.

Generally speaking, religious and royal institutions were mutually supportive in South and Southeast Asia. Royal patronage of the Buddhist monastic order was reciprocated by institutional loyalty and the construction of religious cosmologies and mythologies that valorized the king as propagator of the Buddha's religion (*sāsana*) and as the key to the peaceful harmony and well-being of the universe. Heinz Bechert suggests six ways in which religious authority legitimated political power within the Southeast Asian context (1) the identification of the ruler with the mythological world monarch (*cakkavattin*), (2) ascribing to the ruler the moral and spiritual perfection of bodhisattvahood, (3) describing the 'ideal king' as the promoter and protector of Buddhism, (4) attributing to the ruler the authority of one who governs by the *dhamma*, that is, the *rājadhamma*, (5) the ruler as *devarāja*, an apotheosis or appearance of a divine being, that is, a Hindu god or a Buddha, and (6) the coexistent support of Southeast Asian monarchs by both Buddhist and non-Buddhist cults.[2] We shall explore these forms of what Bechert refers to as "legitimization of political power by religious authority" in the remainder of this chapter.

ASOKA, THE EXEMPLARY BUDDHIST RULER

Buddhist chronicles of Theravāda Southeast Asia often begin their legendary histories with the Buddha's visit to the country of the chronicle's origin. Before recounting the history of Buddhism in that area and the support particular kings rendered the Buddhist monastic order, the chronicles may outline the history of Theravāda Buddhism in India and Sri Lanka. In the chronicles, one monarch stands out: Asoka Maurya. He becomes the exemplar par excellence for all Buddhist monarchs, embodying the virtues of righteousness and justice, materially supporting the monastic order, and ensuring both religious and political harmony within the realm. In effect, the Buddhist tradition constructs Asoka as the historical embodiment of the mythic Buddhist world ruler (*cakkavattin*), one who embodies the *dhamma* and rules by it and who personifies the Ten Royal Virtues (*dasarājadhamma*): generosity, moral virtue, self-sacrifice, kindness, self-control, nonanger, nonviolence, patience, and adherence to the norm of righteousness.[3]

Asoka was the grandson of Candragupta, the founder of the Mauryan dynasty (317–189 B.C.E). Building on his forebearers' expansionist policy, Asoka forged the most far-reaching political unity India was to know until the colonial period, ruling over this vast empire from 270 to 232 B.C.E. Our knowledge of Asoka derives, in part, from commemorative pillar edicts the king erected throughout his kingdom.[4] These edicts, together with the *Aśoka Avadāna* (The Story of King Asoka) in Sanskrit and three Pali works—the *Dīpavaṃsa* (The Island Chronicle), the *Mahāvaṃsa* (The Great Chronicle), and Buddhaghosa's commentary on the *Vinaya* (Book of Discipline)—provide us with a significant, although historically problematic, fund of information about this great Indian ruler. Each of these three sources constructs Asoka from its own distinctive perspective.[5]

Asoka's conversion to Buddhism and its consequences becomes the seminal event in the institutional history of Theravāda Buddhism, not simply for the development of Buddhism in India but for the normative influence of his example on the way monarchs in the Theravāda cultures of Southeast Asia were depicted. Rulers such as Kyanzittha of Pagan (eleventh century) and Tilokarāja of Chiang Mai (fifteenth century) emulate Asoka, or at least the chronicles in Burma and Thailand report events in this manner. By following the example of King Asoka, these rulers not only lend their reign legitimacy and authority in a particular location, they also become part of a more universal Buddhist history. The religion they support literally has its roots in the person of the Buddha, whose physical presence magically resides in his relics, and their political rule is grounded in the legendary career of Asoka who, in turn, is a historical embodiment of the first world ruler.[6] We shall briefly explore the story of Asoka, looking first at the king's reputed conversion to Buddhism for insight into the nature of Buddhist kingship.

In the ninth year of Asoka's reign, war broke out between Magadha, the Mauryan heartland, and Kaliṅga, the most powerful kingdom in India still independent of Asoka's rule. According to the thirteenth rock edict, Asoka was moved to remorse and pity over the horrors he inflicted on Kaliṅga. The killing, death by disease, the forcible dislocation of noncombatants including monks and priests resulted in his conversion. Asoka came to the opinion that the only true conquest was not by force of arms but by the force of religion (*dhamma*). Cynics, of course, have observed that Asoka came to this conclusion after he had defeated by military might all those who had opposed him.

Just exactly what this *dhamma* was is a matter of some debate. The legends in the chronicles portray Asoka as an active patron of the monastic order;

the convenor of the Third Buddhist Council which purged the *sangha* of 60,000 heretics; a promoter of the Buddha's teachings; and they claim that in his old age he became a monk. The *dhamma* of the rock edicts, however, presents an idealistic, humanitarian philosophy with few Buddhist doctrinal interests.[7] Asoka advocates docility to parents, liberality to friends, economy in expenditures and avoidance of disputes (rock edict 3). He urges self-mastery, purity of heart, gratitude, and fidelity (rock edict 7). Like the *Sigālaka Sutta*, a treatise on lay ethics to which the *dhamma* of the rock edicts is sometimes compared, Asoka advises right conduct toward servants, honor toward teachers, liberality to brahmans and recluses, and self-restraint toward all living things (rock edicts 9 and 11). His moral advice is inspiring but not specifically Buddhist: "Man sees but his good deeds, saying: 'This good act have I done.' Man sees not all his evil deeds, saying: 'That bad act have I done that act is corruption.' Such self-examination is hard. Yet, must a man watch over himself, saying: 'Such and such acts lead to corruption, such are brutality, cruelty, anger, and pride. I will zealously see to it that I slander not out of envy. That will be to my advantage in this world, to my advantage, verily, in the world to come.' "[8] Even so, there is little doubt that Asoka was influenced by Buddhist teachings. He commends certain Buddhist texts, the Buddha's teaching in general, and condemns sectarian schism; he also visited the Buddha's birthplace and supported the monastic order. As a comparison of the structure of the Buddha and Asoka legends demonstates, even the story of Asoka's so called conversion to Buddhism mirrors the pattern of the Buddha's life story.

It is informative to compare the structure of the Buddha and Asoka legends. The Buddha's life story exemplifies two modalities: the transformation of a life characterized by ignorance and attachment to one of freedom and knowledge. Even though one modality (*nibbāna*) supercedes the other (*saṃsāra*), the former presupposes the latter; in this sense, the two sides of the story are necessarily interdependent. In a similar manner, Asoka's life story moves from the pole of cruelty, wickedness, and disorder (*Caṇḍa-Asoka*) to justice, righteousness, and order (*Dhamma-Asoka*). This same polarity is evident in two Pali Sutta texts from the *Dīgha Nikāya* (The Long Discourses of the Buddha) which treat kingship, the *Aggañña Sutta* (On Knowledge of Beginnings), and the *Cakkavatti Sīhanāda Sutta* (The Lion's Roar on the Turning of the Wheel). The first justifies the selection of a king, "the great elect" (*mahā-sammata*), as a necessary means to overcome political, economic, and social disorder brought about by human greed and avarice.[9] The second, "presents two apocalyptic images of life under the rule of evil and of life ruled by *dhamma*. The one is a picture of injustice, disorder, and confusion; the other portrays liberation and reciprocity. Both are extended images of the human potential, kept in balance as with Asoka. From the Buddhist standpoint, neither one can be fully appreciated except in relationship to the other."[10]

The legendary chronicle narratives of the great South and Southeast Asian Buddhist monarchs embody the same polarity: Anawrahta[11] (eleventh century) kills his brother to rule Pagan and then becomes a patron of Theravāda Buddhism; Tilokarāja (fifteenth century) revolts against his father, the king of Chiang Mai, and subsequently convenes a council to purify the religion (*buddha-sāsana*); Duṭṭhagāmaṇi (thirteenth century), the great warrior hero of the *Mahāvaṃsa*, defeats the Tamils, unites the island kingdom of Sri Lanka, and then builds many of the great religious edifices of Polonnaruva including the Lohapāsāda and the great *stūpa*.

The legend of King Asoka does more than establish a structural, bipolar framework for royal biography, however. His story functions in an exemplary manner, inspiring other monarchs of Southeast Asia to follow Asoka's example of contributing lavishly to the monastic order. Reflecting Asokan initiatives, monarchs such as Tilokarāja also convene councils to purify the *dhamma*, sponsor a new redaction of the Pali scriptures, and settle sectarian disputes. Finally, Southeast Asian monarchs build *stūpa* reliquaries as loci of popular Buddhist cult and symbolic axial centers of both cosmos and kingdom. As we shall see, material artifacts of Buddhism—*stūpas*, Buddha images, even votive tablets—become emblems of a ritually based galactic polity linking subordinant states to dominant ones.

The primary Buddhist symbol throughout Buddhist Asia has been the *stūpa*. It was a cultic center in the early rock-hewn temples in western India; it commemorated miraculous events attributed to the Buddha and Buddhist saints;[12] it became the locus of popular piety and relic veneration of monastic establishments in Sri Lanka and mainland Southeast Asia; and the *stūpa* was closely associated with royal patronage of Buddhist monastic institutions.[13] The architectural form, historical development, cultic context, and symbolism of the Buddhist *stūpa* has been the subject of considerable study in recent years.[14] The *stūpa* has been described by the architect-Indologist Adrian Snodgrass as a network of homologous symbols, myths, rituals and doctrines that include the *stūpa* as reliquary and memorial, as cosmic mountain and navel of the universe, as *maṇḍala*-field from which demonic forces have been expelled, as generative womb (*gabbha*), and as an ascending pathway to liberation. Snodgrass acknowledges his debt to the interpretation of Borobudur by Paul Mus, who posited the microcosmic signification of the *stūpa* as an image of the universe, a view also developed by his contemporary A. M. Hocart, working in Sri Lanka.[15]

Building on the work of Mus and Hocart, John Irwin suggests that, although Buddhism associated the *stūpa* with the death (i.e., *parinibbāna*) of the Buddha, the archaic, pre-Buddhistic meaning of the *stūpa* as life engendering and cosmogonic still prevaled—"[the *stūpa*] is an image of the the *creation* of the universe, dynamically conceived."[16] On the basis of archaeological evidence discovered in the nineteenth and twentieth centuries and the theories of the renowned American Indologist W. Norman Brown, Irwin argues for the primacy of the *stūpa*'s axis as an *Indra-kīla* or World Pillar, reflective of the Vedic myth of Indra's demiurgic act of creation: "Indra's demiurgic act was to slay the demon [Vṛtra] and to release the waters, while at the same time separating heaven and earth by 'pushing them apart' and 'propping up the sky' at the world's axis, commonly visualized in India as well as in other traditions as World Tree or World Pillar. . . . [W]ith his raising of the heavens, Indra 'pegged' the floating Primordial Mound to the bottom of the Cosmic Ocean, thus 'fixing' or 'stabilising' our universe; the peg he used was the '*Indra-kīla*,' metaphysically synonymous with the World Pillar."[17]

Irwin's interpretation of the centrality of the axial-cosmogonic symbolism of the *stūpa* receives further validation from the association of Buddhist *stūpa*s with kingship. The appearance of Buddha relics and their enshrinement by the Buddhist monarchs of South and Southeast Asia represented not only an act of piety but, more important, associated the king with Indra's cosmogonic act that ordered the universe.

Sponsoring *stūpa* construction was a major activity of Buddhist monarchs in South and Southeast Asia. The prevalence of *stūpa* worship was one of the marks of Indian cultural unity during the 200 year period between 270 and 50 B.C.E., the age of the later Mauryas, the Sungas, and the later Andhras of the south. Although the claim that Asoka enshrined relics at 84,000 sites is fictional, its symbolic value points to a basic truth; namely, that in the Asokan period the cult of relics became a basic expression of Buddhist piety as well as part of Asoka's policy of using Buddhism as an instrument of imperial unity.[18] Indeed, the very inauguration of the cult of relics described in the *Mahāparinibbāna Sutta* may have been a product of the Mauryan age. Although some kind of *stūpa* cult was pre-Buddhistic, the veneration of a mound of earth or brick containing the remains of nobles and holy men gained greater prominence in Buddhism than in other Indian

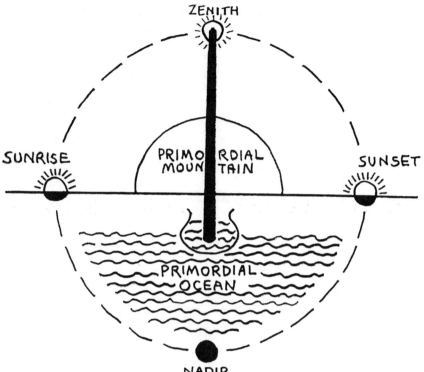

Figure 2.1. The *stūpa* as microcosm. Drawing adapted from John Irwin, "The *Stūpa* and the Cosmic Axis: The Archaeological Evidence," *South Asian Archaeology*, 1977, vol. 2. ed. Maurizio Taddei. Naples: Instituto Universitario Orientale, 1979, p. 843.

religious traditions. Asokan patronage, as Benjamin Rowland suggests, may have been at least partially responsible for this development.

One of the best known Indian *stūpas* is Sāñcī (also known as Caityagiri) located in modern Mahārastra State. Sāñcī is part of a central Indian group of *stūpas*, which extended along a commercial trunk route from the imperial capital of Pāṭaliputra to Ujjain and on to the seaport town of Bharukacha. The association of Sāñcī with Asoka is suggested by an inscribed Asokan pillar thought to have originally stood at the south gate, although this claim is a matter of scholarly debate.[19] Even though Sāñcī has been studied primarily by art historians, it should be remembered as a vital center of Buddhist learning and pilgrimage. From the third century B.C.E. to the tenth century C.E. Sāñcī served as an active center of Buddhist monastic and lay religious practice.

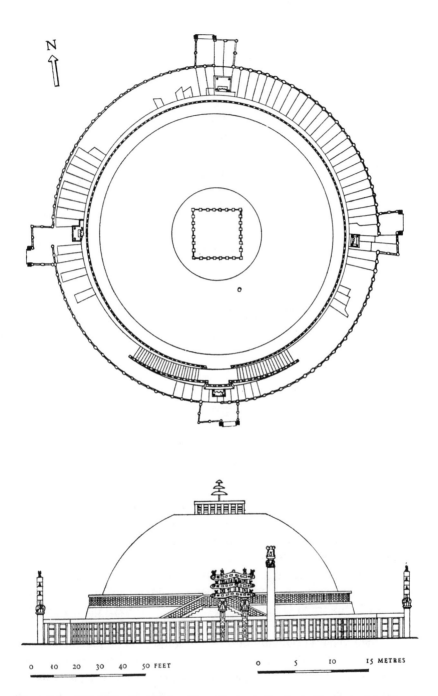

N

0   10   20   30   40   50 FEET   0   5   10   15 METRES

Figure 2.2.   Sâñcī. The Great Stūpa. From Benjamin Rowland, *The Art and Architecture of India*. London: Penguin Books, 1953, p. 53. Reprinted by permission of Mrs. Benjamin Rowland.

Sāñcī's prototypical *stūpa* is composed of three major parts: a mound or dome, a raised platform above the base of the dome for circumambulation, and a stone balustrade encircling the mound at ground level. Gateways are located in the balustrade at the four cardinal points. A quadrangular terrace was added to the top of the dome, over which was placed a parasol symbolizing imperial power. The four gateways at the cardinal directions indicate the cosmic symbolism of the *stūpa*, as do the terms for the dome: *aṇḍa*, meaning "egg," and *gabbha*, meaning "womb," which contained the "seed" (*bīja*), namely, the relic.[20] In addition to this basic architectural structure, the three Sāñcī *stūpa* sites abound in stone sculpture and decorative relief carving, representational scenes from the former lives of the Buddha (*jātaka* tales), and other folk themes.

Such a proliferation of popular art prompted Sukumar Dutt, an Indian scholar of an earlier generation, to see the *stūpa* and the cult associated with it as a "vulgarization" of the tradition: "Shuffling somehow out of the precocity of monkish learning, the religion has taken on a popular aspect. It seems to find in this age a new, perhaps a little 'vulgarised,' expression in its unclerical ritualistic worship, in its motives of art, in attitudes of mind and spirit, often at odds with the approved system of the religion."[21]

The German Indologist Heinrich Zimmer modifies Dutt's interpretation of the Buddhist *stūpa*-reliquary. He sees the *stūpa* as a marriage between the highest ideals of Buddhism and local folk religion: "on the gates and railings, we find a thronging world of forms. Their joyous yet respectful animation is the counterpole to the unembellished quiet of the surface of the dome, illustrating the opposition of *saṃsāra* and *nirvāṇa*." Far from being a vulgarization of the tradition, he argues that the "*stūpa* and its form became the highest symbol of the Buddhist faith. It represents the essence of enlightenment, transcendental reality, *nirvāṇa*. Therefore, instead of remaining simply a reliquary memorial filled with sacred bones, ash, or crumbled wood, the silently eloquent structure became a signal of the highest human goal and of the Buddha's attainment."[22]

Although Zimmer may overly romanticize the meaning of the *stūpa*, Dutt's conception of the *stūpa* as a vulgar expression of popular piety draws too sharp a contrast between monastic and lay Buddhism, between Buddhism's highest ideals and popular practice, and presumes an "original," essentialized Buddhism that, in fact, never existed. Irwin's cosmogonic interpetation of the Buddhist *stūpa*, offers an alternative view, one more compatible with the close association between the *stūpa* and Buddhist kingship. In short, although the Buddhist *stūpa* should not be restricted to a single meaning, for our purposes it represents the symbiotic relationship between sacred cosmology and kingship. The *stūpa*, then, suggests that the ruler is empowered (or legitimated) by his association with the creative-ordering-liberating forces of the universe be they Brahmanical deities or the Buddha and that by this very association the ruler, himself, becomes an active agent for the maintenance of the universe.

Because Buddhist monarchs of Southeast Asia enshrined Buddha relics in *stūpas* (known as *dāgoba*, i.e., *dhātu-gabbha*, in Sri Lanka, and *cedi*, i.e., *cetiya*, in Thailand), they came to represent a magical or supernatural center for the kingdom. In this interpretation, the reliquary mound becomes one modality of the Buddha as cosmocrator, one closely associated with the monarch as world ruler. *Stūpas*, however, not only enshrine the relics of the Buddha but are also associated with other holy and noble personages including kings (*cakkavatti-rāja*). The *Mahāparinibbāna Sutta* refers to the *stūpa* of a "person-of-dhamma/king-of-dhamma" (*dhammika dhammarāja*), which may be an allusion to King Asoka.[23] Furthermore, the legend that Asoka redistributed the Buddha's relics in 84,000 *stūpas* throughout India, each located in a political division of his domain, suggests that Asoka governed his realm through a ritual hegemony rather than actual political control.[24] The *stūpa*-reliquary, then, can be seen as the material representation par excellence not only of the Buddha but of the traditional Southeast Asian Buddhist ruler as well. Hence, the *stūpa* embodies the close interrelationship between religion and the state on both historical and symbolic levels.

KINGS AND COSMOLOGY

Theravāda Buddhism informed the construction of the classical conception of kingship in various ways. One, as we have seen, was the example of King Asoka valorized as the paradigmatic *dhammarāja*, the righteous monarch who, although a powerful world ruler (*cakkavattin*), governed justly and righteously embodying the ten royal virtues. According to the Theravāda chronicles of Southeast Asia, successful rulers—at least in the eyes of those who composed the chronicles—were those who emulated King Asoka. This suggests that the Asokan model had a mimetic potency: to imitate King Asoka legitimated a ruler as a *dhammarāja*. In particular, Buddhist monarchs built Buddhist edifices, especially *stūpas/cetiyas*, and purified the *dhamma* and the *sangha* in self-conscious imitation of King

Figure 2.3. The *cetiya* (Thai: *ŏhedi*) at Wat Phra Buddhapāt Dakphā enshrining the ashes of a revered former abbot. Pasang, Thailand. Photo by Donald K. Swearer.

Asoka. Such mimesis, it was hoped, would guarantee peace and prosperity in the realm and enable the king to rule as a universal monarch (*cakkavattin*).

Theravāda Buddhism informed the classical conception of Southeast Asian kingship in other ways as well. In his study of conceptions of Burmese kingship during the Pagan period, Michael Aung-Thwin cites three essential elements to the ideology of classical kingship—the *dhammarāja*, the *kammarāja*, and the *devarāja*. He likens these elements to human, superhuman, and divine attributes of the king:

> By aiding the public's desire for salvation and upward spiritual mobility as a *bodhisatta*; for ruling earthly Tāvatiṃsa—known as Jambudīpa [generally associated with India], paradise on earth—as Sakka [Indra]; and for guarding the supernatural dimensions of society as a *nat* [Burmese guardian deity]—for these roles the king acquired

a divine image. For administering the state efficiently and morally in the tradition of Asoka and the Mahāsammata...he acquired the image of a *dhammarāja*. For successfully conquering the familiar world as a *cakkavatti[n]*, a "universal monarch," he enjoyed the image of superhuman. Yet, because he achieved all this by the merits derived from his past actions, he was, above all, a *kammarāja*.[25]

Aung-Thwin's analysis summarizes several of the Buddhist concepts that informed the political ideology of the classical Buddhist monarchies of Southeast Asia. These concepts were propagated in various ways. The Buddhist *sangha*, for example, was consulted by kings; monks also composed texts that promoted these ideals. Underlying the human, superhuman, and divine dimensions of classical Buddhist political ideology, however, is the notion of mimesis. By imitating Asoka, the ruler actually represents the "great elect" (*mahāsammata*) or "world conqueror" (*cakkavattin*). It appears, moreover, that in the construction of palaces, temples, and capitals, as well as the organization of state and society, a similar mimetic principle was at work. That is, these structures and their polities were not merely microcosmic symbols of the macrocosmos; in their imitation of the macrocosmos they—in a virtual reality sense—became the cosmos.

This emphasis on the mimetic import of classical Southeast Asian religio-political centers is a variation of Robert von Heine-Geldern's construction of the parallelism between the suprahuman macrocosmos and human microcosmos in which the kingdom represents the cosmos.[26] Heine-Geldern refers to a "magical" relationship between the human realm and the universe, between terrestrial manifestations on the one hand and the points of the compass and the heavens on the other. In this schema everything has a "magical position" and a "magical moment" in the structure and movement of the universe: "Humanity was forever in the control of cosmic forces. This concept was applied to social groups....Kingdom, city, monastery, nothing could prosper unless it was in harmony with these universal forces. In order to achieve this harmony, men tried to build the kingdom, the capital, the palace, the temple, in the form of microcosmos...replicas of the structure of the universe."[27]

We shall apply the aforementioned mimetic perspective to three major Southeast Asian religio-political centers: Angkor in Cambodia, Pagan in Burma, and Sukhothai in Thailand.[28] These centers and the structures contained therein represent high points in the development of their respective cultures. They can and should be assessed as expressions of increasingly powerful and centralized states "which were the foci of intensified central-isation, incorporation of surrounding groups by force. . . .The indigenous inhabitants incorporated into their culture Indian-inspired ideas of statehood. These included a legal system, calendrics and the establishment of a *maṇḍala*-wide religion."[29] Paul Mus and Stanley Tambiah concur with such a characterization. Mus, a seminal interpreter of the religion and culture of Southeast Asia, argues that the imposition of Buddhism or Hinduism as a state religion and the creation of a sacred capital city were crucial elements in a sovereign's strategy to create a centralized state that unified cadastral cults and plural communities into a unified pattern.[30] The anthropologist S. J. Tambiah suggests that Buddhism forged a macro-conception that yoked religion and the sociopolitical order in which kingship was the articulating principle.[31]

To interpret these centers and their monuments simply as material evidence of powerful, centralized political states would be to ignore their symbolic value and mimetic potency as sacred space—representations in the *maṇḍala* form of vertical and horizontal world-planes regulated from the pinnacle of the central axis by embodiments of both divine and royal power. As proposed by various scholars, Heine-Geldern, Coedès, Mus, and Tambiah, these monuments reflect Hindu and Buddhist polities modeled on cosmo-logical notions and parallelism between the suprahuman macrocosmos and the human microcosmos: "The Kingdom was a miniature representation of the cosmos, with the palace at the center being iconic of Mount Meru, the pillar of the universe, and the king, his princes and ruling chiefs representing the hierarchy in Tāvatiṃsa heaven—Indra, the four *lokapāla* (world guardians), and twenty-eight subordinate *devas*."[32]

Utilizing the research of S. Moertono on medieval Java and H. L. Shorto's study of the medieval Mon kingdom in Burma, Tambiah characterizes classical Southeast Asian polities modeled on this mandalic scheme as "galactic," a dynamic structure of peripherial and tributary states subject to a dominant center. In particular, Tambiah contends that a thirty-three unit galactic polity reached its most complex development in Buddhist Southeast Asia. For example, he refers to the Mon scheme of thirty-two townships organized around the capital of Haṃsavati (Pegu, Burma) and a thirty-three unit Burmese hierarchical political structure including the king, four ministers, and twenty-eight regional chiefs.[33] These schemes reflect the Buddhist notions of the thirty-three heavenly realms as well as the divine hierarachy of Indra (Sakka), the four world guardians, and the twenty-eight *devas*.

In the following study of kingship and religious cosmology we shall explore Angkor, Pagan, and Sukhothai primarily as unique combinations of three interrelated symbol systems: the cosmic, the divine, and the royal. Concepts enhancing royal status—the world ruler (*cakkavattin*), king of righteousness (*dhammarāja*), a Buddha-to-be (*bodhisatta*), and the god-king (*devarāja*) or Buddha-king (*buddharāja*)—lurk in the background of the meanings attributed to these centers and to their palaces, temples, and *stūpas*. The meaning of the *devarāja* concept, associated primarily with Khmer imperial rule, has been a particular focus of study and debate.[34] Consequently, we shall look first at this notion which has figured so prominently in discussions of religious cosmologies and kingship in Southeast Asia.

In its basic formulation the *devarāja* concept stands for the divinization of a ruler; that is, at death the ruler becomes the apotheosis of a divine being, be it the Hindu gods Śiva or Viṣṇu, or the Buddha Lokeśvara. George Coedès, the noted French doyen of Southeast Asian culture, gives this interpretation of the *devarāja* in his study of Angkor: "From all evidence it is safe to say that it was the king who was the great god of ancient Cambodia, the one to whom the biggest groups of monuments and all the temples in the form of mountains were dedicated."[35] Lawrence Briggs holds the same position, asserting that the central divinity of the state cult of ancient Cambodia was the king himself, and that he was looked upon as a manifestation of Śiva, a god-king (*devarāja*) whose visible symbol was a *liṅga* located upon the central altar of a pyramidal temple, the symbolic center of the empire, in imitation of Mount Meru.[36] Other scholars qualify such a specific claim, asserting that in the case of Hinduism the ruler was considered to be either an incarnation of a god or a descendant from a god or both. In the case of Theravāda Buddhism, the king became a representative of the god Indra, through good *karma* acquired in past lives.[37] This formulation of the *devarāja/buddharāja* concept has the virtue of giving wider latitude in interpreting the specific nature of the association between the "rāja" (king) and "deva" (god) or "buddha."

The major challenge to identifying the *devarāja* concept with kingship comes from those scholars who contend that the notion of the *devarāja* in Angkor refers to Śiva as the "king of the gods" rather than to a divine monarch (i.e., the god-king).[38] Others argue for a separation of the *devarāja* concept from the cult of royal *liṅgas* (phallic representation of the god Śiva), which became the basis for the Angkorian state cult from the eleventh century onward.[39] Although a concensus has yet to be reached regarding the precise meaning of the *devarāja* and its related concept, the *buddharāja*, we presume that the terms link king and god (e.g., Śiva, Viṣṇu) or king and Buddha at the center of a mimetically potent replica of the universe.

Angkor

The monuments of the Khmer empire, constructed between the ninth and fourteenth centuries, have captured the imaginations of European travelers and scholars because of their extent, as well as the overwhelming size and dynamism of Angkor Wat and the last great Khmer capital, Angkor Thom, dominanted by its central temple, the Bayon.[40] The awesome grandeur of Angkor Wat prompted A. K. Coomaraswamy to comment that the observer could not help but be overwhelmed by a feeling of the monument's "nervous tension" and "concentration of force."[41] The association of the *devarāja* concept with the religious cosmology of the Khmer empire, furthermore, has enhanced the significance of Angkor for the historian of religion who studies the relationship between sacred cosmology and political authority.

From a historical point of view scholars speculate that the notion of *devarāja* first originated in Funan, a kingdom founded in the first century C.E. in the lower Mekong valley. The Chinese word *Fu-nan* may be derived from the Mon-Khmer word *bnam*, meaning "mountain," with specific reference to a cult of a national guardian spirit established by the founder of the state.[42] Under the Khmers this cult acquired a Hinduized meaning during the reign of Jayavarman II (accession, 802 C.E.) when Śaivism became the state religion, a transformation that may have been mediated through Java. Jayavarman linked Śiva worship with kingship, assuming the role of a universal monarch who governed both the spiritual and temporal. He made his royal chaplain the chief priest (*purohita*) of the *devarāja* cult on a hereditary basis. This ensured continuance of this tradition until the reign of Sūryavarman I (C.E. 1002–1050) who added Mahāyāna Buddhist elements to the state *devarāja* cult.

H. G. Quartich Wales interprets the *devarāja* cult as a synthesis of an an indigenous Southeast Asian worldview with Hinduism, but he gives primacy to the chonthic significance of autochthonous mountain symbolism. Wales suggests that the Khmer *devarāja* cult is a synthesis of Indian-Śaivite ideas of divinity and kingship with older Southeast Asian megalithic beliefs. He contends that when the pre-Indianized peoples of Southeast Asia erected stone megaliths they recognized the consubstantial presence of the first ancestor-earth god in the stone as themselves.[43] Wales finds evidence for

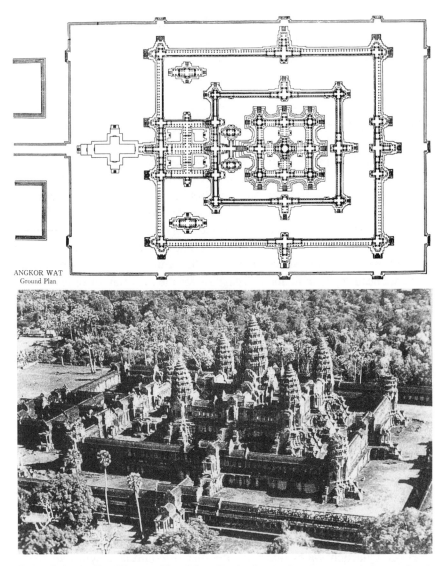

ANGKOR WAT
Ground Plan

Figure 2.4.   Angkor Wat near Siem Riep, Cambodia. Angkor Wat ground plan reprinted by permission of Oxford University Press.

this chthonic character of Śiva among the Khmers in such epithets as Girisa, "the mountain Lord," and Gambhireśvara, "Śiva of the depths." He argues that the development of the temple mountain in Khmer architecture up to the construction of the Bayon points to a displacing of the Hindu Mt. Meru by a more realistic and primordial representation of the sacred mountain. In Wales' interpretation, then, the Khmer temple mountain represents a revival, albeit one transformed by Indian thought, of the chthonic source of divine and royal power.[44]

Mahāyāna Buddhism spread to Angkor in the eleventh century. Sūryavarman II built a central Buddhist temple on the site later to become the Bayon, the great temple that Jayavarman VII (reignal dates 1181–c. 1219) constructed to Buddha Lokeśvara at the end of the twelfth century. In short, what appears to be a full-blown *buddharāja* cult during the reign of Jayavarman VII was rooted in an earlier infusion of Mahāyāna Buddhism. Whether or not the *buddharāja* cult that the Bayon Temple appears to embody represents a cult of a divinized ruler or veneration of the Buddha as divine ruler may be a matter of debate; nonetheless, the mandalic structure and iconography of the monument bear testimony to a complex interrelationship between sacred cosmology, the Khmer state, and Jayavarman's political authority.

We shall first look at Angkor Wat and then the Bayon as exemplifications of the Khmer synthesis of cosmology and kingship. Sometimes known as the Great Temple, Angkor Wat proper covers an area of approximately 500 acres; furthermore, it is part of an extensive complex of buildings of over 10,000 acres. Constructed under the reign of Sūryavarman II (C.E. 1113–1150), the monument was dedicated to the Hindu god Viṣṇu. Subsequently it was used as a sacred Buddhist site, especially after the Thai conquest in the fifteenth century.

Angkor Wat rises from the ground in its mandalic form, an embodiment of the suprahuman macrocosmos and the human microcosmos. It represents simultaneously the image of the universe, the celestial paradise of Viṣṇu, and the heavenly palace of the spirit of the king.[45] The moat surrounding the structure is approximately 200 yards wide and 25 feet deep. The temple itself, symbolizing the earth in its quadrangular plan and guarded by four massive enclosures, rises as Mt. Sumeru, the central mountain of the universe, to the celestial spheres of *Viṣṇuloka*, the realm of the god Viṣṇu. The bridge crosses the moat on the west leading through the main gate of the outer wall and gallery. The pilgrim walks across a paved causeway to a cruciform terrace in front of the main entrance to the temple. The temple itself ascends in three successive terraces to a height of over 180 feet. In the center of the innermost terrace stands an enormous pyramidal foundation supporting the five ultimate towers accessible only by steep stone stairways.[46] The three basic cosmological components of Angkor Wat are the central

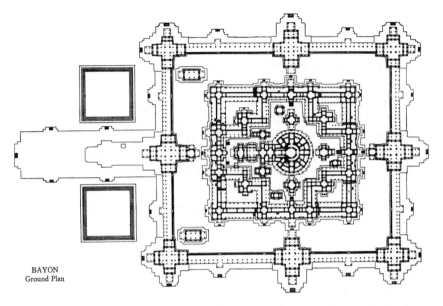

BAYON
Ground Plan

Figure 2.5. The Bayon Temple of Angkor Thom near Siem Riep, Cambodia. Reprinted by permission of Oxford University Press.

tower or *axis mundi*, the wall, and the moat. The latter two represent the alternating mountain ranges and oceans that divide the horizontal plane of the Indian cosmology.[47]

In comparison with other Khmer classical monuments Angkor Wat has garnered the greatest share of both popular and scholarly attention; however, for our purposes the Bayon is an even more apt example of the complex, intricate interweaving of Buddhism, state, and kingship. The splendor and mystery of the Bayon has been noted by all who have seen it: "an architectural wonder of the first order" (Doudart de Lagée), "the most extraordinary of all the Khmer ruins" (Louis Delaporte), "a structure absolutely unique of its kind" (Tissandier), and Pierre Loti's memorable, "I looked up at the tree-covered towers which dwarfed me, when all of a sudden my blood curdled as I saw an enormous smile looking down on me and another smile over another wall, then three, then five, then ten, appearing from every direction."[48] To be sure such romantic characterizations come from an earlier generation of scholars, but I, too, found the Bayon overwhelmingly mysterious and fascinating during a visit to Angkor Thom in 1968.

The Bayon is located at the geometric center of the greatest and last of the Khmer capitals, Angkor Thom. It dominates an extensive array of

Figure 2.6. Jayavarman VII. The Bayon, Angkor Thom, Cambodia. Sketch by Mano, Chiang Mai, Thailand.

religious and royal, stone structures located within the huge walls of the capital. According to Coedès, the Bayon evolved over time from a cruciform shaped temple in the capital to a rectangular temple mountain crowded with towers surrounding a central pediment. Emerging from each of the four sides of the towers just below their lotus crowns is the benign, smiling visage of the human face that caught Pierre Loti's imagination when he first saw the temple. Western scholarly debates over the significance of the faces on the towers of the Bayon have included the four faces of Brahma and the five faces of Śiva. Coedès and Mus are among those scholars who interpret the temple and its faces as symbolizing royal power blessing the four quarters of the country.[49] Furthermore, Coedès contends that the discovery in 1933 of a large Lokeśvara image in the central sanctuary of the Bayon not only proves that the structure was a temple dedicated to Lokeśvara, but also that the face of the image as well as that on the towers represents an apotheosis of King Jayavarman VII in the form of the Buddha. In a more extended analysis of the entire structure, moreover, Mus, contends that the temple represented a galactic, mimetic *maṇḍala*: "Perhaps each tower corresponded to. . .a religious or administrative centre of the province. Thus. . .the four faces symboliz[ing] the royal power spreading over the land in every direction. . .signified that Jayavarman II's royal power was as strong in the provinces as at Angkor itself. . . .We now begin to understand this mysterious architecture as the symbol of the Great Miracle of Jayavarman VII. It represents his administrative and religious power extending to every corner of Cambodian territory by means of this unique sign."[50]

The galactic interpretation of Mus receives further confirmation from an Angkor inscription indicating that Jayavarman dispatched twenty-three stone images of himself portrayed as the Buddha (the Jaya Buddha Mahānātha) to Khmer outposts as far flung as Sukhothai in central Thailand. Jayavarman's extensive empire, like King Asoka's kingdom 1,500 years earlier, was conjoined not only by such symbolic gestures as the installation of Jaya Buddha Mahānātha images of the *buddharāja*, but also by material services as well. For example, the king sponsored the building of an extensive system of roads equipped with more than 100 rest houses.

Pagan

In our exploration of kingship and cosmology in Southeast Asia we now move to the Burmese and Thai kingdoms of Pagan (eleventh–thirteenth centuries) and Sukhothai (thirteenth–fifteenth centuries) where the influence of Theravāda Buddhism eventually overshadowed other Buddhist and Brahmanical influences.[51] Theravāda Buddhism also played a dominant role in other classical Southeast Asian kingdoms, notably Autthaya and Chiang Mai in Thailand, Lan Chang/Luang Prabang in Laos, and Pegu in Burma, but these examples lie beyond the preview of our consideration.[52]

Pagan became the capital of a Burma unified under King Anawrahta[53] (1044–1077). Located in central Burma in a plain near the confluence of the Irrawaddy and the Chindwin Rivers, the city eventually covered an area of approximately 16 square miles where the remains of over 2,000 extant sites can still be seen. While no single monument at Pagan may match the majestic grandeur of Angkor Wat or the iconographic complexity of Borobudur, the size and extent of its monuments are overwhelming and

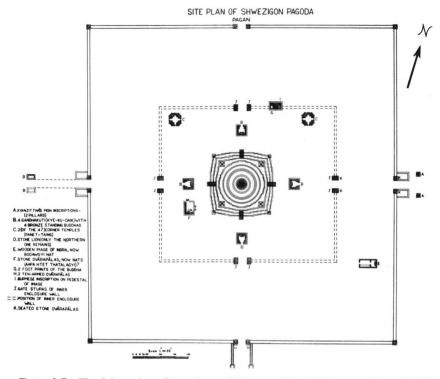

SITE PLAN OF SHWEZIGON PAGODA
PAGAN

A.KYANZITTHA'S MON INSCRIPTIONS-
(2 PILLARS)
B.4 GANDHAKUTI(KYE-KU-DAIK)WITH
4 BRONZE STANDING BUDDHAS
C.2(OF THE 4?)CORNER TEMPLES
(PANE T-TAING)
D.STONE LION(ONLY THE NORTHERN
ONE REMAINS)
E.WOODEN IMAGE OF INDRA, NOW
BODAWGYI NAT
F.STONE DVARAPALAS, NOW NATS
(AHPA HTET THATALAGYI)?
G.2 FOOT PRINTS OF THE BUDDHA
H.2 TEN-ARMED DVARAPALAS
I.BURMESE INSCRIPTION ON PEDESTAL
OF IMAGE
J.GATE STUPAS OF INNER
ENCLOSURE WALL
= = POSITION OF INNER ENCLOSURE
WALL
K.SEATED STONE DVARAPALAS

Scale 1" = 32'

Figure 2.7. The Schwe-zigon *Stūpa*. Pagan, Myanmar. Reprinted by permission of J. J. Augustin.

incomparable.[54] That Pagan was situated only 30 miles from Mt. Popa, the home of some of the most powerful guardian deities (*Mahāgiri nats*) worshipped by the Burmese, also suggests an assimilation between the Mt. Meru symbolism of Indian Buddhist cosmology and an ancient cult of mountain spirits.[55]

The temples and *stūpas* of Pagan vary greatly in architectural style, reflecting Indian, Pyu, Mon, and Sinhalese influences as well as the unique genius of the Burmese. The Shwe-zigon *stūpa* begun by Anawrahta and completed by his grandson, Kyanzittha, in 1086, enshrines three sacred Buddha relics, his collarbone, his frontlet bone, and a tooth.[56]

Anawrahta brought one of the relics from the Baw-baw-kyi *stūpa* in the Pyu center of Thaton. In return he left a votive tablet, a custom he practiced throughout his kingdom. By this dual action Pagan as the sacred center of the Burmese kingdom incorporates peripherial states into its orbit.

Anawrahta enshrined Buddha relics and brought Buddha images, monks, and texts from conquered states. He reciprocated by leaving a portion of himself—votive tablets and *jātaka* plaques.

During the Pagan period, the Shwe-zigon, located near the king's palace (named Jayabhūmi, Place of Victory), functioned as a national shrine. In the tradition of the *stūpa* reliquary described earlier, it represents by its relic not only the person of the Buddha but also the qualities of the *cakkavattin*, as well. Inscriptions refer to Anawrahta as a *cakkavattin* and ascribe to his grandson successor, Kyanzittha, an even more grandiose title—Sri Tribhūvanādityadhammarāja, The Blessed Buddhist King, Sun of the Three Worlds. Paul Strachan's interpretation of the Shwe-zigon suggests the mimetic potency of the *stūpa*. With its three circumambulatory terraces, bell-shaped dome, and four stairways facing in the cardinal directions, the Shwe-zigon is not simply an architectural imitation of a cosmic mountain; rather, in its own right it is the cosmic mountain.[57]

The Shwe-zigon as well as several other Pagan *stūpas*, like the Mingala-zedi (1274 C.E.), share with the Borobudur *stūpa* (see Appendix 3) a basic structure: a truncated pyramidal terrace base with angle towers and a central stairway on each side supporting a central circular dome. As is true of Borobudur, the terraces of the *stūpas* of Pagan serve a practical as well as a symbolic function. There are open air galleries where the pilgrim can view depictions of Buddhist scenes, in the case of Pagan's monuments, usually taken from the *jātakas*. The monuments invite the pilgrim "to ascend the tower gradually, moving clockwise around its terraces in a symbolic pilgrimage of ascent rising from the ground level of earthly everyday life to higher and higher spheres."[58]

The centerpiece of Pagan is not a *stūpa*-reliquary, however, but the Ananda Temple completed by King Kyanzittha who reigned from 1084 until his death in 1113.[59] Made of brick and plaster according to a cruciform plan, the main base is surmounted by two receding curvilinear roofs and four receding terraces, crowned by a spire in the form of a miter-like pyramid known as a *sikhara*.[60] The core of the interior is dominated by an enormous cube rising to the spire, which is surrounded by two galleries. On each side of the cube stands a colossal figure representing the four Buddhas of this world age. Their huge size in a relatively confined place conveys a sense of the Buddha's omnipresence throughout space and time. The Ananda, like the Dhammayangyi Temple and several others, combines both cave and cosmic mountain symbolism. According to the *Glass Palace Chronicle*, the Ananda temple is a replica of an ascetic's cave located on

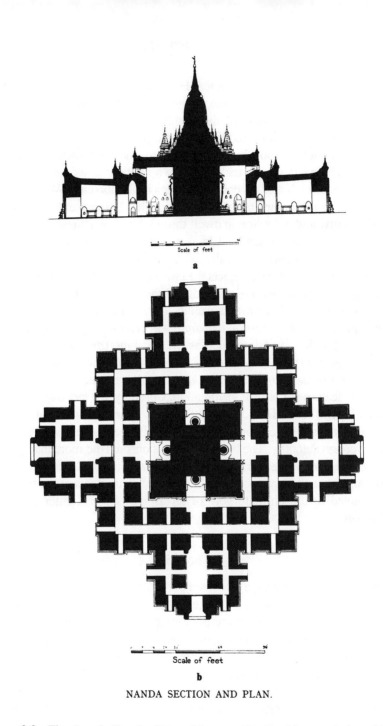

Scale of feet

a

Scale of feet

b

NANDA SECTION AND PLAN.

Figure 2.8. The Ananda Temple, Pagan, Myanmar. Reprinted by permission of J. J. Augustin.

Mt. Gaṇḍamadana in a mythological Himalayan setting. The gilded spire suggests not only the top of a magic mountain but also flames of fiery energy generated by the meditation of the Buddha inside the cave.

The Ananda temple links Buddhist cosmology and kingship. In the opinion of one interpreter of Southeast Asian culture, the monument symbolizes King Kyanzittha's desire to realize his own apotheosis as a divine being in a way similar to that of his contemporaries in Cambodia: "We can. . .see the Ananda as a funerary temple for Kyanzittha. It represents a model of cosmic reality, a world wherein dwell those who have achieved enlightenment. Kyanzittha has spent his life as a *bodhisattva* and on his death he achieves translation into the realm of the Buddhas."[61] A small image of Kyanzittha inside the temple depicts the crowned monarch as a pious devotee of the Buddha, and inscriptions indicate that he saw himself both as a *bodhisattva* and a *cakkavattin* as well as an incarnation of the god Viṣṇu.

The power of Southeast Asian monarchs was enhanced by various religious and cosmically based notions such as the god-king (*devarāja*), the world ruler (*cakkavattin*), and the Buddha-to-be (*bodhisattva*). Indeed, in the Khmer empire *devarāja* and *buddharāja* cults appear to have been a significant feature of political legitimation. Certainly, the fact that monarchs such as Jayavarman VII and Kyanzittha were claimants to extramundane status and at death were apotheosized into divine beings served to enhance their sovereign authority. The buildings they sponsored did more than glorify their own person, moreover; they were magical centers of the state as well as the cosmos, and in symbolizing the spiritual attainments of the monarch they pointed to the ultimate goal of all aspirants to enlightenment and perfection.

Sukhothai

Sukhothai (Pali, Sukhodaya), located some 280 miles north of Bangkok in north central Thailand, was one of the first major Thai capitals.[62] Originally a Khmer outpost, it was conquered by Tai tribes led by Si Indradit in the mid-thirteenth century. Together with its twin city, Si Satchanalai, Sukhothai remained a center of Tai power until the end of the fourteenth century when it was controlled by the neighboring Tai state of Ayutthaya.

The city plan was derived from the formal layout of royal Khmer cities at Angkor—an inner city surrounded by three concentric earth ramparts separated by moats covering an area of nearly two square miles—but it evolved as a distinctively Tai religio-royal center. In the late thirteenth century

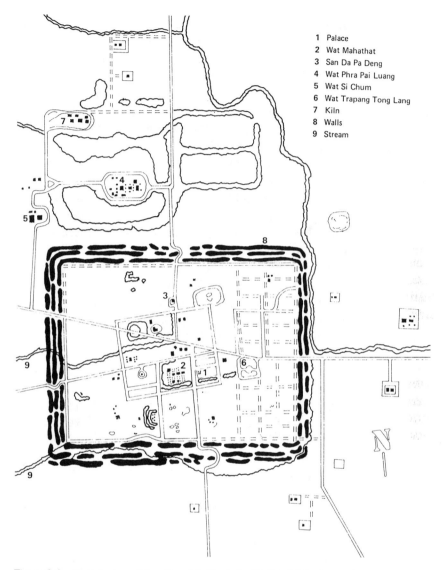

1 Palace
2 Wat Mahathat
3 San Da Pa Deng
4 Wat Phra Pai Luang
5 Wat Si Chum
6 Wat Trapang Tong Lang
7 Kiln
8 Walls
9 Stream

Figure 2.9. Sketch plan of the city of Sukhothai with Wat Mahāthāt at the center. From Carol Stratton and Miriam McNair Scott, *The Art of Sukhodaya. Thailand's Golden Age.* Oxford/Kuala Lamphur: Oxford University Press, 1989, p. 11. Reprinted by permission of the Stratton/Scott Archives.

under King Ram Khamhaeng the axial center of the city was the Manaṅsilāpātra, a stepped pyramid where the king granted audiences and also where monks preached the *dhamma*. The structure may have been a transformation of the Kon Laeng, a stepped altar on which offerings were made to the city's guardian deity (Thai, *phī muang*) during the reign of Si Indradit.[63] The Manansilāpātra represented a sacred, mythical plateau in the Himalayas and was the center of the ceremonial city defined by its triple ramparts, four large gates at the cardinal directions, and various Buddhist monuments marking other directions. The transformation of Sukhothai continued during the reign of Ram Khamhaeng's successor, King Dhammarāja (Loethai), when the capital was restored as a ceremonial center under the direction of Somdet Phra Mahāthera Si Satha, a former prince become monk.

Around 1330 C.E. a slender, lotus bud tower enshrining a Buddha relic was built atop Ram Khamhaeng's pyramid in the center of the city, transforming it into a Buddhist *stūpa*.[64] In the early 1340s Si Satha expanded the *stūpa*, enshrining two Buddha relics he had brought back from Sri Lanka where he had been residing for a decade. He also added four axial towers. More than 200 large and small buildings were constructed around the *stūpa* itself, which became known as Wat Mahāthāt, the Monastery of the Great Relics. This pattern of building a reliquary *stūpa* or *cetiya* as the symbolic and ceremonial center of the kingdom typifies the development of Tai city-states (*muang*).

Although the story of the material representations of kings and cosmology that we have pursued in this section culminates in Thailand in the great capital of Ayutthaya (fifteenth–eighteenth centuries), it is fitting that we close our study of this topic with a brief look at King Lu'thai who reigned at Sukhothai from 1347 to 1361. He was the author of the *Traibhūmikathā* (The Three Worlds), perhaps the first systematic Theravāda cosmological treatise and the first truly literary work written by a Thai author.[65] Lu'thai's treatise is as much a discussion of Buddhist kingship as it is a picture of the thirty-one realms of the Buddhist cosmology.

Lu'thai was most interested in the fifth and seventh levels of this cosmo-logical scheme—the realms of the four great continents and Tāvatiṃsa, the heavenly abode of the thirty-three gods. Both of these realms are ruled by kings who, as we noted in our discussion of King Asoka, served as models for Southeast Asian Buddhist monarchs. Indra reigned in Tāvatiṃsa heaven: "In emulation of Indra, whose palace is regally situated at the exact tip of the cosmic Mount Meru, Theravāda kings traditionally build their palaces at the symbolic centres of their kingdoms. Thus, the earthly king himself becomes Indra. 'Indra' appears twice in the official name of Thailand's present-day capital. . ."[66] Lu'thai, however, was most influenced by the image

World Without Form

Absolute Nothingness
Nothingness
Infinite Mentality
Infinite Space

World With Partial Form
Supreme Brahmas
Clear-sighted Brahmas
Beautiful Brahmas
Serene Brahmas
Prosperous Brahmas
Brahmas Without Perception
Brahmas with Great Rewards
Brahmas with Steady Aaura
Brahmas with Infinite Aura
Brahmas with Limited Aura
Radiant Brahmas
Brahmas with Infinite Luster
Brahma with Limited Luster
Great Brahmas
Brahma Ministers
Brahma Attendants

World of Desire
Delight in Others' Creations
Delight in Own Creations
Full of Joy
King Yama
**Indra's Heaven
Four Guardian Kings
**Humans including the *cakkavatin* King
Demons
Hungry Ghosts
Animals
Hells

Figure 2.10. The Cosmological Scheme of the Three Worlds in the *Traibhūmikathā* attributed to King Lu'thai of Sukhothai. Permission granted by Oxford University Press.

of the *cakkavattin* who attained his position through the virtues of his past meritorious lives and who rules justly and compassionately in accordance with the *dhamma*. Like the mighty *cakkavattin* who conquers the four continents with his armies, Lu'thai conquered Sukhothai and sought to establish his authority over a widespread territory. Over half of the fourteen years of his reign was spent outside of the city. He built distinctive lotus bud *ceitya* towers in outlying centers as tangible signs of the spiritual links binding capital, province, and vassal states.[67] A giant wheel (*cakka*) and the Phra Buddha Singha, a palladium image, accompanied the king on his travels.[68] These practices parallel Jayavarman VII's installation of the Jaya Buddha Mahānātha image in outlying centers of his empire and Anawrahta's custom of enshrining votive tablets and *jātaka* plaques throughout the territories over which he exercised suzerainty.

Stūpas and relics legitimated Lu'thai's territorial rights; the wheel and the Buddha image that accompanied him further reenforced his claims over the network of states beyond the royal capital. Lu'thai also sought to unite his newly reforged kingdom by distributing Buddha images, relics, and Buddha footprints with the 108 cosmologically potent supernatural signs. In effect, he created a ritual unity joined together by a cult of sacred relics, images, footprints, and monks in which "the monks who accompanied a sacred relic [and image] in its passage through the country helped strengthen the nexus between outlying centers and the capital."[69]

The legacy of King Ram Khamhaeng and his grandson Lu'thai, have been very influential in the processes of national integration and political legitimation in the modern period. It has been argued, for example, that King Ram Khamhaeng's famous stele inscription depicting a strong, benevolent, *dhammarāja* king holding audiences with his subjects and presiding over a prosperous realm was in fact created during the reign of King Mongkut on the eve of Thailand's political and economic modernization.[70] It has even been argued that King Lu'thai's *Tribhūmikathā* (Three Worlds of King Ruang) was not authored by Lu'thai as a Buddhist political charter before he overthrew the usurper of the Sukhothai throne and restored the kingdom's fortunes, but rather that this cosmological treatise on the ethics of kingship was written during the reign of Rāma I (1782–1809) to help bolster a Thai monarchy devastated by the Burmese sack of Ayutthaya.[71] Although these particular historical reconstructions have been rejected by most scholars, it is certainly the case that at those two critical transitional periods in modern Thai history—the late eighteenth and late nineteenth centuries—Buddhism provided a critical basis for maintaining a sense of Thai identity in the face of severe challenges. In more recent times the *Three Worlds of King Ruang* has been used both by conservative neotraditional groups to support the maintenance of the power of the ruling Thai elites and by liberal voices urging greater and more rapid democratization. These voices reconstruct the political institutions and cultural products of Sukhothai as providing for a "true Buddhist model of participatory, liberal form of government."[72]

In concluding this section, a brief postscript about the disjunction between the period of the cosmologically grounded Southeast Asian states and our own age is in order. In his lectures on Angkor at the Musèe Louis Finot in Hanoi before World War II, George Coedès observed, "I hope I have made it clear. . .that the arrangement of a Khmer city and its architecture and decoration were governed by a whole series of magic and religious beliefs, and not determined by utilitarian or aesthetic aims. To understand these monuments one has to be acquainted with the mythological images on which they were modelled."[73] Does the fragmentation that characterizes our postmodern worldview undermine our ability to truly understand the supernaturally charged, symbolically integrated cosmos of Jayavarman VII, Kyanzittha, and King Lu'thai? Possibly, for a broad and deep comprehension of the religiously grounded worlds of Angkor, Pagan, and Sukhothai requires both empathy and imagination. To enter into their cosmological milieux demands not that we suspend critical rationality but that we integrate such analysis into an emphathetic, holistic understanding of these classical cultural, political, and religious centers and what they represented in the lives of those who lived, worshipped, and ruled there. These splendid sites are not only great architectural and artistic monuments; they are also systems of mimetic empowerment.

THE BUDDHA AS COSMOCRATOR

Despite the tensions and conflicts that arise between religious and political institutions, a cooperative relationship more often pertains between religion and the state. Among the great historical religions—Judaism, Christianity, Hinduism, Islam, and Buddhism—aspects of this interrelationship include state support of religious institutions, a religious cosmology that legitimates political status, such as divine right of kings, and a similitude between the mythologized portraits of political and religious leaders. In short, in classical religious cultures the lines between the secular and the sacred, or between the political and the religious are complimentary and are often blurred.

Imperial support of Buddhism during the Mauryan period, especially during the reign of King Asoka, inevitably coupled Buddhism and political rule; in particular, linking the institutional fortunes of the monastic order with the state. As a part of this process, the Buddha and king become virtual mirror images of one another. In various Pali texts we find the following: The Buddha appears as a king in previous lives; at Prince Siddhattha's birth sages predict that the royal child will be either a world ruler or a fully enlightened Buddha; the Buddha predicts King Asoka's appearance, thereby legitimating his rule; Asoka becomes a model for Buddhist kingship throughout Southeast Asia by his conversion to Buddhism, by calling a council to purify the *dhamma* and the *sangha*, and by building *cetiyas* to enshrine Buddha relics; kingship in Theravāda Buddhism presupposes many lifetimes of preparation as does Buddhahood; the ten royal virtues share much in common with the moral perfections associated with the spiritual achievement; and finally, in the Theravāda tradition bodhisattahood is associated with both Buddhahood and kingship.

In one sense both the king and the Buddha bear primary responsibility for the well-being of their respective realms—the worldly (*lokiya*) sphere of proximate goods and the religious sphere (*lokkuttara*) of ultimate goods, a relationship that has been referred to as "the two wheels of *dhamma*."[74] On a more subtle level, however, the Theravāda tradition constructs kingship in the image of the Buddha and Buddhahood in the image of the king with power as the key denominator.

In our earlier examination of the consecration of a Buddha image we saw the crucial significance of the sacred power associated with the person of the Buddha. This power manifests itself in several other ways. In classical Theravāda texts like the *Mahāparinibbāna Sutta* (The Buddha's Great Decease) we find the themes of the Buddha as teacher and supernatural miracle worker interwoven. The cult of Buddha relics and their association with ruling monarchs discussed in this important text bear testimony to the sacred power believed to be latent in the physical remains of the great teacher. As we shall see, the cult of relics figures prominently in a consideration of this topic. The Buddha as consecrator of the land plays an even more central role, however; that is, the Buddha's physical presence serves to establish a "holy land" (*buddhadesa*). This motif occurs consistently in Southeast Asian Theravāda chronicles in the form of the Buddha's miraculous visits to these regions.

Both the *Island Chronicle (Dīpavaṃsa)* and the *Great Chronicle (Mahāvaṃsa)* begin with an account of the Blessed One's three visits to Sri Lanka in the first eight years of his enlightenment.[75] The *Island Chronicle* states in its opening line: "Listen to me. I shall relate the Chronicle of the *Buddha's coming to the island*." The same construction appears in Burmese, Thai, and Laotian chronicles. For example, the oldest extant Burmese chronicle, *The Celebrated Chronicle*, written by Samantapasadika Sīlvavaṃsa (fifteenth century) follows the typical Theravāda chronicle pattern of moving from a discussion of the kings of Buddhist India, to the Buddhist conquest of Sri Lanka, and then to the Buddha's visit to Lekaing village in the Tagaung kingdom of Burma, a story repeated in the famous *Glass Palace Chronicle of the Kings of Burma*, commissioned by King Bagyidaw in 1829 C.E. In this legend two brothers, Mahapon and Sulapon, request the Buddha to visit their country and then build a sandalwood monastery for him: "the Lord foreseeing that in time to come his religion would be established for a long time in Burma, came many times with. . . five hundred saints until the monastery was finished. And when it was finished he gathered alms for seven days, enjoyed the bliss of mystic meditation, and refreshed the people with the ambrosia of his teaching (*dhamma*)."[76]

The story continues with the conversion of 500 men and 500 women to the Buddha's teaching and their attainment of sainthood (*arahant*). By tracing the origin of the establishment of Buddhism in Burma to the Buddha himself, the chronicler not only legitimates the tradition but also imbues it with an absolute authority beyond the historical. As the *Celebrated Chronicle* contends, "in Sri Lanka the religion did not begin to arise before the year C.E. 236 [the date of the conversion of King Devānaṃpiyatissa by Mahinda, King Asoka's son]. But in our land the religion that arose since the time the Lord came to dwell in the sandalwood monastery."[77]

Thai Buddhist chronicles tell a similar story with miraculous elaborations. In the *Epochs of the Conqueror* the Buddha takes his bowl and robe and flies from Vārāṇasī to Haripuñjaya in northern Thailand, where he preaches the *dhamma* and instructs the people in the three refuges and the five moral precepts.[78] In the chronicle *The Buddha Travels the World* [*Phrachao Liep Lok*], the Buddha's visit initiates the establishment of towns and monasteries, constituting a kind of sacred geography. Virtually all the chronicles of major northern Thai monasteries begin with a founding visit by the Buddha.

Political units also develop around material representations of the Buddha; namely, his relics and his image. For example, when the Buddha made his legendary visit to northern Thailand, he predicted that one of his relics would be discovered by King Adicca of the kingdom of Haripuñjaya. This discovery coincides with the growth of the kingdom of Haripuñjaya and undoubtedly points to royal patronage of Theravāda Buddhism that abetted integration of the expanding kingdom.

The Buddha relic symbolizes political authority in two ways. First, when enshrined in a *cetiya* or reliquary mound, the relic functions as a magical center or *axis mundi* for the kingdom. The enshrined relic or *cetiya* becomes the symbol par excellence of the monarch as *cakkavattin* or "wheel turner." Literally, the king becomes the "hub" of a cosmosized state. Second, from

a historical perspective the enshrinement of a relic usually entails legitimation of the monarch by the monastic order. Thus, King Anawrahta of
Pagan (eleventh century) justified his conquest of the Mon kingdom of Lower
Burma (Pegu) by expropriating the Mon *sangha* and by building great
monuments. Anawrahta's religious edifices symbolized his power as world
ruler. Patronage of the monastic order helped to guarantee popular support.

Buddha images also function as symbols of political authority, linking
the person of the monarch with the Buddha. A brief look at the Emerald
Buddha image, the palladium of the Chakri Dynasty in Thailand, will
illustrate the power of the Buddha as cosmocrator.[80]

The story of the origin of the Emerald Buddha image or the Holy Emerald
Jewel is told in the northern Thai chronicles as follows:

> Some 500 years after the death of the Buddha the holy monk, Nagasena,
> counselor to the famous king Milinda (or Menander), wanted to make
> an image of the Buddha to propagate the faith. Fearing that an image
> of gold or silver would be destroyed, he decides to make one from
> a precious stone endowed with special power. Sakka (i.e., Indra),
> becoming aware of this wish, goes to Mt. Vibul to obtain a suitable
> gem from the great *cakkavatti[n]* king or Universal Monarch who has
> in his possession seven precious stones with supernatural powers. Since
> only a *cakkavatti[n]* king can possess such a gem, the guardians of
> Mt. Vibul offer an Emerald Jewel which is of the same essence and
> comes from the same place as the gem requested by Sakka. The god
> takes the Emerald Jewel to Nagasena. Vissukamma, the divine
> craftsman, then appears in the guise of an artisan and fashions the Jewel
> into a Buddha image. When it is completed, the holy monk invites the
> seven relics of the Buddha to enter into it. Finally, he predicts that the
> image will be worshipped in Cambodia, Burma, and Thailand.[81]

The chronicles then proceed to narrate the travels of the image from India
to Sri Lanka, Angkor, and various Thai principalities. The Emerald Buddha
emerges onto the pages of history in the fifteenth century during the reign
of Tilokarāja of Chiang Mai. In the mid-sixteenth century it is taken to
Laos where it remained until 1778 when it was brought to Bangkok. Today
it resides in the chapel of the grand palace, venerated as the protector of
the Chakri dynasty.

The Emerald Buddha possesses a power inherent in the precious stone
itself, but its supernatural character is enhanced by its association with such
cult objects as the *Indra-kīla*, the guardian deity of the capital city of Chiang
Mai, and moreover, its identification with the *cakkavattin* king or the Buddha

in his *cakkavattin* aspect. Possession of the Emerald Buddha endowed a monarch with special power and authority:

> Through the proper veneration of the Jewel the king gained the support of sovereign power in its most potent and beneficent form. And, on a deeper level, the king's meditation on the Jewel imbued him with that power and thereby enabled him to exercise authority to establish order, and to guarantee the protection for the kingdom. Moreover, it was this identification between the Jewel and the Buddha-Cakkavatti[n] which provided the ultimate justification for one of the most important functions associated with the Jewel in the Thai and Laotian kingdoms where it was venerated—namely, its role as the sovereign ruler before whom the various princes of the kingdom swore their fealty to the reigning monarch who possessed it.[82]

The relationship between the person of the Buddha and political authority has many fascinating symbolic and historical dimensions. The central theme that emerges from the traditional Southeast Asian Theravāda Buddhist chronicles, however, is the power of the Buddha as cosmocrator. The Buddha sacralizes the land; he becomes the ground of political order and power through his *physical* presence, his actual visitations, or through signs of his physical presence; that is, his relics, footprints, and images. But, the presence of the Buddha is only latent or potential. A royal monarch is the only person with sufficient power to actualize it in the mundane world. Although such notions may seem antithetical to the statement in the Theravāda Suttas attributed to the Buddha that only his teaching (*dhamma*) was his legitimate successor, the canonical Pali texts make abundantly clear there are two "wheels of *dhamma*": one is the Four Noble Truths and the Noble Eightfold Path given in the Buddha's First Discourse; the other is the righteous political ruler (*dhammarāja*) with power and authority to order an otherwise fractious society.[83] In short, the Buddha and the king are mirror images or two sides of the same coin: the mundane (*lokiya*) and the transmundane (*lokuttara*); the princely and the ascetic; power and compassion. Rather than being antithetical, the two poles are fundamentally interrelated and mutually supportive.

MODERN NATIONALISM AND BUDDHISM

Traditional religion plays a crucial role in the modern histories of many of the developing countries. One of the most dramatic recent examples has been in the Islamic countries of the Middle East, an Islamic resurgence also felt in Southeast Asia, particularly Indonesia and Malaysia. In the post-World War II period Mohandas K. Gandhi tapped the rich reservoir of Indian religio-cultural values in the service of his independence movement. In a similar way, Buddhism has figured importantly in various nationalist movements in Sri Lanka, Myanmar (Burma), Thailand, and Vietnam. Buddhism has also become a factor in the national rebuilding process in Laos and Cambodia, two countries economically, politically, and socio-culturally crippled by the Vietnam war.

Given the close identification between Buddhism and the traditional states in colonially dominated countries such as Myanmar and Sri Lanka, it is not surprising to find Buddhism being exploited for the purposes of enhancing nationalistic political forces and new forms of national integration under indigenous leadership. U Nu of Burma and S. W. R. D. Bandaranaike of Sri Lanka provide the most striking examples of political leaders in the immediate postcolonial period who became modern representations of the Buddhist tradition of the "ruler of *dhamma*" (*dhammika dhammarāja*). More recently the militarily controlled government of Myanmar established by General Ne Win in 1963 has sought to legitimate its autocratic, repressive policies through its support of Buddhism. Various forms of Buddhist civil religion have also figured prominently in Thailand's rapid economic development over the past several decades. We shall study the relationship between modern nationalism and Theravāda Buddhism by exploring the particular cases of Burma, Sri Lanka, and Thailand.

Burma

In January 1948 U Nu became the first prime minister of the newly independent Union of Burma. He espoused a political ideology that blended Buddhism and socialism. In essence it was based on the theory that a national community could be built only if the individual members were able to overcome their own selfish interests. U Nu argued that material goods were not meant to be saved or used for personal comfort but only to provide for the necessities of life in the journey to *nibbāna*.[84] He contended that property and class distinctions should be transcended in the spirit of Buddhist self-abnegation for the good of the larger community. Not unlike the *dhamma* of Asoka, U Nu espoused an ideology of a welfare state rooted in a *cakkavattin*'s superior knowledge about the causality of deliverance from suffering (*dukkha*) directed toward the humanitarian ideal of the benefit of all sentient beings. He preached a socialistic doctrine of a classless society without want in which all members would strive for moral and mental perfection to overcome the constant rounds of rebirth (*saṃsāra*).[85]

U Nu's political ideology blended Buddhism and socialism. Moreover, his personal lifestyle embodied elements of the traditional ideal of the righteous Buddhist monarch. Approximately six months after taking office an insurrection nearly toppled the government. His response to that threat was to take a vow of sexual abstinence so that by the power of his personal example the insurgents would be defeated: "On July 20, 1948, when the insurrection was causing anxiety, I went into my prayer room and before the Holy Image took the vow of absolute purity, making a wish at that time that if I kept that vow the insurgents would be confounded."[86]

In 1950 U Nu created a Buddhist Sāsana Council to propagate Buddhism and supervise monks; he appointed a minister of religious affairs and ordered government departments to dismiss civil servants thirty minutes early if they wished to meditate. In the manner of King Asoka and later Southeast Asian Buddhist monarchs he called a *sangha* council to purify the *dhamma* and produce a new redaction of the Pali canon. For that council he constructed a large *stūpa* and assembly hall at the cost of $6 million, emulating the meritorious acts of earlier kings on the behalf of the Buddhist *sangha*. U Nu's overthrow in 1962 at the hands of General Ne Win was partially justified on the grounds of U Nu's insistence on Buddhism as the basis of national identity. In August 1961 he introduced in the Burmese Parliament an amendment establishing Buddhism as the state religion. Because the modern nation state of Burma contains sizable non-Buddhist and non-Burman minorities, such as the Shan, Karen, Mon, and Chin, these groups resisted his policies. Furthermore, Donald E. Smith may be correct when he suggests that U Nu escaped from the hard requirements of political leadership through his many religious activities and that his continual preoccupation with religious matters robbed him of a rational approach to political, economic, and social problems.[87] Despite these criticisms, U Nu still can be interpreted as a modern approximation of the traditional Theravāda Buddhist ideal of the righteous monarch.

U Nu's successor, General Ne Win, proposed to create a secular, socialist state in which Buddhist institutions within the state's superstructure would be dismantled.[88] The Buddhist Sāsana Council was dissolved, and the Burmese Socialist Program called for the freedom of religion. The secular direction of the Ne Win government shifted in the closing years of the 1970s as the government sought to unify and purify the *sangha*. In the face of

Figure 2.11. Aung San
Suu Kyi.

mounting economic and political problems, Myanmar's military government,
called the State Law and Order Commission (SLORC), has attempted to
fashion a policy of Buddhist civil religion more systematic and authoritarian
than that of U Nu.

General Ne Win's policy of isolationist Burmese socialism, now gradually
changing as a result of both internal problems and external pressure, has
impoverished most of the Burmese and other minority peoples in the country
with the exception of the ruling military elite. Not only has the country's
industrial development been stifled, Burma's agricultural production has
declined and the country's transportation and communications infrastructure
has deteriorated. Furthermore, basic freedoms of speech, assembly, and
the press have been greatly restricted. The military refused to step down

in the face of their defeat in the 1989 elections, imprisoning or killing opposition leaders. Aung San Suu Kyi, recipient of the 1991 Nobel Peace Prize, led the major opposition party to the ruling military regime and as of 1995 continues to live in Yangon (Rangoon) under house arrest.[89]

In 1980 the government restructured the monastic *sangha* in an effort not only to assert greater control but also to ensure the support of senior monastic leaders. In April of that year more than a thousand *sangha* representatives from each township attended an assembly in Yangon. Various national, regional, and local monastic structures were created; numerous regulations were passed enforcing monastic discipline and the state control of the monastic order including issuance of identification papers "to provide for the scrutiny of individuals entering the monkhood and to systematically control and supervise members after their admission into the monkhood."[90] The state has sponsored countrywide lecture tours by renowned religious teachers and the government has promoted missions to propogate Buddhism among non-Buddhist populations in the six states and divisons of the country.

On the symbolic level Ne Win ordered the construction of the Mahāvijaya Pagoda in Yangon. The monument virtually abuts the Shwe-dagon Pagoda, Burma's most venerated pilgrimage center and one of the holiest sites in Theravāda Buddhist Southeast Asia. Several articles about the pagoda published in *The Light of the Dhamma*, a journal of the Ministry of Home and Religious Affairs, promoted the Mahāvijaya *cetiya* as a symbol of unity and peace.

The Burmese government's symbolic and practical promotion of Buddhism is reminiscent of classical as well as modern forms of Buddhist civil religion, in which religion and the state are inexorably linked. A 1981 article in *The Light of the Dhamma* likens the relationship between Buddhism, the people, and the state to three strands of a single rope:

> Both the worldly affairs of the people and the governmental affairs of the State are mundane aspects. In the performance and execution of these mundane aspects men must be fully equipped with good conduct, spiritual maturity, and meaningful hope for the happiness in the life hereafter. All these supramundane issues are collectively known as "Religious Affairs."
>
> To carry out, supervise and patronize all these religious affairs, the full-fledged clergy-members of the Monastic Order (Sangha) are entirely responsible.
>
> As a matter of fact, the full-fledged cleric members of the Sangha Order and the officials of the government are the products born out of the nation. Therefore, they have to render their services for the

welfare and happiness of all the people. As such, the working people, the government and the members of the Order (in other words, the People, the State and the Church) must be in harmony and conformity with one another in the establishment of the blissful and meaningful living world. Indeed, they are like three strings twisted properly into one strong durable rope.[91]

In the case of Myanmar, the construction of a contemporary Buddhist civil religion serves to support a repressive military regime—a far cry from the benevolent idealism of a King Asoka.

Sri Lanka

S. W. R. D. Bandaranaike, elected prime minister of Ceylon (Sri Lanka) in 1956, represents another notable example of the symbiotic relationship between Theravāda Buddhism and a political state in the immediate postcolonial period. Like U Nu, Bandaranaike exploited the symbols and institutional power of Buddhism to come into office. Unfortunately, these same forces provoked the severe communal strife that eventually led to his assassination in 1962, an act engineered by a disgruntled Buddhist monk. Despite this disastrous consequence, there is little doubt that "a prominent feature of the movement led by Bandaranaike consisted in the large-scale participation of Buddhist monks in the political struggle, and there can little doubt that approval by the Sangha was a major factor in legitimizing the political actions taken by him in terms of the living Buddhist tradition of Ceylon."[92]

Like U Nu, Bandaranaike espoused an ideology of Buddhist socialism. As he characterized this ideology in a speech before the World Fellowship of Buddhists in 1950, "I believe in democracy because I believe in the Buddhist doctrine that a man's worth should be measured by his own merit and not some extraneous circumstance and also that human freedom is a priceless possession. The Buddha preached that ultimate freedom of man when the human mind need not be subject even to the will of God, and man was free to decide for himself what was right or wrong. . . . In economics I consider myself a Socialist, for I cannot reconcile, with the spirit of the doctrine of Maitreya, man-made inequalities that condemn a large section of our fellowmen to poverty, ignorance and disease."[93]

In his personal lifestyle Bandaranaike did not symbolize the righteous monarch ideal in the same way as U Nu. Still, there is little doubt that his justification for both his democratic political beliefs and socialistic economic philosophy rested in Buddhism. He attempted to fashion a Middle Way ideology that was neutralist in international policy and uniquely Sinhalese in national policy. In the eyes of many Sinhalese Buddhists, Bandaranaike is a national hero who stands with the Anagārika Dharmapāla as one of the two great leaders in the modern period who, like the ancient kings Duṭṭhagāmaṇi (101–77) and Parakrama Bāhu I (1153–1186), sought to establish the preeminence of Buddhism in Sri Lanka.[94] His espousal of a Buddhist civil religion, however, also contributed to a Sinhalese Buddhist chauvinism that exacerbated the violent conflict between the Sinhalese majority and Tamil minority populations on the island.

Since 1983 the island nation of Sri Lanka has been caught in the maelstrom of a fratricidal conflict between the majority Sinhala population (75 percent) and the Tamils. Most of the Sinhalese are Buddhist whereas Tamils are either Hindu (18 percent) or Muslim. As the Sinhalese chronicle, the *Mahāvaṃsa*, suggests, the conflict between the Sinhalese Buddhists and Hindu Tamils has ancient roots. King Duṭṭhagāmaṇi, for example, is lionized for defeating King Elara, a Hindu Tamil who ruled much of the island in the first century of our era. More proximate causes of the conflict stem from three centuries of Dutch and British economic exploitation, which disrupted the island's traditional way of life by challenging the ancient cultural synthesis fostered through royal and religious institutions, especially the Buddhist monastery. Recent Sri Lankan history has also abetted the conflict, especially the following: the chauvinistic Buddhist ideology of the early twentieth century reformer, the Anagārika Dharmapāla; the Buddhist civil religion promoted by S. W. R. D. Bandaranaike; and, the economic policies of J. R. Jayawardena, prime minister from 1977 to 1989, which created an increasing disparity between urban wealth and rural poverty.[95] Chauvinistic nationalism was further exacerbated by the militant policies of Jayawardena's successor, Ranasingha Premadasa, who was assassinated in the Spring of 1993. Premadasa even sought to undermine the work of A. T. Ariyaratne's Sarvodaya Shramadāna movement, which since 1958 has worked in over 8,000 villages throughout the island for the uplift and well-being of all people, regardless of religion or ethnicity. In January 1994, Ariyaratne visited Jaffna, the stronghold of the Tamil Elam, in an effort to act as a mediator between the Sinhalese controlled national government and the Tamil separatists. The Sarvodaya movement has been the most important Buddhist force seeking reconciliation between the two sides.

It is probably the case that historical distance has given traditional Buddhist kingship a more benevolent cast than was actually the case. Nevertheless, the current Buddhist nationalisms in Myanmar and Sri Lanka, have taken the fervor of mid-twentieth century Buddhist nationalist movements to extremes of violent conflict and repression.[96]

Thailand, Cambodia, and Laos

Unlike Myanmar and Sri Lanka, Thailand was never ruled by a Western colonial power, consequently, Buddhism has played a somewhat different role in defining and legitimating national identity in the modern period.[97] Under the leadership of King Rāma V (King Chulalongkorn, 1865–1902), the Buddhist *sangha* was organized along national lines governed by a Supreme Patriarch (*sangha-rāja*).[98] Via the network of Buddhist monasteries throughout the country, Rāma V promoted the first scheme of national education. Monastic education itself was regularized under the control of the national government. Under Rāma V's successor, King Vajiravudh (reign 1910–1925), religion and government became increasingly integrated. Vajiravudh blended the concepts of "nation," "religion," and "king" into a governing ideology for modern Thailand. He fashioned a civil religion in which "nation" seemed to supercede "religion," a process that has increasingly accelerated. Since that time, shifts in the government have led to revisions in the legal code governing the monastic order first in 1941 and again in 1962, but the integration of the *bhikkhusangha* into a national, bureaucratic system and its control by a central government has not changed. Since 1962 the legal structure of the *sangha* has tended to support a hierarchical, status quo oriented, civil religion.

From time to time controversial monks, such as Khrūbā Sivichai in Chiang Mai in the 1930s or Phra Phimonatham in Bangkok in the 1950s, have threatened the compliant cooperation between the *sangha* and the government but the hand-in-glove mutuality between religious and political orders has never been significantly altered. The Buddhist religion (*sāsana*) has enjoyed the material support of powerful government, military, and economic elites; in turn, the *sangha* has rendered assistance to various national development schemes. Field Marshall Sarit Thanarat, who exploited the symbolism of the monarchy and Buddhism to legitimate his 1957 coup d'état, promoted national integration through the creation of the Thammathūt and the Thammachārik Programs under the control of government ministries and bureaus. In the 1960s and 1970s one of the main aims of the Thammathūt

Figure 2.12. A Rama V (King Chulalongkorn) Shrine. Restaurant, Chiang Rai, Thailand. Photo by Donald K. Swearer.

Program was to promote rural development in areas of the country threatened by political unrest. The Thammachārik Program sends monks to work among the animistic hill tribe peoples of northern Thailand. Propagating Buddhism among non-Thai peoples with limited loyalty to the national government has been one of the principal means of their integration into the Thai nation-state.[99]

One of the striking developments in Thailand in the early 1990s has been the emergence of a cult of King Chulalongkorn, Rāma V, the Thai monarch principally responsible for overseeing the changes that challenged Thailand at the end of the nineteenth century. It is not unusual to see a bronze image of Rāma V on a restaurant altar shelf; Rāma V's equestrian statue in front of the parliament building in Bangkok has become a shrine visited by thousands of people daily; and there are shops in new shopping malls devoted exclusively to Rāma V memorabilia. One is tempted to interpret this phenomenon in *devarāja* terms. Although it may be legitimate to ask whether Rāma V has become a type of divine apotheosis, the social, economic, and political reasons for this apparent apotheosis are quite complex; they have to do with the rapidity of economic and social change in the country, increasing affluence accompanied by the frustration of the expectations of an expanding educated, urban, professional class, and I would argue, the general decline of Buddhism as a determinant of cultural and social values. From a political perspective it has been suggested that the Rāma V cult is orchestrated to shore up the power of the monarchy, increasingly criticized by Thai intellectuals. Primarily, however, the cult seems to reflect a nostalgia for the early days of the twentieth century when—as popular belief has it—the monarchy was strong, the country relatively prosperous, and traditional values informed the progress of modernization.

With the establishment of a legitimate Cambodian government in 1993, in which Prince Norodom Sihanouk and his son Prince Norodom Ranariddh were key players, Buddhism resumed a central role in Cambodian social and political life. Politicians seek the blessing of high-ranking monks much as they do in Thailand, and monks are invited to chant at various large public gatherings. In short, the current revival of institutional Buddhism in Cambodia parallels the revival of the Cambodian state. To be sure, there are other aspects of the revival of Buddhism in Cambodia. Mahāghosānanda, a monastic leader in the pre-Vietnam war days, currently headquartered in Providence, Rhode Island, organized a massive Buddhist peace march prior to the Cambodian elections in 1994 and has been active in the "engaged Buddhist" movement that includes the Dalai Lama and the Vietnamese Zen monk Thich Nhat Hanh. This movement has articulated a Buddhist social activism based on a reformed Buddhist worldview and Buddhist meditation practice. It remains to be seen how this reformist, social activist wing of Cambodian Buddhism led by Mahāghosānanda might affect the shape of a resurgent Buddhist civil religion.

Although the socialist regime in Laos never sought to destroy the Buddhist *sangha* per se, the government did place severe restrictions on the monastic order, including the freedom to enter the monkhood and the content of the monastic curriculum. Furthermore, in a material sense the *sangha* suffered from an economy greatly weakened by the Vietnam war and the economic policies of a socialist government. With the gradual political and economic transformation of Laos, Buddhism is also seeing signs of revival. As the speed of the economic recovery of Laos continues in the 1990s fueled especially by Thailand, one hopes that the accompanying prosperity of the *sangha* will also lead to a revival in monastic education and spiritual practice. Laotian and Cambodian monks in the United States and in Europe will play a crucial role in the revival of Buddhism in their respective countries.

In this chapter we have studied some of the ways in which political authority and power in Southeast Asia are grounded in or related to religion, especially Buddhism and its institutions. We found that the centrality of the person of the Buddha in the rituals, rites and festivals studied in the first chapter emerged within the context of the classical Southeast Asian states in the form of the Buddha as cosmocrator. We explored how sacred history came into play in the context of traditional Southeast Asian monarchies in the form of the exemplary, righteous ruler King Asoka; we also examined the relationship between religion and the state, kingship and cosmology within the context of classical Southeast Asian states and monuments dating from the tenth through the fifteenth centuries. Our interpretation of King Asoka and classical Southeast Asian monarchical states was informed by the notion of mimesis; namely, that Southeast Asian rulers and their states were empowered by the imitation of the paradigmatic Buddhist world ruler, on the one hand, and the cosmology of the Indian worldview, on the other. Subsequently, we analyzed the proposition that in the modern period leaders of independence movements in Burma and Sri Lanka consciously sought to legitimate their new nations in the face of Western colonialism through the symbols and ideology of Theravāda Buddhism; and, furthermore, that within the contemporary nation-states of Myanmar, Sri Lanka, and Thailand, at both symbolic and institutional levels, Buddhism continues to figure prominently in government policies, programs, and strategies. Finally, Buddhism has become an important factor in the slow and painful process of national renewal in Laos and Cambodia, countries devastated both economically and politically by the Vietnam war and its aftermath. In short, in this chapter we have explored the various and diverse expressions of religion in Southeast Asia as a key factor in dynamic processes of the construction of political states, political legitimation, and national integration.

THREE

Modernization

The Dynamic of Tradition and Change

R eligious traditions are not static. They respond to social, economic, and political change; indeed, they help shape such change. They challenge foreign ideologies and in doing so are influenced by them. In stable periods of history, religious traditions seem to change only imperceptibly, but in more volatile times the disruption and transformation of religious institutions and worldviews keeps pace with and sometimes outstrips changes in other areas of life. Since the end of World War II, Southeast Asia has undergone rapid change dramatized by war, political revolution, the overthrow of colonially shaped governments, the impact of the world market economy, and the rapid erosion of many traditional institutions.[1]

The most extreme case in point has been Cambodia. Under Pol Pot's (Saloth Sar) reign of terror the Communist Party of Kampuchea (CPK) sought to eliminate virtually all vestiges of its colonial and traditional past, including Buddhism. Between 1975 and 1979 the CPK "wanted to exercise absolute control and hoped to preside over the destruction of Cambodia's past."[2] In doing so over a million Cambodians were killed and over a half a million fled the country. The population of Phnom Penh, the capital, was forced to evacuate the city within twenty-four hours. The country witnessed the wholesale destruction of monasteries and temples. Buddhist monks were either killed or forced to disrobe and return to lay life. The consequences for religious institutions were disastrous. It appeared that Theravāda Buddhism as an institution had been effectively eliminated, surviving only in the Cambodian refugee camps along the border in Thailand or among refugee communities in North America and Western Europe. However, when the Vietnamese established the People's Republic of Kampuchea (PRK) in 1979 the fortunes of Buddhism improved somewhat. The creation of a new coalition government in 1992 brought hope for renewal for the Cambodian Buddhist *sangha* and in 1993 Norodom Sihanouk was restored as king of Cambodia, a position closely associated with Buddhism.

In Laos the Pathet Lao who came to power in 1975 restricted and regulated the Buddhist *sangha*. Unlike the Pol Pot regime, however, the Laotian government did not try to destroy Buddhism. Monastic education suffered, monastic recruitment declined, and the primacy of Buddhism for Laotian national identity was challenged by a Socialist government supported by the Soviet Union. Buddhism, however, continued to be important in Laotian social and cultural life and today thrives among expatriate Laotian communities in the United States and Europe. By 1994 the material fortunes of the Lao *sangha* benefited from the rebounding Lao economy.

Contemporary challenges to traditional Theravāda Buddhism have not been as dramatic in Myanmar, Thailand, or Sri Lanka, but severe strains have occurred and institutional Buddhism has had to adapt in various ways. This chapter will examine the nature of these adaptations and the challenges to the present and future well-being of Buddhism in Cambodia, Laos, Myanmar, and Thailand as well as in Sri Lanka. We shall focus on the changing roles of the monk and of the laity, and on reform movements within the Buddhist *sangha*.[3]

THE CHANGING ROLE OF THE MONK

As the following examples demonstrate, the Pali scriptures provide relevant background information about the place and role of the Buddhist monk in the Indian society of the early centuries B.C.E. In one of the *Majjhima Nikāya* (Middle Length Sayings of the Buddha), dialogues between the Buddha's blessed disciple Ānanda and a military general, the latter expresses his appreciation for the presence of the *sangha*; Ānanda, in turn, thanks the general for his protection, which enables monks to pursue their practice in a peaceful society. In the Future Dangers Sutta in the *Aṅguttara Nikāya* (Gradual Sayings of the Buddha) the factors that jeopardize *dhamma* practice are listed as famine, war, and social unrest as well as specifically religious issues; viz., schisms in the *sangha*, lax practice among the monks caused by desire for material comforts, and living in too close an association with laity or nuns. In the frame story of the Dangers of the Palace *paritta* people disapprove when a monk visits a king too frequently. Finally, in several Pali *suttas* the Buddha expresses a preference for a republican form of government but accommodates himself to the emerging monarchies of his time.

The picture that emerges from this limited selection of canonical references is the following: The practice of Buddhism depends on peaceful, prosperous social conditions; the *sangha*'s involvement in politics was on the personal level, advising individual rulers to promote more enlightened policies; monks were not forbidden from advising rulers but were warned about the dangers of such a role; and finally, the Buddha did not agitate for structural changes in the form of government although he preferred republics to monarchies. In short, the Theravāda scriptures provide us with a picture of the *sangha* actively involved in the social, economic, and political life of its day, not merely an institution pursuing narrowly construed religious ends. The major issue was not whether the *sangha* should be involved in various human affairs but, rather, what determines the appropriate role played by the monk in society and in politics.[4]

To what degree has the role of the monk in modern Buddhist Southeast Asia changed? Or, has the role of the monk remained essentially the same within a significantly altered social, economic, and political environment? These questions offer no easy answers and are debated by both adherents and scholars of Buddhism. It is certainly the case that monks engage in a range of activities previously seen as being outside the realm of legitimate monastic activity. They provided leadership in the independence movements in Burma and Sri Lanka in the early twentieth century. Vietnamese monks protested against the corrupt Diem regime in the late 1960s through dramatic acts of self-immolation.[5] In the mid-1970s Thai monks became active on both the political left and the right. Theravāda monks in Southeast Asia are speaking out on a variety of contemporary social and economic issues, including the increasing gap between the rich and the poor in the developing world, the exploitation of women in the workplace and as prostitutes, the scourge of AIDS, and the destruction of the natural environment.

Buddhist monks in Southeast Asia take part in a wide range of activities with both direct and indirect political consequences. On the surface such involvement may seem antithetical to the traditional role of the Theravāda monk. Or is it? Although the monastic order provides an alternative to the householder's pursuit of mundane goals, as just suggested the monkhood has never been isolated from politics or from society. Indeed, by its very existence the monastery unavoidably participates in the political realm. Throughout its history, Theravāda monks have advised political leaders with varying degrees of influence. Aspects of the symbiotic relationship between traditional monarchies and the monastic order were explored in the last chapter. Contemporary monks have justified political activism on the grounds of historical precedent and sociological inevitability. Even so, as the contrasts between scenarios from the Pali canon and contemporary Southeast Asia demonstrate, the form of political and social involvement by monks has changed dramatically from the days of the formation of the monastic order.[6]

Today if monks are perceived as political manipulators or as performing roles that are more secular than religious, they risk undermining the symbolic status of the *sangha* as an embodiment and propagator of the Buddha's *dhamma*.[7] For example, in 1958 a disgruntled Sinhalese monk was held responsible for the assassination of S. W. R. D. Bandaranaike, the prime minister of Sri Lanka. This act led to a strong public reaction against monastic involvement in politics, although, today, Sinhalese politicians continue to solicit support from influential monastic leaders. A typical negative sentiment against monastic involvement "in the world" was expressed in a letter to the monthly publication of the Colombo Young Men's Buddhist Association: "the Buddhist public are naturally embarrassed and dismayed to find bhikkhus in vehicles, with briefcases tucked under their arms, looking quite brisk and business-like, meticulously handling money, haunting shops, cinemas and public places, with all the materialistic fervor of dedicated worldlings."[8] Whether or not the spiritual status of the monk is jeopardized by monks moving beyond the confines of the monastery walls depends on both the kinds of activities monks undertake and the ways they engage them. Monks who are perceived as self-serving and having worldly goals will inevitably lose the respect of fellow monks and the laity whether they are carrying out traditional roles or fashioning new ones. By way of contrast, monks who personally embody the moral and spiritual ideals of Buddhism and who speak to political and social issues with the authority of dhammic insight will most likely retain the respect and win the admiration of their monastic peers and thoughtful lay persons even though their activities may trouble traditionalists. We shall explore these issues under three topics: the monk and politics, the monk and society, and *sangha* reform.

The Monk and Politics

In the contemporary period Theravāda monks have played various roles within the context of the modern nation-state. The following examples

Figure 3.1. Monks at typing class. Chiang Mai, Thailand. Photo courtesy of Thomas Borchert.

illustrate some of them. By and large monks have willingly supported traditional legitimation processes. The *sanghas* in Thailand, Laos, Cambodia, and Myanmar have been organized under the aegis of their governments. Monks may receive government stipends and be rewarded with ecclesiastical honors by their governments. We shall look at some specific examples of the interaction between monks and the state to illustrate the social and political complexities of this symbiotic relationship.

In Thailand in 1962, the government expelled from the *sangha* Phra Phimontham, the popular pro-democracy abbot of Wat Mahāthāt in Bangkok, the largest Mahānikai monastery in the country, on fabricated charges that he was a communist.[9] The Kampuchean (Cambodian) government under Pol Pot not only disestablished the *sangha* but also tried to destroy it. Burmese monks in Yangon and Mandalay were imprisoned and some were killed in 1989 as they protested the military government's repression of political freedom. In Sri Lanka many Sinhalese monks have supported the government's battle against the Tamil Elam, a Tamil liberation group who wish to secede to form an independent state on the island. A smaller minority of monks has actively pursued reconciliation between the

two sides. In Laos, the late Venerable Anantasounthne, the abbot of Wat
Thāt Luang in Vientiane, presided over the Lao *sangha* that suffered greatly
during the post-Vietnam war years. The socialist government restructured
monastic education, discouraged ordination into the monkhood, and imposed
restrictions on traditional lay support of the monastic order. In Thailand
during the politically volatile period between 1973 and 1976, Buddhist monks
joined farmers, students, and workers to demand greater freedom of
assembly and expression, more just and equitable economic policies, and
greater government accountability. Yet, other monks publicly support
entrenched military authorities and right-wing political organizations. One
of the most controversial of these monks is Bhikkhu Kitthiwuttho.[10]

Kitthiwuttho was born in 1936 and ordained in 1957. Very early in his
monastic career he proved himself an able public speaker and administrator.
He established a foundation for the study and propagation of Buddhism
at a major Bangkok monastery, and he opened a school for novices and
monks located about a hundred kilometers from Bangkok in Chonburi
Province. Between October 1973 and October 1976, a period that began
and ended with two massive student demonstrations, Kitthiwuttho spoke
out on political issues and even helped to lead a quasi-political demonstration
in Bangkok. Generally he strongly supported the government with anticommunist speeches and writings critical of radical groups and social
disruption. He was identified with a right-wing political movement known
as the Navaphala (New Power Movement).

In a speech on August 16, 1975, entitled *"Sing Tī Khuan Kham Nu'ng"*
(Things We Should Reflect On) Kitthiwuttho argued for Thai national unity
in the face of divisiveness at home and threats to Thailand's border areas.
He urged support for the government, obedience to the law, and he criticized
disruptive tactics by pro-democracy groups. In particular he offered three
solutions to the political and social problems faced by Thai society: the
practice of moral virtues (*sīla*), the training of the mind (*samādhi*), and
the attainment of knowledge (*paññā*). On the surface, these solutions seem
to be conventional, mainstream Theravāda Buddhist teachings, but Kittiwuttho
gave each of them a uniquely nationalistic interpretation.

Sīla is interpreted in general terms by Kitthiwuttho as the five precepts
every Buddhist should follow, such as not to take the life of sentient beings.
He emphasized the prohibition against lying, especially with the intent to
sow the seeds of dissension. For the individual, *sīla* means being morally
pure and avoiding wrongdoing, but on the societal level Kitthiwuttho
interpreted *sīla* as the law of the nation. If everyone embodies *sīla*, concluded

the monk, all will automatically obey the law (i.e., support the status quo) and peace and civil order will reign.[11]

Training the mind means, in Kitthiwuttho's interpretation, to have a mind that is loyal to the country and does not easily waver and bend in the winds of this or that ideology. Both the practice of mindfulness (*sati*) and attainment of wisdom (*paññā*) assume a practical, political orientation. Thailand's problems, he stressed, stem from citizens' failure to understand their duties and responsibilities to society. Only by such an understanding can the people correct social ills and build a happy, peaceful, and orderly nation. Kitthiwuttho then concluded his speech with an appeal to the symbols of Thai national unity, "nation, religion, king" as represented by the three colors (red, white, and blue) of the Thai flag. "The Buddha taught us," stated the monk, "that whenever we are frightened we should look at the flag and have steadfast hearts."[12]

In July 1976 Kitthiwuttho addressed an audience of government and religious leaders at the college he had founded. This address was an elaboration of an interview with a liberal Thai magazine, *Caturat*, in which Kitthiwuttho developed his ideas about the role of the monk in the context of the political crisis brought about in part by the student-led revolution of 1973, the subsequent creation of a parliamentary system of government in Thailand, and the communist victories in Laos, Cambodia, and Vietnam.[13] In the speech entitled "Killing Communists Is Not Demeritorious," he marshalled several arguments to justify his claim that killing communists would not produce negative *kamma*, that is, suffering in this life or some future life. In his interview he stated that, because communists attack the nation, the religion, and the king, they are subhuman. To kill them is akin to killing Satan (i.e., Māra).[14] Furthermore, he argued, the merit accrued from protecting the nation, the religion and the monarchy was greater than the demerit from taking the life of a communist.

In his speech, later printed as a pamphlet by his foundation, Kitthiwuttho reiterated his statement that soldiers who kill communists gain more merit for protecting the nation, the religion, and the king than the demerit from taking life. Citing the Buddha and scripture as authority for his position, he argued that some people are so worthless that to kill them is, in fact, to kill *kilesa* (impurity).[15] Killing communists is like purging the body of impurities and the ideologies responsible for the horrible deaths of millions of people in China, Laos, and Cambodia, he asserted.[16] In addition to these arguments Kitthiwuttho cited the scriptural criteria which define the first precept (*sīla*), the prohibition against taking life: The being must be alive, knowledge that the being has life, intent to kill, acting in order to kill, and finally, death. Kitthiwuttho argued that those who kill with the intention of protecting the nation, the religion, and the king are exempt from the necessary conditions that prohibit taking the life of a living being. Such casuistic reasoning prompted his Thai Buddhist critics to contend that Kitthiwuttho was at least as anti-Buddhist as he was anticommunist.

Kitthiwuttho has continued to be a controversial figure. His support by conservative, right-wing political groups has been criticized by political liberals and thoughtful Buddhist lay persons who argue that he has subverted the *dhamma* for his own political purposes. His entrepreneurism has also come under attack. His school and, more recently, a retirement center in Cholburi have attracted millions of baht in investment, and in 1994 his foundation came under government scrutiny. Whatever the truth of the accusations against Kitthiwuttho, his politicization of the *dhamma* and his controversial personal example contribute to an undermining of the symbolic status of the Thai monk as an exemplar of the Buddha's *dhamma*.

Kitthiwuttho has also been a supporter of Wat Dhammakāya, Thailand's fastest growing Buddhist movement.[17] Officially registered with the government in 1978, Wat Dhammakāya has attracted the backing of the military and political leaders as well as the patronage of the royal family. The Dhammakāya movement was established in the early 1970s by Chaiyaboon Sitthiphon (Phra Dhammajayo) and his friend Phadet Phongasawad (Phra Dattajīvo). As students at Kasetsart University in Bangkok, they studied with a meditation teacher in the lineage of the late Venerable Monkhon Thepmuni (Luang Phọ Sot), abbot of Wat Paknām Phasī Charoen in Bangkok. In 1969 they were ordained at Wat Paknām after completing advanced degrees in business administration and marketing. Dhammajayo pledged to work for the worldwide renewal of Buddhism, beginning in Thailand.

Among its many distinctive features, the Dhammakāya movement has sought to create a new national Buddhist center at Pathum Thani near Bangkok. From an original site of approximately 100 acres Wat Dhammakāya now encompasses well over 1,000 acres; furthermore, its assertive assistant abbot, Dattajīvo, has been quoted as claiming that Wat Dhammakāya intends to expand to over 100,000 acres.[18] On this site the movement has built an impressive, modern temple and other facilities to accommodate thousands of supporters who visit the *wat* on weekends and for major festivals. The celebration marking the end of the Buddhist Rains Retreat (the giving of *kaṭhina* robes) in 1986 was attended by over 100,000 people, many of them bused from various parts of the country. The Dhammakāya movement,

Figure 3.2. Main Sanctuary. Wat Dhammakāya. Prathum Thani, Thailand. Courtesy of Wat Dhammakāya.

furthermore, has become the controlling influence in the Buddhist Associations of most major Thai universities. Through its national headquarters, its network of *dhamma* practice centers throughout the country and influence on university student groups, Wat Dhammakāya seeks to restore a Buddhist civil religion under threat from an increasingly fragmented Thai society and a political environment continually beset by corruption and factionalism that undermines the symbolic power of the monarchy and the practical significance of Buddhism.

Critics of Wat Dhammakāya point out that the strategies and goals of the movement are excessively worldly. With assets of over $40 million, using aggressive recruiting methods, and a commercial approach to evangelism, the movement has been characterized as "religious consumerism."[19] Critics also argue that the movement has been controlled by the economic and ruling elites, that it has done little to address Thailand's increasing social and economic problems, that the leaders of the movement lack knowledge of the *dhamma*, and that the movement has made exaggerated claims for the spiritual attainment of its founder. Despite these criticisms Wat Dhammakāya maintains a broad and strong visibility in the midst of the challenges to the Thai monastic order.

The Monk and Society

The contemporary Theravāda monastic order is inextricably imbedded in the modern social fabrics of Buddhist Southeast Asia even though the *sangha* defined its social role primarily in the context of a traditional, largely rural environment. In most rural areas the monastery has been and continues to be the most important social organization beyond the family. Because traditionally the majority of young men in Theravāda Southeast Asia ordained briefly as a monk, families participated directly and personally in the life of the *bhikkhu sangha*. Furthermore, the doctrines of *kamma* and rebirth undergirded the moral ethos of Theravāda cultures and the philosophy of merit making gave meaning to most lay religious activities. In a practical sense, furthermore, the monastery served local communities as school, orphanage, nursing home for the elderly, bank, pharmacy, and counseling center.

The centrality of the monk and the monastery to Theravāda societies has been undermined in the past few decades in the face of rapid economic, political, and social change. Theravāda societies have become more urban and modern. Central governments have assumed many of the roles once undertaken by monks as diverse as educator, pharmacist, doctor, agricultural consultant. In some places war and armed conflict have jeopardized not only the traditional place of the monastery but also its safety, as in Pol Pot's Kampuchea (Cambodia). Furthermore, the increasingly pervasive atmosphere of modern rationalism and materialism threatens the values of nonattachment and nibbanic goals represented by the Theravāda world-view and its moral ethos. In the face of these challenges Buddhist monks have sought new ways to remain relevant to modern society and its distinctive problems. The following examples suggest only the range and types of these activities.[20] We should keep in mind, furthermore, that traditional forms of religious expression and practice as described in the first chapter of this monograph still remain meaningful to large segments of Buddhist populations in Sri Lanka and Southeast Asia.

In Thailand, Myanmar, and Sri Lanka monks have been and continue to participate in programs of rural and urban uplift and social welfare.[21] As with the *sangha*'s political involvement, some of these programs seem more appropriate to the normative teachings of the tradition than others and the nature of the monk's activity less detrimental to the symbolic value of the position of the monk. Regarding monastic sponsorship of and involvement in development and welfare programs, one student of Theravāda Buddhism observed:

Formerly the monk had been, ideally and often actually, a community leader—educator, sponsor of cooperative work activities, personal and social counselor, and ethical mentor—in the nearly static traditional village. Now, if he is to "resume" such a role, he would have to become at least modestly competent in a whole range of "modern" activities, such as literacy campaigns, modern and technical education, agricultural extension and "community development.". . . All of these are activities designed to generate social and cultural dynamism as well as economic change. The important thing to grasp here is that there is some considerable difference between the essentially conservative "traditional role" of the monk in the traditional village and any credible community leadership role today; for many of the activities now proposed are of a radically different character from those to which a monk sometimes gave leadership a century ago.[22]

Modern forms of monastic involvement in social welfare and rural development became increasingly important in Sri Lanka and Burma in the early days of national independence. In Burma projects sponsored by the Buddha Sāsana Council created by U Nu included establishing schools for hill tribe children and vocational training.[23] In Sri Lanka various social service and welfare projects were sponsored by the All Ceylon Buddhist Congress. Other organizations linked monk and laity in similar types of endeavors. The Ceylon Farmers' Association, for example, was established with the general aim of providing "for the spiritual and material welfare of the people of Ceylon throughout the island through the medium of the Sangha dedicated to the service of mankind and the welfare of the country."[24] In recent years Buddhist social welfare in Sri Lanka has been spearheaded by the Sarvodaya Shramadāna movement. Since 1958 it has recruited more than 800,000 volunteers to work in rural uplift and development projects in over 8,500 villages touching a population of over 4 million people. The movement has attracted considerable international attention and financial support. Although founded by A. T. Ariyaratne, a layman, monks have been a significant factor in the success of the movement.[25] George Bond argues that whereas earlier Sinhalese social service movements were patterned after Christian missionary models, more recent social movements such as the Sarvodaya Shramadāna "represent serious attempts to establish and put into practice a socially relevant interpretation of the *Dhamma*."[26]

Thailand in the 1960s and 1970s witnessed the development of several programs that trained monks in the areas of rural uplift, community development, and public welfare. One was the Project for Encouraging the Participation of Monks in Community Development, begun in 1966 under the sponsorship of the two Buddhist universities for Thai monks. By 1973 the program had conducted three training sessions for approximately 250 monk-trainees. The 1973 program focused on the greater Bangkok metropolitan area that posed particularly pressing problems for the monks in 450 monastery-temples (*wats*). The training program centered on three main areas: to improve *sangha* administration in urban areas, to promote knowledge about the conditions and problems of society, and to investigate ways in which monks could contribute to solutions of urban problems.

The main justifications given for the sponsorship by Buddhist universities of monastic training programs in community development during the 1960s and 1970s were based on the premise that the central role played by the *sangha* in Thai society in the past was in danger of deteriorating. In modern times society has changed but the *sangha* has not, the program leaders contended. Phra Mahāchai, a chief administrator of the 1973 training program, observed that traditionally Buddhism was at the heart of Thai society, but that the role played by the *sangha* in contemporary Thailand was being seriously challenged. He cited two main reasons for this development: (1) Recent societal changes have led people to desert Buddhism and its essential values; (2) secular institutions have made adjustments and improvements in recent times, whereas the monastic order as an institution has not changed significantly and has, consequently, declined in the estimation of the people.[27] The solution, argued Phra Mahāchai, is for the monastic order to recognize its role in Thai society: that its responsibilities extend beyond the confines of the monastery and monastery-related activities into the daily and increasingly complex lives of the people.

Several results emerged from the Project for Encouraging the Participation of Monks in Community Development and similar training programs. A significant number of monks became involved in the formal study of subjects in which they had been previously untrained. A constant theme of the monks reporting on the benefits derived from the training program was the practical value of the knowledge gained.[28] This knowledge was put to use in the home districts of monks graduating from the training program where the meetings held bore practical results. New buildings on monastery compounds were constructed, wells dug, new roads built, dams and irrigation channels constructed, and public health programs encouraged.

In most cases the presence of the monk provided the main motivation and guidance for the work. The monk himself, with certain exceptions, did not engage in actual labor on the project. It is especially important to note that the work done by the laity on such projects led by monks was perceived as being religiously as well as practically efficacious. In other words, labor was perceived as meritorious because it was encouraged by the person symbolizing the source of merit; namely, the monk. Although the form of the monks' activity was different, the reciprocal structure of the relationship between the monk and the laity remained intact. However, this relationship is more difficult to maintain when the monk steps outside of traditionally defined roles.

The fundamental issue at stake regarding the involvement of the Buddhist monastic order in rural uplift, social welfare, and community development is whether or not the *sangha*'s symbolic value will be seriously undermined if the monk goes beyond familiar, culturally sanctioned roles. Although the *sangha* has never been "otherworldly," its teachings and disciplines have set it apart as a vocation distinct from mundane vocations. The monk seeks religious (*lokuttara*) rather than worldly (*lokiya*) goals. For this reason, the *sangha* has been perceived as a mediator between the goals of the mundane world and the ideals of spiritual transformation. If the *sangha* loses its power to represent these ideals because of excessive identification with worldly goals, then its symbolic status will be threatened and the reciprocal bonds between the monastic order and the laity will be compromised. In short, a significant reason for the existence of the monastic order will be undermined.

In a similiar vein, Somboon Suksamran makes an important distinction between monks involved in government programs that manipulate the *sangha* for political ends and those monks known as *phra nak patthana* ("development monks") who voluntarily dedicate their lives to liberate rural populations from oppression, exploitation, poverty, and ignorance.[29] Professor Somboon believes that monks who participated in government sponsored rural development programs jeopardized their prestige and position by being associated with policies that, in fact, perpetuated rural underdevelopment. He believes that the latter is an extraordinary response to the rapid social, economic, and political changes of the 1970s that have served to improve the quality of rural life, strengthen self-reliance and self-respect, and preserve community culture. Coincidently, Professor Somboon believes that these development monks are an important factor in the survival of the Thai *sangha*.[30]

Some of the most effective efforts of the Thai monastic order to address problems of pressing social and economic need have been developed by individual monks responding to particular situations and needs rather than as part of any official government program. The vitality of programs begun with government sponsorship in the 1960s and 1970s continues under the able leadership of monks such as Phra Khrū Sakorn in Samutsongkrām Province, Luang Phọ Nān in Surin Province, and Phra Thepkavī who holds the rank of Dhammādiloka in Chiang Mai Province. Of special interest are the forest conservation monks (Thai: *phra nak anurak pā*) such as Phra Prachak, Phra Khrū Pitak, and Āchān Pongsak.[31]

Telling the Story:
Development Monks and Conservation Monks in Thailand

In 1962 Phra Khrū Sakorn Sangvorakit became the abbot of Wat Yokkrabat in Samutsongkrām Province about 40 miles west of Bangkok. At that time the Yokkrabat subdistrict (*tambon*) was poor, dry, plagued by mosquitoes and lacked public transportation. Salt water had infiltrated the ground water supply. The villagers supported themselves by fishing and cutting and selling wood. Crime, drugs, and alcoholism were rife. Phra Khrū Sakorn first addressed the villagers' material problems: "If you have the four basic needs, namely food, . . . [housing], clothes, and medicine, other things will follow. Education, culture, . . . [morality], and [social] unity will follow. Gambling and crime, drugs and misbehaviour will . . . [diminish]."[32]

Teaching by example, Phra Khrū Sakorn solved the water problem by digging wells and constructing small canals from fresh water sources. Paddy lands were banked to protect against the intrusion of salt water. He encouraged villagers to plant coconut palms and when the market price of coconuts fell suggested that they should plant sugar palms. Other community development projects followed: cutting a new access road to the village to ease transportation of goods to the district center, building a dam to prevent the spread of salt water, electrification of the village, promoting new crops. To accomplish these goals the monk not only had to set an example and motivate villagers, he also had to fight against the exploitation of middlemen, traders, and creditors and he brought pressure to bear on government officials. Primarily he acted as a catalyst and coordinator among teachers, village headmen, local admininstrators and the police. By 1984 he had raised hundreds of thousands of dollars to establish a foundation for community development.

Yokkrabat's economic miracle led, however, to other problems. Greater prosperity promoted a heretofore unknown disparity between the middle

Figure 3.3. Phra Khrū
Sakorn Sangvorakit,
Wat Yokkrabat,
Samutsongkram
Province, Thailand.

class and the poor. Villagers became more materialistic and selfish. The
abbot put it this way:

> During the time that there was no road young people came to work
> together transporting sand to the temple, often working till one or two
> o'clock at night. It gave me the opportunity to be close to them. I taught
> them Dhamma at the same time. They had unity. When the work was
> done they would say "our canal, our road."...They participated so
> actively in all [the] work that they could not feel otherwise....Today
> things are different. You have...to have incentives. We can hardly
> find people who are ready to...sacrifice for the community for 4–5
> days. They live much better today. They are no longer so poor. They

have a lot of money and also spend a lot....They are used to comfort,...to going everywhere by car. They cannot walk anymore.[33]

Concerned about the increasing consumerist mentality, the impact of urban values through the mass media, and the abandonment of the village by urban-educated youth, Phra Khrū Sakorn sought to find ways to develop a greater sense of community solidarity and mutual concern. Through the monastery (*wat*) he established a youth group, a women's group, a professional group, and a credit union. The credit union functions as a people's bank: "The principle of the credit union is love and sharing....The rich help the poor and all help one another not to be exploited by outsiders."[34] Through the credit union the abbot has sought to promote two principles: mutual responsibility within the community and the promotion of a locally diversified economy to shield the community from the vagaries of a free market. The latter shares something in common with the Gandhian concept of self-reliance: "[Villagers] should work out what they need in their family first, such as raising fish, growing vegetables and [coconut] trees that can be used in the long term. They can sell the surplus in order to have money to buy things they cannot produce themselves. In such a way the villagers will depend less on the market. At the same time they will live a more simple life..."[35]

Finally, Phra Khrū Sakorn has worked hard to develop the spiritual life of the villagers. He has promoted meditation at the *wat* and through the school and has stressed the relevance of the Buddha's *dhamma* for self-awareness and peace. He, himself, is a tireless teacher conducting seminars and training courses not only in his subdistrict but throughout the province. Yokkrabat is not yet the abbot's hope for a "village of the saints," and probably never will be, but through the wisdom and energy of Phra Khrū Sakorn Buddhism has become a vital force in the lives of many villagers in Samutsongkrām Province.

Many other Thai monks have actively sought to address the social, economic, moral, and spiritual problems in their local communities. Luang Phọ Nān of Wat Sāmakkhī, Surin Province in northeast Thailand, emphasizes the central value of meditation to all aspects of life. While he has sponsored many community development projects from farm cooperatives to rice banks he firmly believes, "We need the spiritual dimension in all development activities. Without spiritual life we cannot start carrying out a real development."[36]

Phra Thepkavī Kusalō in Chiang Mai Province in northern Thailand helps villagers establish rice and water buffalo banks from which farmers can borrow in times of need, founded a secondary school for poor children (Metta Suksa) in 1959, and later established centers for training village youth in modern agriculture and a vocational training center for village girls. As the abbot of Wat Čhedi Luang, Chiang Mai's most prestigious Thammayut monastery, Phra Thepkavī works to solve problems of poverty and improve the quality of rural life from his Foundation for Education and Development of Rural Areas (FEDRA) located at Wat Pā Dārā Phirom monastery in the Mae Rim District of Chiang Mai Province. Supported by the Social Welfare Council of Thailand and by private and government contributions from Thailand and abroad and with the help of both paid and volunteer staff, Phra Thepkavī runs programs throughout the year to train young men and women in marketable skills to supplement their farming income. Because prostitution has become such a pervasive and lucrative industry in Thailand,[37] Phra Thepkavī has been especially concerned to empower young women to earn sufficient income by mastering the skills of native handicrafts, such as weaving, dressmaking, or wicker work, to counterbalance the economic lure of what has become a major social, moral, and health problem for Thailand. Other cottage industries with a guaranteed commercial market are being developed, ranging from ceramics and artificial flowers to the cultivation of medicinal herbs.[38]

The visitor to Phra Thepkavī's monastery in Mae Rim is initially struck by the care with which the compound is being developed and maintained, and the omnipresence of Phra Thepkavī's sayings in Thai script written on small wooden plaques attached to the many trees planted on the grounds. Since 1961 Phra Thepkavī has also presented Dhamma New Year cards that distill his wisdom into Thai verses. The following selections suggest the wisdom, compassion, and humor Phra Thepkavī brings to his work:

> Anxiety poisons life. The past is a dream and the future is uncertain; only the present can be mended.
> To solve the problems of life is neither to multiply the quantity nor to escape; it is to search for their causes. Having found the cause, the problem is half-solved.
> He who does good for self-glorification will be spurned by others; he who does good truthfully will live peacefully.
> Luxurious living turns one into a millionaire on loans.
> Sweating when young is better than repenting when old.
> Nothing is new in the world except constant change.[39]

Figure 3.4. Phra
Thepkavī (Dhammā-
dilōka), Wat Pā Dārā
Phirom, Mae Rim,
Thailand, in front of a
rice bank barn.
Courtesy of Phra
Thepkavī.

We turn now to consider forest conservation monks (*phra nak anurak
pā*), who have grown increasingly concerned about the destruction of the
natural environment by powerful economic and government interests, as
well as the detrimental effects of forest overuse by villagers. Phra Prachak
Kuttachitto in northeastern Thailand has gained considerable notoriety in
his struggle to protect local forests from being converted into eucalyptus
plantations to produce woodpulp for export and the accompanying dislocation of villagers whose economic livelihood depends partially on neighboring
forest habitats. One of his techniques to combat government and private
schemes has been to "ordain" trees by tying saffron banners around their
trunks. His opposition to powerful economic and political interests has led
to severe government harrassment.

Phra Khrū Pitak Nantakhun is another monk who has become actively
engaged in conservation work. He promotes environmental conservation

Figure 3.5. Monks working at a reforestation project, Mae Rim, Northern Thailand. Photo courtesy of Thomas Borchert.

by presenting slide shows on the effects of deforestation throughout the northern Thai province of Nan where his monastery is located. In 1990 he helped establish a community forest on about 400 acres of land in his home village. More recently he has worked to develop community forests along the Nan River to combat problems stemming from drought and pollution.[40]

Some Thai forest conservation monks have gained international recognition. In 1990 Ăchăn Pongsak Techathamamoo, the former abbot of Wat Phālād, a small forest monastery on Doi Suthep mountain near Chiang Mai was a recipient of the Global 500 Roll of Honour given by the United Nations Environmental Programme (UNEP). Working in Mae Soy, a poor, deforested subdistrict of Chọm Thọng, Chiang Mai Province, Ăchăn Pongsak developed an effective forest preservation project.[41] Unfortunately, the story of Mae Soy is not unique to Thailand or to many other parts of the world. Prior to 1950 Mae Soy, like much upland northern land, was covered by a dense, diverse forest. The forest provided the villagers with water, building materials, food, fuel, and medicinal plants. By the mid-1950s a commercial timber company was granted a government concession to cut selectively teak and other large trees in Mae Soy's plain. Instead, most of the timber was clear-cut. In 1973 a tobacco company was permitted to

Figure 3.6. A Yang
tree "ordained" with a
saffron sash. Northern
Thailand. Photo by
Donald K. Swearer.

continue taking trees from the forest for fuel to cure leaf tobacco. In order
to salvage some income from the forest the villagers completed the
destruction of the forest by cutting most of the remaining trees. By 1978
the forest was devastated. To make matters worse a Hmong hill tribe of
100 families was resettled there as part of the Thai government's efforts
to promote commercial crop production by hill tribe peoples rather than
opium production. Extensive use of pesticides on fields of cabbage has
led to pollution of the watershed and conflict with the villagers.

Āčhān Pongsak became familiar with the Mae Soy valley in the 1960s
when wandering as a *dhutaṅga* (ascetical practice) monk. In the mid-1970s
he established a meditation center there for the use of student activists for
whom his monastery, Wat Phālād, had become a refuge and discussion
center. In 1983 the monk began the task of helping the villagers restore

their environment. First he advised them to seek permission from the Royal Forestry Department to register the forest area of the Mae Soy valley as a Buddhist Park as a way of protecting both trees and animals. Second, he sought to change the attitude of the villagers toward the forest by convincing them that environmental problems have a spiritual dimension; that morality is not merely a matter of obeying the Buddhist precepts but also striving for a balance between the physical and spiritual, society and the natural environment:

> The balance of nature in the environment is achieved and regulated by the functions of the forest....It provides a space for humans to live in peace and contentment. Destroying the forest or not recognizing the value of all the benefits we owe to...nature is a lack of morality [sīla-dhamma]. When we destroy the forest, we offend basic morality, both physical and spiritual. [Human]kind may take whatever the natural world provides, but [we] must also exercise responsible action in order to maintain it. To have a sense of gratitude to nature...is to gain an understanding of the essence of Buddhist morality.[42]

Āchān Pongsak convinced the villagers that the forest was a source of life, not merely an object to be exploited. He taught them that forests are their first home and second parents as provisioner of the four requisites of life: food, shelter, clothing, and medicine. Gradually, he has been able to protect and improve the environment of the Mae Soy valley: voluntary labor groups cleared firebreaks, repaired fences, and laid water pipes; through the Thammanāt Foundation at Wat Phālād, organized to receive private donations, Āchān Pongsak established rice and seed banks and a cooperative store; in 1988 the Forestry Department and the Thammanāt Foundation began a reforestation project; and, in 1989 as a response to disastrous floods in southern Thailand, the government banned all logging concessions in northern Thailand. To be sure, many problems still remain, not the least of which is the delicate problem of the resettlement of hill tribes. Nevertheless, the Conservation Group in the Chom Thong district of the Mae Soy valley now claims 97,000 members; a formal association of forest conservation monks with Āchān Pongsak as its head was organized in 1989 to balance conservation and development based on Buddhist principles; and, in 1990, it was proposed that the Royal Forestry Department and the Department of Religious Affairs join together to work for the protection of Thailand's forests. Unfortunately, the success of activist conservation monks like Āchān Pongsak has led to reprisals. Phra Prachak has been accused of harboring Cambodian dissidents in his monastery, and

Pongsak resigned from the monkhood in 1993 on controversial charges that he committed a *pārājika* offense against the disciplinary rules punishable by dismissal from the order. Fortunately, Ăčhān Pongsak has been able to continue his conservation work as a white-robed *anagārika* ("one who renounces the householder life") at his center in Chọm Thọng.

As the preceding stories indicate, forest conservation and development monks are making a difference in the lives of the rural poor. Furthermore, Professor Somboon Suksamran's contention that their work assures the future viability of the *sangha* may be prophetic. For Theravāda Buddhism to remain a vital force in the societies of Southeast Asia, it must address both deeply felt personal problems and social needs. In this regard Buddhism does not differ from other religious traditions. Southeast Asian Buddhism as well as other world religions face the challenge of keeping pace with the times, transforming their traditions into a contemporary idiom without sacrificing their ethical and spiritual foundations. As we have seen by these examples, part of this transformation has meant redefining the role of the monk in society; however, reforming the structures and the teachings of the tradition, itself, is an equally important task. In short, the Buddhist worldview, as well as the work of monks and nuns must adapt to and help guide the social, economic, and social worlds in which it is embedded.

Reforming the Tradition

Theravāda monks in Southeast Asia are redefining their role in relationship to contemporary politics and the pressing social issues and economic problems of the day. Of equal importance, they have also criticized and attempted to reform inherited models of Buddhist thought and practice. All religious traditions move between periods of reformation and counter-reformation. Reformations serve to recall a religious tradition to its normative ideals as well as transform outmoded institutions and teachings.

Although reformation is not new to Buddhist history, Theravāda *sanghas* have experienced major changes in the nineteenth and twentieth centuries, partially in response to Western influence. We shall briefly examine major nineteenth century reformation movements in Sri Lanka and Burma before exploring contemporary Thai reformist movements in greater depth.

Sri Lanka and Burma

Nineteenth century Ceylon (Sri Lanka) witnessed the emergence of two reformist sects (*nikāya*), the Amarapura and the Rāmañña. They arose primarily in response to the domination of the Sinhalese *sangha* by the *goyigāma* caste. In 1800 the Amarapura sect was created when a monk, five novices, and three laymen traveled to the Burmese capital of Amarapura where they were ordained in a ceremony sponsored by King Bodawpaya. In the late nineteenth century monks of the Amarapura sect led the protest against Christian missions, debates that attracted the active support of the Western theosophist Henry Steele Olcott. Olcott, in turn, proved to be a major influence on the Anagārika Dharmapāla, one of the leaders of the renewal of Buddhism in Sri Lanka during the period marking the end of British rule on the island. The Rāmañña monastic fraternity, also begun in the nineteenth century through a Burmese ordination lineage, advocated a return to strict observance of the monastic discipline (*vinaya*) and helped revitalize the forest tradition of Buddhist piety and spiritual practice in Sri Lanka.[43] The revival of the tradition of forest monks in Sri Lanka attracted Europeans to the island, several of whom made significant contributions to Pali scholarship: Nyanatiloka Thera founded the Island Hermitage south of Colombo; Nyanaponika Thera was one of the cofounders of the Buddhist Publication Society and established the Forest Hermitage in Kandy. Both were German. Two British monks, Nyanamoli Thera and Soma Thera, translated important philosophical and meditation texts into English. In Sri Lanka there has been a crucial link between the revival of the forest tradition, the promotion of Buddhist scholarship, and the mutual cooperation of Asian and Western Theravāda Buddhists. Nyanaponika, for example, is known not only for his scholarly work on *Abhidhamma*, (Theravāda scholastic philosophy) but also for his translation and analysis of the Foundation of Mindfulness Sutta (*Satipaṭṭhāna Sutta*).

The late nineteenth century also saw a renewal of Buddhism in Burma. Under King Mindon (1853–1878) Buddhism experienced a considerable revival. Mindon convened the Fifth Buddhist Council in 1871 for the purpose of producing a new redaction of the Pali scriptures. It was engraved on 729 marble tablets erected within the precincts of the Kuthodaw Pagoda located at the foot of Mandalay Hill. During this period several reformist sects also developed. New monastic fraternities, the Dwaya and Shwegyin, advocated a stricter code of monastic conduct than the mainstream Thudhamma tradition.[44] In this respect they were similar to the "puritan" reform movements which arose at the same time in Sri Lanka and Thailand. In Michael Mendelson's view, the fundamental criterion for sectarian differentiation in Burma was "cleaving to the Vinaya."[45] Burmese reform sects objected to what they considered to be the disciplinary laxity of the

Figure 3.7. The German monk, Nyanaponika Thera, at the Forest Hermitage, Kandy, Sri Lanka, in 1967. Photo by Donald K. Swearer.

dominant tradition. Increasingly it became popular for monks to wear silk robes, not to eat directly from begging bowls, to wear sandals, to use umbrellas, to handle money, and to attend public entertainment.[46] As in other Theravāda countries doctrinal differences were less important. In the Burmese context doctrinal controversies tended to focus on whether *kamma* undermined the freedom of the will, a question of great interest to Western thinkers.

The forest dwelling ideal associated with meditation practice has played a major role in promoting reform movements in Sri Lanka, Thailand, and especially Burma. Michael Carrithers has shown that Sinhalese forest monks inspired a reformist tradition in Sri Lanka that emphasized the attainment of liberation in this life, a fundamental theme of reformist Buddhist movements.[47] In Burma under Prime Minister U Nu, meditation practice was encouraged for both monks and the laity. U Nu himself favored the Mahasi Sayadaw and invited him to establish a meditation center in Rangoon. With government favor the Mahasi Thathana Yeiktha center soon attracted thousands of meditation practioners from Burma and abroad. The Mahasi style of insight meditation (*vipassanā bhāvanā*) has been promoted with great success in Thailand and in Sri Lanka. Burmese meditation teachers in the Mahasi Sayadaw tradition were first invited to Sri Lanka in 1955. George Bond argues that this event helped spark one of the major elements in the revival of Buddhism in Sri Lanka.[48]

Thailand: The Forest Tradition and Its Legacy

Like Sri Lanka and Burma, Thailand experienced a major reformist impulse in the nineteenth century when the future monarch, Mongkut (Rāma IV, reign, 1851–1868), initiated the Thammayut Sect while he was a monk (1824–1851). During his monastic tenure Mongkut engaged in intensive study of the Pali scriptures. In 1840 and 1843 he sent monks to Sri Lanka who when they returned to Thailand brought with them seventy volumes of the Sinhalese Pali scriptures. As the name Thammayut (Pali, Dhammayutika) ("those adhering to the law") suggests, Mongkut also advocated a stricter adherence to the monastic disciplinary rules (*vinaya*) in contrast to the Mahānikai (Pali, Mahānikāya) sect of Thai Buddhism. As the abbot of the royal monastery, Wat Bovoranives, which became the center of the Thammayut sect, he formulated a reformist "orthodoxy" that included correct procedures for establishing the sacred boundary (*sīmā*) around the ordination hall and for the ordination ritual itself, for wearing monastic robes (covering both shoulders instead of only one), for holding the alms bowl, for receiving robes presented at the end of the rains retreat (*kaṭhina*), and for chanting in Pali.[49] Through correspondence with Sinhalese monks who were engaged in defending Buddhism against Christian missionaries, he began thinking about Buddhism as a universal religion that could be defended on rational grounds.[50] Protestant missionaries in Thailand hoped to convert the king. Instead, he skillfully exploited their knowledge of Western science, learned English from them, and enjoyed debating with them the comparative merits of Christianity and Buddhism.

In the assessment of S. J. Tambiah, Mongkut's reform emphasized scripturalism, intellectualism, and rationalism.[51] In effect, the future king laid the foundation for modern Thai Buddhism, which became formally institutionalized under Mongkut's son, King Chulalongkorn (Rāma V, reign

1886–1910), and by Supreme Patriarch Vajirañāṇavarorasa (1860–1921), the head of the Thammayut order. Although challenged by a charismatic northern Thai monk in the early decades of this century,[52] the modern Thai Buddhist *sangha* initiated by Mongkut and organized by Vajirañāṇa has dominated Thai Buddhism to the present. Furthermore, as in Burma and Sri Lanka, reformist trends in Thai Buddhism are particularly indebted to the forest tradition (*araññavāsa*) of Theravāda Buddhism.

The 1920s and 1930s witnessed significant changes in Thailand, most notably the overthrow of the absolute monarchy in 1932. During this period two monks, differentially indebted to the forest tradition of Buddhism, began careers that have greatly affected Thai Buddhism. One, Āčhān Mun[53] (1870–1949), became a noted Thammayut meditation teacher in northeast Thailand.[54] His fame attracted many disciples who have continued his teachings and practice in different regions of Thailand: Āčhān Lee in central Thailand, Āčhān Chā and Āčhān Mahābua in the northeast, Luang Pū Waen and Luang Pū Sim in the north.

Prior to Āčhān Mun and his teacher, Āčhān Sao, forest monks in Thailand were noted for their magical powers and lax *vinaya* practice. Āčhān Sao and Āčhān Mun took the Thammayut scholarship on the *dhamma* and *vinaya* and the section on the thirteen ascetical practices (*dhutaṅga*) from Buddhaghosa's *Visuddhimagga* and applied them to the forest monk's life, eschewing magic and adhering strictly to the *vinaya*. In short, they brought together two major reformist elements of late nineteenth century Theravāda Buddhism; namely, strict observance of the monastic precepts and rigorous meditation practice. They also reaffirmed that *nibbāna* was attainable in the present, something that even King Mongkut doubted.

The Āčhān Mun tradition has attracted a wide following in Thailand and beyond. His disciples, in particular Āčhān Chā and Āčhān Mahabua, have attracted many Westerners. An international monastery at Āčhān Chā's *wat* in Ubon is thriving. The ideal of a simple, ascetical life has also had an impact on other, diverse movements in contemporary Thai Buddhism, most notably Santi Asok, to which we shall turn later. The forest ideal, furthermore, inspired the late Bhikkhu Buddhadāsa, Thailand's most original and controversial interpreter of the Buddha-*dhamma*.[55]

Bhikkhu Buddhadāsa[56] began his monastic career in a conventional manner but early on he chose to establish a hermitage in the forest near his home of Chaiya in southern Thailand. He adopted a simple lifestyle in emulation of the early Indian Buddhist tradition, but soon after entering the forest his teachings began to be published, initially with the help of his brother Dhammadāsa, a scholar in his own right. By the 1960s Buddha-dāsa had become the major reinterpreter of Theravāda Buddhism in Southeast Asia. For this reason, whereas Āčhān Mun's reputation has been associated primarily with the path of meditation practice (*paṭipatti*), Bud-dhadāsa's fame rests more on his innovative scholarship and unique interpretation of the *dhamma* (*pariyatti*).

Born in 1906 and ordained a monk in 1927, Buddhadāsa withdrew from the Thai *sangha*'s system of monastic educational advancement after a frustrating experience with the rigid system of Pali language examinations established by Vajirañāṇavarorasa. Deciding that living in the forest and delving deeply into the Pali scriptures on his own would be more conducive to practicing the Buddha's *dhamma*, he founded a forest hermitage, The Garden of Empowering Liberation (Wat Suan Mokkhabalārāma, more commonly known as Suan Mokkh) about four kilometers from Chaiya. He writes, "The place for practicing Dhamma is. . .a matter of great importance. This is because we have to study directly from nature."[57]

Wat Suan Mokkh now has living quarters for over fifty monks, accom-modations for lay visitors, and an international meditation center. All monks live in adequate but modest wooden huts and perform some form of manual labor such as the creation of reproductions of bas-reliefs from ancient Indian Buddhist sites. They spend their time in meditation and study, rather than chanting at merit making ceremonies. When his health permitted, Buddhadāsa lectured at the hermitage. In earlier years he spoke annually at universities and other gatherings of various professional groups including lawyers and medical practioners. Most of these talks have been recorded and printed as a series of collected works.[58]

Specific themes are pivotal to Buddhadāsa's thought. He consistently emphasizes the traditional Theravāda teaching of nonattachment, which he relates to the concepts of not-self (*anattā*), interdependent coarising (*paṭicca-samuppāda*), and emptiness (*suññatā*).[59] Buddhadāsa views essentialism in any form, including language, as obscuring the deeper dhammic meaning of reality. His unconventional, iconoclastic approach to interpreting and propagating Buddha-*dhamma* from his forest monastery embodies the Buddhist principle of impermanence (*anicca*). For Buddhadāsa this concept and its corollaries—not-self, interdependent coarising, and emptiness—are not abstract notions but have a practical, existential import.

Buddhadāsa consistently tackled problems of current political, social, and economic urgency. During the political upheavals of the mid-1970s his *dhamma* talks included such topics as "The Kind of Political Reform that

Figure 3.8.
Buddhadāsa Bhikkhu,
Wat Suan Mokkha-
balārama, Chaiya,
Thailand, 1976. Photo
by Donald K. Swearer.

Creates Problems" and "Democratic Socialism." In the face of aggressive economic despoliation of the environment, Buddhadāsa addressed the issue of a Buddhist approach to nature.[60] Unlike Kitthiwuttho who seems to subordinate Buddhist *dhamma* to the interests of Thai nationalism, Buddhadāsa offers a "spiritual politics" based on the central Buddhist teachings of nonattachment and interdependent coarising (*paṭicca-samuppāda*). Interdependent coarising is interpreted as a situation of mutual balance, a whole composed of interconnected, mutually influencing, and mutually influenced parts. On the individual level, it means that one acts in a nonattached manner on behalf of the whole or on behalf of others. This leads to a middle way ethic of sufficiency, adequacy, appropriateness and normalcy—nothing in excess. When this concept is applied to politics, we have what Buddhadāsa characterizes as "spiritual politics," the proper balance among human beings and nature, an action taking into account the interests of the whole as well as the individual parts.

In more practical terms, spiritual politics is a kind of socialism, or to use the Thai term, a "fellowship of restraint" (*sangha-niyama*). As an economic system, Buddhadāsa contends that socialism is inherently better than capitalism because it is less acquisitive and competitive.[61] Yet, modern socialism is too materialistic for him. A spiritual socialism must be rooted in the practice of truth (*sīla-dhamma*). Its governing principles work for the best balance among individual goods. No policy in one area will be isolated from policy matters in another. Take the problem of overpopulation, for example. Buddhadāsa argues that population growth must be seen in relationship to resource use, production, and distribution. He contends that the earth can sustain an even larger population, but only if there is a better balance among production, distribution, and use. Buddhadāsa concludes that Buddhism's contribution to spiritual politics is to help people see the fundamental interrelatedness of all things (i.e., their *paṭicca-samuppāda* nature).

Most Thais, claims Buddhadāsa, believe that the highest principles of Buddhism demand a separation from the world. Such is not the case, he argues. The principles of *nibbāna* (i.e., nonattachment) are for everyone because (1) the state of nonattachment was our original state and (2) a state we strive to recover from our present unsatisfactory (*dukkha*) condition: "To be nonattached means to be in one's true or original condition—free, at peace, quiet, nonsuffering, totally aware."[62] Although some may think that this teaching is more appropriate for the monk than the lay person, just the opposite is the case says Buddhadāsa. Lay people are usually more harried than the monk: "Those who are hot and bothered need to cool off." For this reason the Buddha taught that emptiness (*suññatā*) is the basis for the action of ordinary people.[63] Indeed, in Buddhadāsa's view, emptiness and nonattachment are at the heart of a truly socialistic society where people work for the benefit of the whole and overcome their acquisitive interests.

In the thought and example of Bhikkhu Buddhadāsa we see an attempt to emulate the highest teachings of Buddhism and apply them to political and social life to promote interpersonal and civic well-being.[64] He urges a political involvement based on dhammic insight that sees all forms of political, social, and economic organization not as ends in themselves but in serving spiritual goals. Buddhadāsa also applies Buddhist doctrine to a wide range of social-ethical issues such as the environment. At the heart of his innovative interpretations is the conviction that the transmundane (*lokuttara*) is not opposed to the mundane (*lokiya*); as Buddhadāsa puts it, "*nibbāna* is in *saṃsāra*." Practically speaking, Buddhadāsa's forest hermitage in southern Thailand is very much a part of "the world."

Buddhadāsa, however, has not been without his detractors. From one side, his constructive interpretations of Buddhist thought have been criticized for being too abstract and impractical; from another side, scholarly monks see his creative reinterpretations as being too cavalier with the Pali canonical and commentarial texts. Others accuse Buddhadāsa of propagating an eclectic blend of various Buddhisms, Zen, and Taoism. They are especially suspicious of his interpretation of "nature" as an ideal state of peace and harmony. Buddhadāsa's admirers, however, far outnumber his critics. His death on July 8, 1993, was an occasion of national mourning.

Buddhadāsa's influence has led Suchira Payulpitack to refer to a "Buddhadāsa movement" characterized principally by a return to the original meaning of Buddhist doctrine coupled with a strategy to adjust Buddhism to meet the needs of the modern world.[65] Payulpitack's statistical data supports Peter Jackson's socio-political analysis of Thai Buddhism. Jackson sees the rationalistic reformism of Buddhadāsa as a vehicle for modern, urbanized politico-religious dissent associated primarily with a college-educated professional class, rather than as a medium of middle-class aspirations to which some new religious movements in Thailand appeal.[66]

Several well-known activist monks either have spent time at Suan Mokkh or claim to be followers of Buddhadāsa. In early 1994, one of Buddhadāsa's disciples, nationally renowned Phra Payom Kalayāno, abbot of Wat Suan Kaew on the outskirts of Bangkok, created a disciplinary crisis for the Supreme Sangha Council by spearheading an attack on worldliness in the Thai *sangha*. He directed his attack against Phra Yantra Amarō, a popular, charismatic monk who frequently travels abroad in luxurious style and has been photographed with religious and secular notables around the world.[67] Lay social activist leaders, in particular Sulak Sivaraksa, Praves Wasi, and Chatsuman Kabilsingh are also great admirers of Buddhadāsa and are indebted to his modernist interpretation of the Buddhadhamma.[68]

Santi Asok, a radical sectarian movement in Thailand, also reflects the forest tradition's ideals of simplicity and its founder, Phra Bodhirak, claims to have been influenced by Buddhadāsa, a claim he later recanted. Unlike Āčhān Mun and Bhikkhu Buddhadāsa, however, Phra Bodhirak did not spend his early years as a wandering forest monk nor did he live in a forest hermitage. He was, rather, a television entertainer and songwriter[69] who was ordained after a conversion experience: "At two o'clock in the morning

Figure 3.9. Bodhirak.
Founder of Santi Asok.
Reprinted by
permission of Santi
Asok Foundation.

of Tuesday 17 January 1970, I woke up and walked from my bedroom into
the bathroom to relieve myself. Suddenly a brilliant flash occurred within
me—a brightness, an openness, and detachment which could not be
explained in human terms. I know only that my life opened before me and
that the whole world seemed to be revealed."[70]

Bodhirak was ordained at Wat Asokārām of the Thammayut sect in 1970,
but from the very beginning of his monastic career he has forged his own
way. He developed a following at Wat Asokārām and Wat Mahāthāt in
Bangkok which he called the Asoka group. He soon established a center
near Nakorn Pathom about thirty miles from Bangkok which he named
Asoka's Land (Dan Asok) where monks and lay people, both Thammayut
and Mahānikai, could practice the *dhamma* together. Forced to disrobe as
a Thammayut monk because of his unorthodox activities, he was reordained

Figure 3.10. A Santi Asok publication pokes fun at the Tourist Organization of Thailand comtemplating the destruction of a Buddhist site in order to build a motel.

into the Mahānikai sect in 1973. However, the Thai *sangha* hierarchy continued to object to his independent ways and ordered him to disband Dan Asok. In response, Bodhirak and his fellow monks cut all ties with the national Thai *sangha*.

Santi Asok continued to expand. They established a foundation to manage its many publishing ventures and founded three communities where monks and laity observe a moderately ascetic regime. They live in simple wooden thatched huts, eat one vegetarian meal daily, and eschew intoxicants, stimulants, and tobacco. The Santi Asok movement defines itself in terms of a simple, disciplined lifestyle reminiscent of the forest tradition ideal of Theravāda Buddhism; moreover, it has adopted a highly critical, moralistic stance over against Thai society. It is very critical of the laxity of the Thai *sangha*, immorality and violence in Thai society, and corruption in the government.

General Chamlong Srimuang, the former governor of Bangkok and a highly visible national politician has had an on-again-off-again association with Santi Asok.[71] He formed the Phalang Dhamma party (Power of Dhamma party), which elected over twenty members to the Thai Parliament in October, 1992, Chamlong among them. He follows an ascetical lifestyle, wears traditional Thai clothing, lives in a converted storefront, sleeps on a thin mattress on the floor, eats one vegetarian meal a day, and eschews sexual relations with his wife. In short, his lifestyle seems to translate the ideals of the forest tradition into a modern, urban, political context.

Santi Asok's moral critique of Thai society and laxity in the Thai monastic order appeals to many Thais, but the strident tone of its attacks has repelled others. Phra Bodhirak's outspoken manner and flagrant disregard for Thai ecclesiastical law and certain *vinaya* rules led the Supreme Sangha Council to take punitive measures against him and the movement. On June 19, 1989, Bodhirak and seventy-nine ordained followers were arrested by the police. As of 1994 hearings continue to be held around the country with no end in sight. Some observers believe that Bodhirak and his followers will never be brought to trial and that the intention of the government is simply to keep the movement off balance.[72] Santi Asok continues its advocacy of a simple, morally upright, communitarian ideal over against mainstream Thai Buddhist culture. Its future is uncertain as government prosecution may have irreparably damaged the movement.

Traditionally the "work" of the monk in Theravāda Buddhism has been defined as study (*ganthadhura*) and practice or meditation (*vipassanādhura*), the latter often being associated with forest monasteries. Although we have seen that various permutations of the Theravāda forest tradition have influenced the shape of Buddhist reformism in Southeast Asia, we should not be surprised that reformist tendencies are also indebted to new developments in education and scholarship.[73] Changes in this area have resulted, at least in part, from the impact of modern, Western education. Although monastic education is still based in the study of Buddhist texts, doctrine, and the Pali language, the curricula of monastic colleges and universities reflect subject matter and disciplines we associate with Western education. These include the former monastic colleges in Sri Lanka, Vidyōdaya and Vidyalaṅkara, and Mahāmakut and Mahāchulalongkorn Buddhist Universities in Thailand. Buddhist scholarship, in may cases, has also broken out of the confines of traditional, exegetically based approaches. In the best instances this transformation has resulted in a scholarship grounded firmly in Pali texts and Buddhist doctrine, but fashioned to speak to an urban, educated audience.

In the case of Thailand, P. A. Payutto, whose current monastic title is Phra Dhammapiṭaka (formerly Debvedi and Rājavaramunī), has emerged as the unrivaled dean of Thai Buddhist scholarship. His magnum opus,

Buddhadhamma, and his two Buddhist dictionaries match or surpass the Pali erudition of Vajirañāṇavarorasa, the head of the Thai *sangha* in the early twentieth century who built the modern monastic educational system still in place today.[74]

Dhammapiṭaka, formerly an administrator at Mahāchulalongkorn Buddhist University, has not limited himself to dictionaries and exegetical tomes. He has written in both Thai and English on a wide variety of philosophical, social, and cultural matters. An example is the paper he prepared for the October 1993 Parliament of the World Religions in Chicago, "A Buddhist Solution for the Twenty-First Century."

Dhammapiṭaka begins his essay with an analysis of the three basic perceptions he believes are at the heart of today's global problems: that humankind is separated from nature and consequently needs to control and manipulate nature; that fellow human beings are seen as "other" rather than as sharing a common human nature; and, that happiness depends on an abundance of material possessions.[75] After analyzing the problems resultant from these perceptions, Dhammapiṭaka argues that Buddhism challenges these beliefs with three counterclaims; namely, that human beings are only one element within a natural system of cause and effect, that all beings are co-dwellers within this system of natural laws (e.g., birth, suffering, death), and that true happiness is external freedom (sufficiency of four necessities—food, clothing, shelter, and medicine), freedom from social harassment because of class, race, gender, and so forth, and in particular, the inner freedom that comes from true wisdom and equanimity. Living in terms of these truths results in a balanced harmonious life working for the benefit of oneself and of others.[76] Dhammapiṭaka's essay integrates a typically Buddhistic mode of cause and effect argumentation and a doctrinally grounded analysis of the nature of things with an informed understanding of the problems of the contemporary world.

Theravāda Buddhism has experienced various reforms during the past century. Some of them were promoted by enlightened monarchs (e.g., King Mindon) or nurtured by national governments. Reform movements have taken the form of new sects or denominations (e.g., Rāmañña Nikāya). Over time they have tended to lose the earlier reformist impetus from which they arose, but not before influencing mainstream traditions. Other reformers have been particularly indebted to the ideals of the forest tradition of early Buddhism. In some cases meditation has been the raison d'être of the movement (e.g., the Mahasi Sayadaw and Āchān Mun traditions). Others, however, developed primarily as innovative voices for doctrinal and institutional renewal (e.g., Bhikkhu Buddhadāsa) with some being more radically sectarian than others (e.g., the Santi Asok movement). Changes in the traditional patterns of monastic education and scholarship have also transformed Buddhist traditions, especially in Sri Lanka and Thailand. In Thailand, Phra Dhammapiṭaka—abbot, university administrator, scholar—personifies this dimension of modernist reformism.

THE CHANGING ROLE OF THE LAITY

Are Theravāda monks in Southeast Asia losing their distinctiveness and coming to resemble their lay constituents? Perhaps, but it may be equally true that some lay persons are becoming more like monks. The ideal of *nibbāna* and the practice of meditation associated with its attainment, once rather exclusively identified with the monastic vocation, are becoming part of the religious life of the devout lay person. Earlier we saw how U Nu encouraged Burmese civil servants to pursue the practice of meditation. In fact, the impetus for the development of lay meditation centers in Theravāda Southeast Asia comes largely from Burma. In this section we shall examine the emergence of lay meditation organizations as one of the distinguishing features of contemporary Theravāda Buddhism.

Another significant development in Theravāda countries in the modern period has been the formation of various lay Buddhist associations that have partially assumed the social service responsibilities formerly associated with the monastery. In recent years lay Buddhists increasingly have come to define the shape of Buddhist ethical concerns ranging from the place and role of women in the tradition and in society to the destruction of rural habitats and the natural environment by corporate economic interests. Finally, lay Buddhists have played the major role in shaping an emerging international Buddhism. Each of these topics will be explored in the remainder of this chapter. At the outset, however, as this chapter suggests, in my view one of the most challenging and problematic issues facing Buddhism in the modern period is the nature of the roles of the "almsperson" and the laity and questions relating to this issue, such as the reform of the monastic code or *vinaya*.

Meditation and the Revival of Theravāda Buddhism

The practice of meditation, once largely the exclusive purview of monks, has played a central role in the revitalization of Buddhism in Sri Lanka,

Figure 3.11. Monk in
meditation. Chiang Rai,
Thailand. Photo by
Donald K. Swearer.

Burma, and Thailand.[77] Lay interest in meditation in Burma can be traced
to at least four factors: Westerners attracted to the practice of insight
meditation; the revival of interest in Buddhism as part of the rise of nationalism in the late colonial period; the personal example and encouragement
of the prime minister, U Nu; and finally, the appearance of outstanding
monastic and lay meditation teachers who developed simple methods of
practice. Three of the best known meditation masters in Burma were two
monks, Ledi Sayadaw and Mahasi Sayadaw, and one layman, U Ba Khin.[78]
U Nu invited Mahasi Sayadaw to come from Shwebo to Rangoon in 1949
to establish a meditation center. In December of that year the center was
formally opened. Since that time branches have been opened elsewhere
in Burma and other Theravāda countries. The Mahasi Sayadaw's methods
of instruction in mindfulness (*satipaṭṭhāna/vipassanā*) have been published
in Burmese, English and several other languages.[79]

U Ba Khin holds a special interest, partly because he was a layman but
also because *vipassanā* meditation centers in the United States were founded
by Americans who studied with his students. U Ba Khin was accountant

general in the Burmese government under U Nu and became an advocate of meditation practice on the basis of his own personal experience. When he was nearly fifty years old, he developed a cancerous growth on the bone and in the tissue immediately below his right eye. In the course of some years of meditation he cured himself completely. "To him the moral was obvious; a calm and pure spirit produces a healthy body and furthers efficiency in one's work."[80] To promote these goals he established the International Meditation Center (IMC) in Rangoon, which continues to flourish as a center of meditation practice for both Burmese and Western practioners.

Winston L. King, who spent a ten day retreat at the IMC in 1960 when U Ba Khin was still living, described the *guru ji* as "a fascinating combination of worldly wisdom and ingeniousness, inner quiet and outward good humor, efficiency and gentleness, relaxedness and full self-control."[81] The daily schedule at the center was rigorous but not excessive, beginning with meditation at 4:30 A.M. and alternating two and three-hour periods of meditation with an hour of rest, an hour for breakfast and for lunch, and an evening talk by U Ba Khin. King characterized the method as concentration without tension, a middle way between sloth and a focused tension of mind. Although many of his own personal objectives for embarking on this experience were realized, King was unable to decide whether U Ba Khin was "a kind of genius who makes his 'system' work or whether he represents an important new type in Burmese Buddhism—the lay teacher who combines meditation and active work in a successful synthesis. . ."[82] Although that particular question may be open to debate, U Ba Khin, a layman, encouraged the practice of meditation as part of the daily routine of the Buddhist (and non-Buddhist) lay person.

The lay Buddhist meditation movement has been equally important in Sri Lanka and Thailand. Lay as well as monastic meditation teachers have developed sizable followings. In Sri Lanka lay meditation organizations such as the Saddhamma Friends Society have been organized specifically to promote meditation for lay persons.[83] In Thailand several lay meditation teachers have attracted wide attention, and meditation centers in which monks, nuns, lay men and women practice together are becoming almost commonplace.

Khun Mae Dr. Siri Krinchai, a seventy-five year old retired teacher from Nakorn Sawan conducts insight meditation workshops in cities countrywide throughout the year. Numbers participating in each of her workshops held in 1986, 1987, and 1988 ranged between 50 and 300.[84] In 1994 she scheduled forty-six workshops in the four major regions of Thailand. Various other centers of meditation practice also attract hundreds of practioners. Wat Dhammakāya's popularity stems in part from a unique visualization meditation technique promoted as a common practice for both monks and laity. In northern Thailand, Wat Rampung has become a major meditation location, in particular for Thai women and foreigners. The monastery has founded over twenty-five branch meditation centers in northern Thailand, and in the past nine years nearly 500 hundred young men and women from more than a dozen countries have completed a month's meditation training course. Several of these graduates have now established meditation centers in Europe, North America, and Mexico.

Wat Rampung was built in 1492 as a royal monastery at the foot of Doi Kham mountain on the outskirts of Chiang Mai.[85] The monastery was abandoned for many years and occupied by Japanese troops during World War II. Rebuilding began in 1971; a year later a meditation center was founded there by Phrakhrū Pipat (known as Āchān Thọng), the abbot of Wat Muang Man, a historic monastery in Chiang Mai. Āchān Thọng studied insight meditation in Burma for two years with Mahasi Sayadaw and has been one of the principal teachers of the Mahasi method of breathing meditation in northern Thailand.[86] Although male monks and novices reside at the monastery, the largest population—ranging between twenty-five and fifty at any given time—are women. They take either full renunciant vows (chī or mae chī)[87] or ordain as a yogī. The chī take the eight precepts observed by laity on Buddhist sabbath days (the five precepts plus abstaining from eating after noon, from entertainment, and from wearing perfume or jewelry), shave their head and eyebrows, and wear white robes. Yogī, both men and women, observe the five precepts and dress in white. As a rule, women do not shave their heads. In addition to residences for monks, mae chī, and Thai yogī, there is also a dormitory for the foreign yogī who commit themselves to a month's practice. Āchān Thọng's method focuses on the development of insight in two primary postures, sitting and walking as well as bowing or prostrating.[88] All meditation practioners follow the same intensive meditation schedule: 4–6 A.M., 7–10:30 A.M., 12:00–4 P.M., 5–10 P.M. Practice is informal. Most of this time is spent in private meditation with one or two daily consultations with a meditation teacher.

Meditation is also being promoted in Thailand as a treatment for patients with AIDS.[89] Beginning in 1989 a team of psychologists, social workers, and nurses utilize meditation techniques as part of a hospital training program to help health care workers who treat HIV and drug dependent patients. Trainees participate in a seven day insight meditation course taught by an

Figure 3.12. Mae Chī Ruthin Hotikaew, head of the group of nearly fifty *mae chī* at Wat Rampung, Chiang Mai, Thailand. Photo by Donald K. Swearer.

experienced meditation teacher. Adhering to the basic principle of insight meditation—to understand the nature of the psycho-physical phenomena taking place in the body—the trainees' practice focuses on becoming as aware as possible of all bodily and mental acts, feelings, and thoughts while sitting, walking, and in other settings. The purpose of the training is to develop patience, self-understanding, concentration, and the qualities of empathy and altruism. The week's training is followed by discussions relating the intensive meditation experience to cognitive categories at the core of Buddhist mental and moral development, such as mindfulness (*sati*), compassion (*karuṇā*), neutrality (*upekkhā*). The training program concludes with clinical supervision. Results from questionnaires, self-reports, and observations of colleagues show positive results among the majority of health care workers: higher altruism and empathy among trainees, less verbal abuse toward clients, and a greater personal sense of tranquility, happiness, and patience.[90]

Cumulative evidence from Sri Lanka and Southeast Asia supports the view that meditation has been a major factor in the revitalization of Theravāda Buddhism in the modern period. This feature of modern Buddhism is even more striking when coupled with the resurgence of the forest tradition in its various forms in Sri Lanka, Burma, and Thailand. Three related inferences might be drawn from the modern revival of the monastic forest tradition and of meditation practice by laity: (1) that traditional mainstream, institutional religion no longer suffices to define personal meaning and social identity; therefore, (2) there is a desire to recapture an enduring core or essential Buddhism in one's personal life and (3) that insight meditation, in particular, is less bound to specific cultural forms and, hence, is more adaptable to modern settings than other more parochial forms of Buddhist practice.[91]

Lay Buddhist Movements and Associations

Another major aspect of the changing place of the laity in Theravāda Southeast Asia has been the active leadership role taken by lay men and women in the formation of various movements and associations devoted to education, public welfare, social service, and political activism. Some groups incorporate monks into their programs, although lay people usually remain the driving force. Several of these movements and associations were established at the turn of the century. The Young Men's Buddhist Association of Colombo, Sri Lanka was founded by a layman, D. D. Jayatilaka, one of the early leaders in the movement to revive Buddhism in Sri Lanka through education. He was the principal of two Buddhist colleges in Colombo, Ānanda and Dharmarāja, and served as the general manager of the schools sponsored by the Theosophical Society. The Colombo YMBA continues to conduct Dhamma Schools and give Dhamma Examinations aimed at providing "the youth of the land with the same standard of religious instruction and Buddhist education as was imparted by the Maha Sangha in the temple schools in times before foreigners destroyed that great national institution."[92] From a beginning of twenty-seven schools in 1919, by 1966 it had established 3,000 educational centers throughout the island. Other prominent Buddhist lay organizations devoted to various kinds of educational institutions in Sri Lanka and other countries include the Mahābodhi Society, founded by the Anagārika Dharmapāla, and the Buddhist Publication Society headquartered in Kandy, Sri Lanka.[93] The latter has been a major publisher and distributor of essays on Theravāda doctrine and translations of Pali *suttas* into English. German, British, and American monks have contributed significantly to the work of the society, in particular, Nyanaponika Thera, one of its founders.[94]

Lay Buddhist social service organizations that have been established in Theravāda countries since the 1950s function much like lay associations in the West that grew out of religious institutions. Many are national or regional in scope. In Sri Lanka several lay organizations have sponsored social welfare projects. The National Council of Social Services funded under the All-Ceylon Buddhist Congress has supported orphanages, homes for the deaf and blind, and centers for the aged and for delinquents. The Sāsana Sevaka Society, begun in 1958 has worked primarily in the areas of Buddhist education and village uplift.

The Sarvodaya Shramadāna, a rural self-help program also begun in the late 1950s, has developed the most ambitious volunteer service organization in any Theravāda Buddhist country. It has conducted training programs and work projects in over 8,500 villages. The projects have included agriculture, village infrastructure, health, preschool education, and women's health and welfare.[95] To date the Sarvodaya movement has involved over 800,000 volunteers in its programs. Its founder, A. T. Ariyaratne, claims that his efforts are inspired by the Buddha's teaching to strive for awakening. For Ariyaratne the primary meaning of *sarvodaya* is liberation, first from "the defilements within one's own mind...and secondly, from unjust and immoral socio-economic chains."[96] Ariyaratne grounds awakening or liberation in individual transformation, but expands the concept to a universal utopian vision that moves from individual to village, and from community to nation and finally to encompass the world.

Although Ariyaratne has been influenced by the philosophy of Gandhian nonviolence, especially as mediated through Gandhi's activist disciple Vinoba Bhave, the philosophy of Sarvodaya is grounded in basic Theravāda teachings: the three characteristics of existence (suffering, impermanence, not-self), the mutually interdependent and coarising nature of reality, the Noble Eightfold Path encompassing moral virtue, meditation, and wisdom, the mental perfections of loving-kindness, compassion, sympathetic joy, and equanimity, and the moral precepts (*sīla*). However, Ariyaratne extrapolates classical Buddhist teachings as practical action guides to meet current needs. For example, equanimity (*upekkhā*), often linked with *nibbāna*, is transformed into the ability to look at "both sides of life" rather than primarily as a mental state associated with the attainment of higher states of consciousness.[97] The Four Noble Truths are given social correlates:

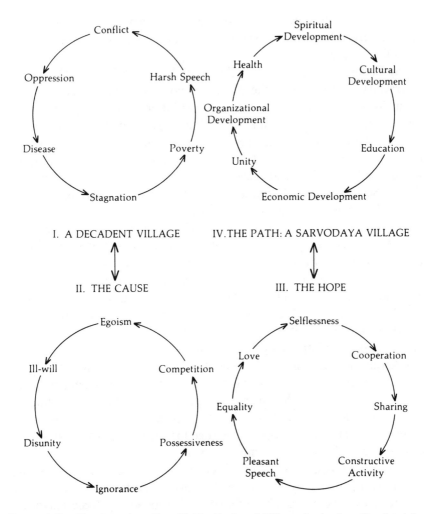

Figure 3.13. The Sarvodaya Four Noble Truths of Village Awakening. Reprinted by permission of Kumarian Press, Inc.

(1) there is an unproductive village; (2) there is a cause for this lack of productivity; (3) there is a hope that the village can renewed; and (4) there is a way to the renewal of all.[98] In short, Ariyaratne's view of Buddhism is consistent with the modern, reformist tendency to interpret the tradition in pragmatic, ethical terms.

Some lay Buddhist social activists criticize the Sarvodaya movement for becoming too success oriented and too dependent on financial support from the government and Western foundations. Yet, Ariyaratne has steadfastly resisted being co-opted by the national government. His refusal to join the Premadasa administration in 1990 prompted the government to attack Sarvodaya's activites, restrict contributions to the movement from outside of Sri Lanka, and even to threaten Ariyaratne's safety.[99] With Premadasa's death in 1992, Sarvodaya's relationship with the Sri Lankan government has improved and the work of the movement continues to expand.

In Thailand, the driving force behind many NGOs (nongovernmental organizations) is the controversial lay Buddhist social activist Sulak Sivaraksa.[100] S. Sivaraksa launched a career as teacher, intellectual gadfly, moral critic, and Buddhist social activist in 1961 upon his return from studying in England. He started several journals including the *Social Science Review* (*Sanghomsat Parithat*), and *Seeds of Peace*, the English-language publication of the International Network of Engaged Buddhists. The organizations that Sulak has founded or helped direct include the Asian Cultural Forum on Development (ACFOD), which has consultative status with the Economic and Social Council of the UN; the Coordinating Group for Religion and Society (CGRS), an ecumenical Buddhist and Christian human rights organization; and the Thai Inter-Religious Commission for Development (TICD), which has sought to encourage Buddhist student associations to participate in social service and social change programs, to act as a bridge between rural and urban groups, and to cooperate with various organizations in short-term educational and recreational projects for children in slum areas.

Upon founding his first NGO in the early 1970s, S. Sivaraksa characterized his Buddhist social activism as follows: "Our main objective was to promote idealism among the young so that they would dedicate themselves to work for the people. We tried to revive Buddhist values. . . .We [also] felt that the monkhood could play a role again through education and public health. . ."[101] Currently the most visible of S. Sivaraksa's NGOs is the Santi (Peace) Pracha (Democratic Participation) Dhamma (Justice) Institute (SPDI). Its projects include the Thai Forum Program to provide information to the mass media on matters of alternative approaches to peace and justice, the Thai-Indochinese Dialogue Project to facilitate dialogue among Thai, Lao, Khmer and Vietnamese, and an organization, Sekiyadhamma, to assist and support the work of monks dedicated to developing a constructive Buddhist challenge to the rapid destruction of the natural environment and the dissolution of religious and cultural values.[102] In particular, the SPDI has supported the efforts of forest conservation monks to challenge the

Figure 3.14. Sulak
Sivaraksa, Thai
Buddhist Social
Activist. Reprinted
courtesy of Sulak
Sivaraksa.

government's attempts to resettle farmers in northeast Thailand for the
purpose of taking over thousands of acres of forest lands assessed by the
government as degraded. The philosophical basis of SPDI's approach to
its mission owes much to Buddhadāsa's holistic vision of spiritual or
dhammic socialism.

S. Sivaraksa has also taken a leadership role in several ecumenical,
international organizations. He serves on several advisory boards including
the Society for Buddhist-Christian Studies, the Buddhist Peace Fellowship,
and the Gandhi Peace Foundation. He cofounded the International Network
of Engaged Buddhists (INEB). In addition to INEB's annual international
conference, the organization sponsors human rights and welfare projects
for Buddhists in Sri Lanka, Myanmar, and Bangladesh. As this list of
organizations suggests, S. Sivaraksa not only carries out his activities in
Thailand, but has developed a worldwide network of projects.

Together with A. T. Ariyaratne, S. Sivaraksa stands as one of the most
visible international lay Buddhist social activists. Like Ariyaratne, he bases
his philosophy of social activism on Buddhist teachings and seeks to
reinterpret them in a personally and socially relevant manner. For example,

S. Sivaraksa contemporizes the Five Precepts as social criticism. He applies the first precept of nonkilling to the use of chemical fertilizers and insecticides that deplete the soil of rich microorganisms, the destruction of forests that contributes to the loss of biodiversity, and to the contamination caused by the dumping of nuclear and chemical waste. He uses the fourth precept of nonlying to advocate truth in advertising and to attack the mindlessness of commercial television and the sensationalism of newspapers.[103] Nor is the *sangha* exempt from S. Sivaraksa's criticism. In an article in the *Bangkok Post*, he used the traditional monastic vow of chastity to question the increasing affluence of Thai monastic life. He argues that, in a consumerist society, seeking for endless sensory pleasures and possessions has become an end in itself while Buddhism advocates nonattachment. When society is driven by lust and greed, S. Sivaraksa contends, living a chaste life becomes absurd: "Unfortunately, this kind of thinking is also pervasive among monks. They have mistaken a chaste life as meaning only celibacy. Senior monks are then living in luxurious quarters similar to those of millionaires. They are riding in Volvos and Mercedes. They are fierce[ly competitive]. They are strict on rules and forms which show that they are pure. But their way of life directly violates the pious existence prescribed by Buddha."[104] Although S. Sivaraksa articulates his philosophy of social action primarily by reinterpreting classical Theravāda philosophical and ethical teachings, he has also been influenced by Buddhist activists from other traditions, most notably the Vietnamese Zen monk Thich Nhat Hanh. Furthermore, he also admires Christian liberation theologians and the spiritual activism of the American Cistercian monk Thomas Merton.

S. Sivaraksa's outspoken criticism of the Thai goverment and Thai society has brought reprisals. In 1984 he was arrested but released after four months in prison. In September 1991, the military government, stung by his attacks, again issued a warrant for his arrest. S. Sivaraksa, fearing for his life, lived in exile for a year, lecturing in Europe, the United States, and Japan. Although the resignation of the military government and the parliamentary elections in Thailand in October 1992, seem to vindicate Sulak's criticism, as of March 1995, his case continues with no imminent resolution in sight.

S. Sivaraksa has not only been attacked by military and government leaders; he has also been criticized by sympathizers who contend that his outspoken style has blunted the effectiveness of his work. Others argue, however, that S. Sivaraksa's biting sarcasm enhances the effectiveness of other Buddhist social critics by allowing more moderate voices to be heard.

Yet even his critics acknowledge that S. Sivaraksa has been an effective agent in promoting idealism and public service, has revived Buddhist values, and has built cooperative networks of religiously committed and motivated people—clergy and lay, Buddhist and non-Buddhist.

Women and Buddhism

In Buddhist texts authored by male monastics women are depicted in various guises: female renunciants attain arahantship and renowned lay women give generously to the *sangha*, yet women are also seen as threatening the stability of the male renunciant order and are often depicted as greedy, weak in wisdom, and inferior to men.[105] Exploring a wide range of classical Indian Buddhist texts, Alan Sponberg distills four diverse attitudes toward women. He characterizes these attitudes as soteriological inclusiveness, institutional androcentrism, ascetic misogyny, and soteriological androgyny.[106] In general Sponberg argues that the early Indian Buddhist tradition acknowledged gender differences but saw them as soteriologically insignificant (i.e., soteriological inclusiveness). As the Buddhist movement became larger and cenobitic monastic traditions became the norm, women's renunciant lives were more and more carefully regulated (i.e., institutional androcentrism). As class and caste differences came to be determined by constructions of purity and pollution, women were defined as a threat to the purity of the male monastic vocation (i.e., ascetic misogyny). Finally, in the Vajrayāna tradition Sponberg argues that gender differences become insignificant relative to the goal, and that ultmately they are perceived as unreal or mutually complimentary (i.e., soteriological androgyny). Although Sponberg's analysis attempts only a broad thematic overview, his schema suggests the complexity of the place of women in the Buddhist worldview and the cultural society it reflects.

The Buddhist women's movement in Theravāda Buddhism, especially in Thailand and Sri Lanka, has assumed an increasingly important place in the changing role of the laity in the contemporary period. The traditional role of women in Southeast Asian society reflected the values of a patriarchial society. Women's roles were defined primarily by men in relationship to men.[107] The ideal woman was a loyal wife and devoted mother. Translated into the Buddhist monastic context, as mothers they produced sons who became monks and as homemakers they prepared the food donated to monks. In the legendary story of the life of the Buddha, this latter role is valorized by the tale of the young woman Sujātā, who offered milk and honey-sweetened rice to Prince Siddhattha while he sat under the Bodhi tree just before his enlightenment. In the same legendary life of the Buddha it was the earth portrayed as a woman who bore witness to the accumulated virtues of the Buddha when the evil Lord Māra challenged the Buddha after his *nibbāna*. Other stories in the Pali texts uphold female exemplary donors (viz. Visākhā) as well as men (viz. Anāthapiṇḍika). These various images of the feminine in the Pali texts are reflected in the roles played by Buddhist women in Southeast Asia. Primarily, women have provided material support for the male monastic order, especially the preparation and donation of food. Lay women also play institutional leadership roles, ranging from managing the preparations for various Buddhist rituals to membership on boards of temples as deacons and trustees. Furthermore, without the participation of women, Buddhist sabbath meetings would be sparsely attended.

Students of Thai Buddhism, in particular, have debated the complicity of Buddhism in constraining the development of women, devaluing them as persons, and even promoting violence against women, much as similar questions have been raised by critical scholars of Christianity and Judaism. Thomas Kirsch has suggested that in Thailand the Theravāda worldview constrains women to be more worldly and more attached than men to the realm of desire that hinders the attainment of salvation.[108] Kirsch bases his view, in part, on occupational specialization; namely, that women tend to be involved in economic-type activities, such as market vending, which are perceived as more worldly. Extending this argument, Khin Thitsa argues that this "materialistic" image of women legitimates prostitution as the place where women can most fulfill their role expectations.[109] In short, she argues for a direct link between Buddhism and the promotion of wide-scale prostitution in Thailand.

Several critics see these interpretations as simplistic, inadequate, and indeed, erroneous. Charles Keyes, in particular, has countered Kirsch's view.[110] Relying primarily on sources from popular village traditions, Keyes contends that relative to the dominant Buddhist value of overcoming attachment, women are perceived more positively than men. Analyzing the images of women as mother, as suffering lover, and as passionate mistress as constructed in Buddhist sermons, popular legends, and courting songs, Keyes contends that women are depicted as more sensitive to the problem of suffering produced by attachment and, therefore, naturally embody more positive Buddhist values than do men. Because the natural state of men inclines toward immoral acts, males are required to enter the monastery to be taught or trained in virtues that are naturally embodied in women. Whether or not Keyes's sympathetic reading of the rural Thai Buddhist tradition is correct, the differing views represented by Thomas Kirsch or Khin Thitsa, on the one hand, and Charles Keyes, on the other, regarding the impact of Buddhism on women in Thailand suggest the difficulty of arriving at a definitive conclusion to this important issue.

It should be noted that womens' roles in Theravāda Southeast Asia reflect differences among cultural environments. In Myanmar, for example, the adolescent rite of passage, exclusively for males in Thailand, is also accorded females even though the ceremony itself is gender differentiated. Furthermore, although female renunciants (*thilashin*) in Myanmar are technically not nuns (*bhikkhunī*), they are granted a higher social status and cultural respect than their female counterparts (*mae chī*) in Thailand. Not only are their numbers significantly larger, some nunneries have highly regarded courses in the Pali scriptures, and *thilashin* are accorded national honors for high achievement in Pali studies. There has also been a revival of a women's renunciant (*sil matavas*) movement in Sri Lanka and, to a lesser extent, in Thailand.[111]

Although the tradition of a valid ordination for women is generally agreed to have ended in 456 C.E. in the Theravāda Buddhist tradition, there have been efforts to inaugurate a female order (*bhikkhunī*) in Thailand.[112] The first attempt was in 1932 when a monk secretly ordained two women as *bhikkhunī*. The monk who was suspected of conducting the ordination was forced to leave the *sangha*. The Thai monastic order never recognized the ordination as valid and public pressure eventually forced both women to disrobe. In 1956 Voramai Kabilsingh received the eight precepts of the Thai female renunciant (*mae chī*) from Phra Pronmuni of Wat Bovoranives.[113] To distinguish herself from the usual white-robed *mae chī*, she wore a light yellow robe and referred to herself as a *nak-buad* (ordained person). Voramai adopted a strict regime that included continuing the meditation practice she had begun in 1953 and keeping a strict vegetarian diet. As her reputation spread, a few young women joined her in becoming yellow-robed nuns. In 1957 Voramai purchased land in Nakorn Prathom province near Bangkok and after a few years opened Wat Songdharma Kalyani, the first monastery in Thailand established by and for Buddhist women. The monastery also operates a K-8 school for orphans and a printing press and conducts social service activities for the poor and needy. In 1971 Voramai traveled to Taiwan where she received *bhikkhunī* ordination in the Dharmagupta tradition; however, her ordination remains unrecognized by the Thai *sangha*. Although

Sakyadhītā, the name of the International Association of Buddhist Women, means 'Daughters of the Buddha.' The objectives of Sakyadhītā, as expressed at its founding meeting in 1987 in Bodhgaya, India, are:

To promote world peace through the practice of the Buddha's Teachings.

To create a network of communications for Buddhist women throughout the world.

To promote harmony and understanding among the various Buddhist traditions.

To encourage and help educate women as teachers of Buddhadharma.

To provide improved facilities for women to study and practice the teachings.

To conduct research on monastic discipline and the role of women in Buddhism.

We are committed to pursuing the Buddhist ideal of positive human development and especially hope to advance the spiritual welfare of the world's women. (*Sakyadhītā.* International Association of Buddhist Women. vol. 4, no. 1, Winter, 1993, p. 12) [p. 60]

Figure 3.15. Objectives of *Sakyadhītā*

the Theravāda countries do not recognize *bhikkhunī* orders, they do exist in Korea, Taiwan, and Japan. Furthermore, an increasing number of Western women are being ordained as *bhikkhunī*.

Lay Buddhist women as well as nuns have been a major force in the international Buddhist women's movement.[114] Karma Lekshe Tsomo, ordained in the Tibetan tradition, has been an active leader and is one of the cofounders of Sakyadhītā, the International Association of Buddhist Women. Chatsumarn Kabilsingh, the daughter of Voramai, studied in India and Canada, and wrote her Ph.D. dissertation on the *bhikkhunī* monastic discipline. A professor in the Department of Philosophy at Thammasat University in Bangkok, Thailand, Kabilsingh works tirelessly on Buddhist women's issues in both Thailand and internationally as the current president of Sakyadhītā and editor of the *Newsletter on International Buddhist Women's Activities (NIBWA)*. Furthermore, as an active leader in the International Network of Engaged Buddhists, she frequently writes and lectues on "green Buddhism" in an effort to protect Thailand's rapidly disappearing forests.

Examples of other lay Buddhist educational, social welfare, and human rights organizations and movements beyond those mentioned in this section abound. Their proliferation reflects the vitality of lay leadership in the revival of Buddhism in the modern period in Southeast Asia, but also underlines the increasing ambiguity of the leadership position of the monk in the Theravāda tradition. What justification remains for the monastic order if lay persons can become meditation teachers and perform the social services once rendered solely by the monastery when it served as the most important organization beyond the family? Can the dominant male character of the monastic order be sustained when it is challenged by thoughtful Buddhist women's organizations? Such questions are not merely rhetorical but are very real and practical in the Theravāda cultures of Buddhist Asia.

In Cambodia and Laos revolutionary forces viewed the *bhikkhu sangha* either as reactionary or a hindrance to political and economic development, although recent political changes offer more hope for the future of the monastic order in those countries. Whether or not the monk can continue to symbolize values of lasting significance embodied in the ideals of Buddhism and at the same time speak to the needs of societies in radical transition is a fundamental issue not merely for the academic study of Buddhism and society in Southeast Asia but for the very survival of this religious tradition.

BUDDHISM AND THE WEST

The future story of Theravāda Buddhism will unfold not only in Sri Lanka and Southeast Asia, but also in the West. Interrelationships between the West and Theravāda Buddhist countries are not new. Travelers' accounts from the early colonial period often portrayed Buddhism in either unsympathetic or exotic and esoteric terms. By the nineteenth century, however, Western interest in Buddhism had become both intensive and extensive. Westerners not only made many contributions to Buddhist scholarship, they also took a personal interest in the tradition. T. William and Caroline Rhys Davids, for example, founded the Pali Text Society, an organization reponsible for editing and translating Pali canonical and commentarial texts, and also helped organize the London Buddhist Society. These early Western Buddhists and sympathetic scholars helped to create and promote a rationalized, demythologized Buddhism that appeals as much to twentieth century Europeans and Americans as it does to Western-educated Asians.[115] In this section we shall explore three distinct but related aspects of a new ecumenical Buddhism: the emergence of an international *Buddha-dhamma*, the popularity of Theravāda insight meditation, and the expansion of expatriate Buddhism.

In 1959 *What the Buddha Taught*, by the Sinhalese monk-scholar-educator Walpola Rahula, was published in the West. It was to become one of the standard introductions to Buddhist thought in this country. Soundly grounded in the Pali scriptures, the book discusses such seminal teachings as the Four Noble Truths, not-self, interdependent coarising, meditation, and *nibbāna*. Like D. T. Suzuki's idealistic interpretations of Zen, Rahula's scripturally grounded, clearly articulated interpretation of Theravāda thought can be seen as a masterpiece of apologetic literature. This monograph presents a rationalized, demythologized version of Buddhism devoid of reference to various aspects of popular Buddhist constructions, such as the Buddha cult or merit making rituals. To be sure, the Venerable Rahula did not intend for his interpretation of Buddhism to be a comprehensive treatment of the variety of genre in Buddhist literature. Rather, *What the Buddha Taught* represents a tradition of modern, reformist reinterpretations of Theravāda doctrine by both Asian Buddhists and Westerners.

A modern, rationalized Buddha-*dhamma* gauged to a Western-educated audience has many representatives from Sri Lanka, Southeast Asia (e.g., Bhikkhu Buddhadāsa) and the West. This tradition tends to emphasize the compatibility between the teachings of the Buddha, Western empiricism and pragmatism, and Western science. Western-educated Sinhalese scholars are particularly influential. The late K. N. Jayatilleke of Peradeniya University, Sri Lanka, who studied with Ludwig Wittenstein, and several of Jayatilleke's students, most notably David J. Kalupahana, Department of Philosophy, University of Hawaii, and Padmasiri de Silva, University of Singapore, have written sophisticated interpretations of Buddhist thought in dialogue with modern epistemology, British empiricism, American pragmatism, and Western psychology.[116] Western philosophers are also part of this tradition. Nolan Pliny Jacobson, for example, interprets early Buddhist thought through the lens of Humean empiricism.[117] These interpreters differ in viewpoint to be sure; they do not represent a monolithic position. The most comprehensive and philosophically sophisticated corpus of work has been produced by Professor Kalupahana.[118]

This modernized view of the Buddha-*dhamma* demythologizes the tradition in the service of ethical and psychological values. *Nibbāna*, for example, tends to be interpreted primarily as a nonattached way of being in the world that affects how we act, rather than as an extraordinary and difficult to achieve state of enlightenment. Prince Siddhattha, the mythic hero of the Buddha legend, is transformed into a social critic and moral exemplar.[119] This is not to say that the modernized Buddha-*dhamma* misinterprets the inherited tradition of Buddhist doctrine; rather, the tradition is skillfully reinterpreted to make sense to a rational, Western-educated audience. Although critics have faulted this modernized Buddha-*dhamma* for an overemphasis on Buddhism as a philosophical and ethical system while ignoring the rich textures of Buddhist practice and nonphilosophical forms of Buddhist thought, without such reinterpretations a religious tradition loses its relevance and saliency to an educated audience. There is a risk, however, that in the service of rationality and relevance the richly textured and multivalent nature of the tradition is ignored.

The sine qua non of Buddhism in the West has been the practice of meditation. Beginning with the development of Zen Buddhism in America after World War II, promoted by the writings of D. T. Suzuki and the founding of the early Zen centers in New York, San Francisco, and Los Angeles, meditation has been at the heart of Buddhism's appeal to Westerners. The practice of *zazen* continues to flourish in North America and Europe. With the creation of a Tibetan Buddhist diaspora in the West following the Chinese invasion of Tibet in 1958, Tibetan forms of Buddhist meditation, especially as taught by Chogyam Trungpa Rimpoche, further expanded the practice of Buddhist meditation.[120]

The interest in Theravāda insight meditation (*vipassanā*) in the United States is a more recent development. The major *vipassanā* center is located in Barre, Massachusetts, although meditation teachers promoting insight meditation methods are found throughout the United States. Some insight teachers are former Asian Buddhists monks, such as Dhiravamsa, a Thai teacher who maintains a center at Friday Harbor, near Seattle; others are American lay persons who have studied with Burmese meditation teachers, such as Joseph Goldstein of the Barre meditation center; and still others are American monks ordained in Asia who are now teaching in this country, such as Thanissaro Bhikkhu (Geoff DeGraff), the abbot of the Metta Forest Monastery, a meditation center near Valley Center, California. This diversity mirrors the nature of the development of Buddhism in the West.

Finally, a discussion of Theravāda Buddhism in the West is incomplete without reference to the presence of an estimated 300 Thai, Lao, Cambodian and Sri Lankan monasteries in North America. At this writing these Buddhist centers primarily serve the needs of expatriate Southeast Asian populations, many of them refugees. Lao and Cambodian monasteries are cultural outposts for those dislocated from their own culture, dispossessed of their property, many of whom experienced untold hardship in their escape from Laos, Cambodia, and Vietnam in the 1970s and 1980s.[121]

Southeast Asian monasteries in this country serve many functions. Major Buddhist holidays and ceremonies such as Visākhā Pūja virtually transport the participants back to Thailand, Laos, or Cambodia. Classes held in native languages and the arts including classical dance, perpetuate Southeast Asian cultural identity in an alien environment. Informal counseling on issues ranging from family problems to civil rights teach a variety of coping skills. Above all, these centers honor the Buddha and study his teachings. In the coming decades Theravāda Buddhism in America will inevitably undergo major changes to remain relevant to second and third generation immigrant populations. Although Southeast Asian monasteries will continue to function as cultural outposts for Thai, Lao, Cambodian, and Burmese populations, the challenge to adapt to a Western setting will lead to new and creative forms of religious thought and practice.[122]

POSTSCRIPT

We have explored Buddhism in Southeast Asia as a dynamic multiplex and multivalent system of thought and practice imbedded in the respective cultures, societies, and histories of the region. Such a holistic, multifaceted approach belies the possibility of a grand interpretative theory in terms of which we can easily characterize the nature of Southeast Asian Buddhism or predict its future. Certainly, any interpretation of religion and society in Southeast Asia begs a crucial question. Can or will Theravāda Buddhism, which has been such an integral part of the societies of Sri Lanka, Burma, Thailand, Laos, and Cambodia, be sustained in a form resembling the description in the preceding chapters?

The post-World War II years have brought drastic changes to much of Southeast Asia, so drastic that the Buddhist worldview and the institutions fostered there are being severely challenged. In Cambodia and Laos the Buddhist *sangha* has been disrupted by the Vietnam war and its aftermath. The sacred monarchical traditions of Southeast Asia, largely undermined during the colonial period, exist only in vague, vestigial forms. Even Thailand's existing monarchy is no longer immune from challenge or criticism. The traditional religious festivals that once shaped community life are gradually losing their meaning. A smaller percentage of the male population is being ordained into the Buddhist monkhood. Nevertheless, in much of what remains of rural Southeast Asia the traditional rites, rituals and festivals still bind people together in a common identity; Buddhist values continue to play a normative role in a peoples' view of social well-being and personal salvation; and Buddhist institutions are making creative adjustments to economic, social, and political changes. Furthermore, new forms of Buddhist thought and practice emerging from extensive interaction between Asia and the West, men and women, monk and laity hold great promise for the future. Indeed, although the new face of Buddhism will reflect its rootedness in Asia, its visage will reflect a new aspect, one that is increasingly international and broadly multicultural.[123]

Even though this book has not constructed a grand theory of Buddhism and society in Southeast Asia, it has been grounded in a general theoretical perspective; namely, a holistic view of the history of religions as dynamic and inherently multiplex-multivalent. In addition, several major interpretative issues and themes have been highlighted in this study. In conclusion I would like to emphasize one in particular: the traditional social constructions of Theravāda Buddhist cultures, especially of "almsperson" and "lay person"—although plural and dynamic in nature—appear to be on the brink of dramatic change. I assume that there will be a twenty-first century Buddhism, but its forms may differ significantly from the mainstream civil religion Buddhism of Chapter 2 of this book or even from many aspects of the popular Buddhism of Chapter 1, despite the current resurgence of fundamentalistic, simplistic, cultic belief and practice.

At a January 1994 symposium on the impact of "globalization" on Thailand, a professor of Buddhism at Chiang Mai University suggested that a "global" or "international" Buddhism was philosophically realistic, but that it would necessarily be culturally impoverished. He concluded his remarks with the question, "Is this really the kind of Buddhism that we would like to have?" His comments were reminiscent of Gananath Obeyesekere's critical assessment of the "protestantizing" of Buddhism in modern Sri Lanka. At the same symposium a Thai monk with a doctorate from India suggested an even more distressing possibility. Seeing "globalization" primarily as the commercialization of culture, a "globalized" Buddhism would necessarily mean that Buddhism becomes a commodity, a value determined primarily by the idioms of commerce.

These two views offer starkly different visions, one a rationalized, culturally denuded Buddhism taught by philosophers and sloganized by politicians with little meaning to real-life people in Southeast Asia; the other, a Buddhism overwhelmed by the commericalization of culture, a Buddhism devoid of the power to define or challenge a community's moral identity or to transform individual lives spiritually. I see and fear the truth of both possibilities. I hope that the reality will be neither.

The symposium at Chiang Mai University dealt with the impact of globalization on Thailand. The very notion of "globalization," however, implies processes affecting the entire globe, not just Thailand. The possibilities suggested by the university professor and the Thai monk point to realities that confront all religious traditions. The topic of the impact of globalization, therefore, suggests that all religions, not only Buddhism in Southeast Asia, are in the midst of dramatic, unprecedented change.

APPENDIX 1

Sigālaka Sutta

Code of Lay Ethics

In the *Sigālaka Sutta* in the Discourses of the Buddha (*Dīgha Nikāya* III.180), the Buddha ethicizes the Brahmanical custom of worshipping the deities of the four quarters, the zenith, and nadir. In the Buddha's interpretation, the six directions become metaphors for different social relationships: parents (east), teachers (south), wife and children (west), friends and relatives (north), servants and workers (nadir), brahmans and mendicants (zenith). The Buddha outlines their duties and obligations as follows.[1] (The moral admonitions may sound old-fashioned to modern ears but we should keep in mind the historical context—hierarchical and patriarchal—in which they were written. Taking the context into account, one is impressed with the underlying premise of mutual responsibility for social and moral well-being.)

EAST

Forward direction signifying mother and father whom their children should uphold in five ways: (1) they have looked after and brought up their children so they should repay this kindness by looking after them; (2) they should help look after their parents' affairs; (3) they should ensure the endurance of the family name; (4) they should conduct themselves in ways that make them worthy to receive inherited wealth; (5) after their parents have died, they should make merit on their behalf.

The children's mother and father having been upheld in the preceding ways, they should help their children in five ways: (1) by helping them avoid

163

doing evil; (2) by encouraging them to do good; (3) by seeing that they receive an education; (4) by finding a suitable mate for them; (5) by giving over their wealth to them at the appropriate time.

SOUTH

To the right, signifying the teacher whom his pupil should uphold in five ways: (1) by standing up to receive him when he comes (as a sign of respect); (2) by waiting in attendance on him; (3) by paying attention to what he says; (4) by acting as his attendant; (5) by being his diligent student.

The teacher, having been upheld in these five ways should help his pupil (1) by setting a good example; (2) by motivating him to study; (3) by telling him as much as he knows without holding anything back; (4) by praising him among his friends; (5) by seeing he is properly supported and cared for.

WEST

Signifying the wife whom her husband should uphold in five ways: (1) by praising her and upholding the relationship; (2) by not looking down on her; (3) by not being unfaithful; (4) by letting her be in charge of the home and family; (5) by giving her clothing and presents.

The husband's wife having been upheld in these ways should support her husband (1) by organizing family affairs well, (2) by helping her husband's relatives and friends; (3) by not being unfaithful to her husband; (4) by looking after the valuables and property; (5) by being energetic in her duties.

NORTH

Signifying friends, good people whom one should uphold in five ways: (1) by sharing things with them; (2) by talking agreeably with them; (3) by doing things for them that are useful; (4) by being evenminded and without pride; (5) by not speaking pretentiously and by being truthful.

One's friends, having been upheld in the preceding ways, should then help as follows: (1) by protecting them from being careless; (2) by protecting their property and valuables if they are careless and neglectful; (3) by providing shelter when there is danger; (4) by not abandoning them in times of adversity; (5) by taking care of the relatives of one's friends.

NADIR

Signifying servants whom their master should uphold in five ways: (1) by arranging work that is suitable and not beyond their capability; (2) by providing them with food and other compensation; (3) by taking care of them when they are sick; (4) by sharing delicacies with them; (5) by giving them time off.

A master's servants, having been upheld in these ways, should help their master (1) by getting up before their master and starting their work; (2) by quitting work after their master; (3) by not stealing from their master; (4) by constantly trying to do their work better; (5) by praising the virtues of their master.

ZENITH

Signifying *samaṇa* (religious practioners) whom their disciples should uphold in five ways: (1) by acting with loving-kindness; (2) by speaking with loving-kindness; (3) by thinking thoughts with loving-kindness; (4) by always welcoming them into their homes; (5) by providing them with material requisites.

Samaṇas, having been upheld in these ways, should then help their followers (1) by helping them avoid evil; (2) by encouraging them to do the good; (3) by helping them with a compassionate mind; (4) by teaching them what they do not know; and (5) clarifying for them what they might know already.

APPENDIX 2

Audio Visual Bibliography

See *Focus on Buddhism*, ed. Robert A. McDermott (Chambersburg, Pa: Anima Books, 1981) for additional information about the films listed produced prior to 1980. Contains addresses of film distributors.

Angkor: The Lost City 12 minutes, b/w, 16mm, 1961. National Film Board of Canada. Available from The Pennsylvania State University, AV Services. A useful overview of the Angkor complex.

Being the Buddha in L.A. 45 minutes, color video, 1993, WGBH/Michael Camarini producer. Distributor: WGBH, 125 Western Ave., Allston, MA. 02134. An exploration of Buddhism in America focusing on Los Angeles. The film includes scenes from an ordination at a Cambodian monastery.

Blue Collar and Buddha 57 minutes, color, videocassette, 1987, Taggart Siegel Producer. Distributor: Siegel Productions, P.O. Box 6123, Evanston, IL 60602. A realistic exploration of a Laotian community, their monastery, and the reaction of the people of Rockford, Illinois, where it is located.

Borobudur: The Cosmic Mountain 40 minutes, color, 16mm, 1972. Zodiac Films/Brian Brake producer. Available from the University of Michigan, AV Educational Center; University of California at Berkeley, Extension Media Center. Presents Borobudur within the historical and cultural context of Java.

The Buddha: Temple Complex at Borobudur 11 minutes, 16 mm, Sepia, 1960. Film Images/Radim Films/Henre Dore producer. Available from University of Chicago AV Center.

Buddhism in Southeast Asia and Ceylon (slides) 220 slides, color. Asian Religions Media Resources/Charles A. Kennedy producer. Distributor:

Visual Ed. Service, Yale University Divinity School, 409 Prospect St., New Haven, CT. 06511.

Buddhism, Burma, and Neutralism   55 minutes, b/w, 16mm, 1957. Paul Nevin director. Available from University of Michigan AV Educational Center. Presents the interface of Buddhism and politics in U Nu's Burma. Reflects 1950s American attitudes toward Burmese neutrality.

Buddhism: Be Ye Lamps Unto Yourselves   29 minutes, color, 16mm, 1973. ABC/Howard Enders producer. Available from University of Minnesota AV Library Services, University of Missouri Academic Support Center. An effective film on contemporary Thai Buddhism. An introduction to Theravāda Buddhism constructed around an ordination ceremony.

Buddhism, Footprint of the Buddha   54 minutes, color. 16mm and video-cassette, 1977. BBC Long Search Series/Peter Montagnon producer. Distributor: Time-Life Video, Inc. 100 Eisenhower Drive, Paramus, NJ 07652. Buddhism in Sri Lanka narrated by Ronald Eyre. Focuses on monastic life and interaction between monk and laity. Highly recommended.

Cave Temples of India—Buddhist   9 minutes, b/w, 16mm, 1961. Government of India/M. Bhavanani producer. Available from Government of India, Information Services, Washington, D.C. A useful though brief overview of the development of Buddhist cave temple/monastery sculpture in India.

Chiang Mai, Northern Capital   15 minutes, color, 16mm, 1971. Australian Information Services, Our Asian Neighbors Series/John Morris and Thanom Soonaratna producers. Available from Australian Information Services, Australian Consulate General, NY. Presents selected aspects of northern Thai culture including the end of the rains retreat and Loi Krathong.

The Evolution of the Buddha Image   74 slides, 1963. The Asia Society of New York producer. Presents the development of the Buddha image in Buddhist Asia. The Asia Society Exhibition catalogue by Benjamin Rowland and the slide set are available in many university and college libraries.

Gautama the Buddha   78 minutes, b/w, 16mm, 1956. Government of India/Bhimal Roy producer. Available from Government of India, Information Services, Washington, D.C. Uses images and bas-reliefs to portray the life of the Buddha.

The Glory that Remains   30 minutes, color, 16mm, 1969. BBC/Adrian Malone producer. Available from The Pennsylvania State University AV Services. An appreciation of the great artistry of early Indian Buddhist sculpture. Focuses on Asokan pillars, inscriptions, the Sāñcī *stūpa*.

I am a Monk   30 minutes, color, 16mm and videocassette, 1978. Hartley Productions/Elda Hartley producer. Distributor: Hartley Film Foundation, Cat Rock Road, Cos Cob, CT. 06807. Explores the motivations, rewards, and life experiences of an American monk in Thailand.

Image Bank   5,500 color slides cross-indexed by tradition, theme, and geographic area. Distributor: Center for the Study of World Religions, 42 Francis Avenue, Cambridge, MA. 02138. Includes material on Buddhist Southeast Asia.

Immortal Stupa   14 minutes, b/w, 16mm, 1961. Government of India/ Bhimal Roy producer. Available from Government of India, Information Services, Washington, D.C. Focuses on the Sāñcī bas-reliefs. Primarily of art historical interest.

In the Steps of the Buddha   19 minutes, color, 16mm. Government of Sri Lanka/P. Hettarachi director. Distributor: Tribune Films, 38 West 32nd St., New York, NY 10001. Presents episodes from the life of the Buddha found in the *Dīpavaṃsa* as portrayed primarily in the modern mural paintings at Kelaniya near Colombo, Sri Lanka.

The Killing Fields   Commercial film. Available through video rental stores. Powerful depiction of the impact of the Vietnam War on Cambodia.

Land of Enchantment   12 minutes, b/w, 16mm, 1953. Government of India/M. Bhavanani producer. Available from Government of India, Information Services, Washington, D.C. Through the device of pilgrimage to sacred sites this film shows some of the key locations in the sacred geography of Buddhist India.

Life and Work of Buddhadāsa Bhikkhu   25 minutes, color, videocassette, 1987. Children's Foundation producer. Distributor: Suksit Siam 113-115, Fuangnakorn Rd., Bangkok 10200, Thailand. An introduction to the noted Thai monk, Buddhadāsa, filmed at his monastery in southern Thailand.

Little Buddha   Commercial film. Available through video rental stores. An appealing presentation of the life of the Buddha.

Rebuilding the Temple: Cambodians in America   60 minutes, color, videocassette, 1991. Florentine Films/Claudia Levin and Lawrence Holt producers. Distributor: Direct Cinema Limited Library, P.O. Box 135, Franklin Lakes, NJ 07417.

Samsāra   29 minutes, color videocassette, 1992. Ellen Bruno producer. Distributor: Film Library, 22nd Holywood Ave., Hohokus, NJ 07423. Cambodia after Pol Pot.

Sañchi 50 slides. Asian Art Archives, University of Michigan, 1969. Walter M. Spink and Deborah Levine producers. Distributor: Interbook, Inc., 13 East 16th Street, New York, NY 10003. A detailed presentation and explanation of Sāñcī with accompanying notes.

The Smile 20 minutes, color, 16mm, 1963. Tamara Films/Serge Bourguignon producer. Available from the Florida State University Instructional Support Center, the University of Wisconsin/Madison Bureau of AV Instruction. Depicts Burmese Buddhism through the experiences of a young novice monk in Burma.

Temple of the Twenty Pagodas 22 minutes, color, 16mm, 1971. Australian Information Services/John Morris and Thanom Soonaratna producers. Available from Australian Information Services, New York. Presents a day in the life of a Theravāda Buddhist temple-monastery outside of Lampang, northern Thailand.

Thai Images of the Buddha 14 minutes, color, 16mm, 1962. University of Indiana/Arts of the Orient. Available from the University of Indiana AV Services. Informative film tracing the evolution of the Buddha image through various periods of Thai art history.

Thailand 52 minutes, color, 16mm, 1979. Australian Information Services/ John Temple producer. PBS-Views of Asia Series. Available from Australian Information Services, New York. A sympathetic portrayal of Buddhism within a general survey of modern Thailand.

Vejen 22 minutes, color, 16mm, 1971. Carousel Films, Inc./Elsebet Kjolbye producer. Distributor: Carousel Films, Inc., 1501 Broadway, New York, NY 10036. Focuses on the experience of a young boy in his capacity as an attendant to a monk. Culminates in his ordination as a novice.

Vesak 18 minutes, color, 16mm, 1975. Yvonne Hanneman producer. Distributor: Focus International, Inc., 1776 Broadway, New York, NY 10019. A cultural film on the festival of Vesak in Sri Lanka which celebrates the birth, enlightenment, and final *nibbāna* of the Buddha.

APPENDIX 3

Borobudur

The pyramidal terrace known as Borobudur[1] was constructed on the Kedu plain near present-day Jogjakarta between 760 and 830 C.E. by a ruling dynasty called the Śailendras, or "kings of the mountain."[2] Under King Sumaratunga (792–824) the Śailendras controlled most of central Java and enjoyed especially close relations with the Pāla kings of north India, patrons of Mahāyāna and Tantrayāna forms of Buddhism.[3] Borobudur, the only surviving monument of its type in Java, embodies a set of complex meanings: "The monument has multiple layers of meaning which accumulated during its active life, and it therefore represents a process of cultural evolution rather than a single moment in Javanese history."[4] Interpretations variously define Borobudur as a cosmic mountain, a *stūpa*,[5] a *maṇḍala*, and as the stages of development of a spiritual journey.[6]

The structure consists of six square terraces, the lowest being 479 square feet, topped by three circular platforms bearing seventy-two perforated, hollow *stūpas* covering seated Buddha images and a solid central *stūpa* 52 feet in diameter.[7] The walls of the terraces and the lower basement are covered with bas-reliefs. The ground level portrays the operation of *kamma* and rebirth, depicting in graphic detail the punishments that result from evil deeds. The terraces are perambulation galleries. Bas-reliefs carved in stone depict the life of the Buddha according to the *Lalitavistara*, and stories from the *Divyāvadāna, Jātakamālā,* and *Gaṇḍavyūha*. A total of ninety-two Buddha images are situated in niches on the outer walls of the monument's five levels.

Borobudur's terraced pyramid appears to represent a spiritual ascent from the mundane world of karmic action and rebirth to that supreme reality beyond all form. Along the ascending path, pilgrims encounter the Buddha

Figure A.1. Top view of Borobudur. From A. J. Bernet Kempers, *Ancient Indonesian Art.* Harvard University Press, 1959, p. 42. Reprinted by permission of Harvard University Press.

Śakyamuni and Mahāyāna *bodhisattvas* carved in bas-relief on the circum-ambulatory terraces. Borobudur can be constructed in ways other than mapping stages of a spiritual journey. Paul Mus sees the monument as a representation of the upper reaches of a cosmic mountain enclosed by the cupola of the sky.[8] As a cosmic mountain or *axis mundi* it serves to connect the divine source of royal power with the Buddha. From this perspective, Borobudur has been interpreted as merging a chthonous cult of "kings of the mountain" with the Buddha Vairocana, the universal, unconditioned Ādi-Buddha. De Casparis, for instance, has argued that in Śailendra inscriptions the Sanskrit term *gotra* was used to mean both the fundamental element of Buddhahood as well as the "line of the ancestors," thereby identifying the family of the Tathāgata with the Śailendra ancestral line.[9] R. Soekmono agrees with the underlying assumption of this view when he contends that a stepped pyramid with a *stūpa* on top is the most appropriate symbol to depict the virtues successively accumulated by the forefathers along the *bodhisattva* path to Buddhahood.[10]

Although scholarly interpretations of Borobudur differ, there seems to be a consensus that the monument integrates three levels of meaning germane to our study of the symbiosis between political authority and cosmology: cosmic, royal, and Buddhist. At the macrocosmic level the monument connects royal power with the universal Buddha at the center of a complex cosmology; at the microcosmic level Borobudur represents stages of spiritual ascent from the realm of desire, through the realm of form, and finally to the realm beyond form, or—in terms more specifically related to kingship—Borobudur represents stages of *bodhisattva* perfection not only to the unconditioned ground of reality but to the foundation of the royal Śailendra lineage.[11]

Notes

PREFACE

1. See Donald K. Swearer, "Buddhism in Southeast Asia," in *The Encyclopedia of Religion*, vol 2. 385–400, ed. Mircea Eliade (New York: Macmillan Publishing Company, 1987), for a more detailed discussion of the development of Buddhism in Southeast Asia. This article is also reprinted in *The Religious Traditions of Asia*, ed. Joseph M. Kitagawa and Mark D. Cummings (New York: Macmillan Publishing Company, 1989); and *Buddhism and Asian History*, ed. Joseph M. Kitagawa and Mark D. Cummings (New York: Macmillan Publishing Company, 1989). For a discussion of Theravāda Buddhism in Sri Lanka and its legacy in India, see Richard F. Gombrich, *Theravāda Buddhism. A Social History from Ancient Benares to Modern Colombo* (London and New York: Routledge and Kegan Paul, 1988).

Students unfamiliar with the Pali canon of Theravāda Buddhism can consult K. R. Norman, *Pali Literature* (Wiesbaden: Otto Harrassowitz, 1983). The Pali canon and a number of Pali commentaries have been edited and published by the Pali Text Society. Many volumes are available in English in the Pali Text Society Translation Series. Recent English translations of the Long Discourses of the Buddha (*Dīgha Nikāya*) and the Middle Length Discourses (*Majjhima Nikāya*) are *Thus I Have Heard. The Long Discourses of the Buddha*, trans. Maurice Walshe (London: Wisdom Publications, 1987) and *A Treasury of the Buddha's Words. Discourses from the Middle Collection*, trans. Nyanamoli Thera, ed. Phra Khantipalo (Bangkok: Mahāmakuta Rājavidyalaya Press, 1992).

2. Current scholarly convention uses *Tai* or *Dai* as a collective term encompassing various Tai ethnic groups, e.g., the Shan of Burma, the Lue, the Khoen, the Yuan, and uses Thai when referring to the Thais of modern Thailand.

3. See the Introduction to *For the Sake of the World: The Spirit of Buddhist and Christian Monasticism*, by Patrick Henry and Donald K. Swearer (Minneapolis: Augsburg-Fortress Press, and Collegeville, Minn.: Liturgical Press, 1989), for a discussion of the use of the terms monk and nun.

4. See Appendix 2 for an alphabetical listing and description of films referred to in the notes.

INTRODUCTION

1. Wilfred Cantwell Smith, "The Study of Religion and the Study of the Bible," *Journal of the American Academy of Religion* 29, no. 2 (June 1971): 131–140.

2. A good example of this point would be *The Temple of the Twenty Pagodas*. The film focuses on a Thai *wat* (monastery-temple), the activities of the monks there, and the interaction between monks and laity. It includes scenes of monks chanting, on their alms rounds, cleaning the temple precincts, studying, eating a noon meal, and speaking to lay visitors. The camera takes the viewer outside of the monastery compound to farmers in nearby rice fields and follows school children playing inside the compound in an attempt to illustrate the fluid boundaries of the Thai *wat*. Its minimal sound track enhances the visual impact of temple activities seen by the viewer—amulets being purchased by lay visitors, monks prostrating before the image of the Buddha, a monk talking with a group of civil servants. In the hands of a skillful and knowledgeable teacher, a discussion of the film elaborates and clarifies conceptually what has been seen but without detracting from the admittedly more vague, yet possibly more profound level of understanding gained through the film. (Unless otherwise stipulated, bibliographic information about films referred to in the Notes can be found in *Focus on Buddhism*, ed. Robert A. McDermott [Chambersburg, Pa.: Anima Books, 1980]. The films are listed alphabetically in Appendix 2.)

3. See Donald K. Swearer, *Secrets of the Lotus* (New York: Macmillan Publishing Company, 1971).

4. See Robert N. Bellah, "Religious Evolution," in *Beyond Belief* (New York: Harper and Row, 1970).

5. Here I allude to G. Van Der Leeuw's classic study, *Religion in Essence and Manifestation* (New York: Harper and Row, 1963). I believe that Van Der Leeuw's notion of "essence" is primarily epistemic rather than ontological, a sense of essence problematized in poststructuralist thought.

6. *Ethos* and *worldview* are used here in the sense defined by Clifford Geertz in his article, "Ethos, World View, and the Analysis of Sacred Symbols," in Clifford Geertz, *The Interpretation of Cultures* (New York: Basic Books, 1973), p. 127: "A people's ethos is the tone, character and quality of their life, its moral and aesthetic style and mood; it is the underlying attitude toward themselves and their world that life reflects. Their world view is their picture of the way things in sheer actuality are, their concept of nature, of self, of society. It contains their most comprehensive ideas of order."

CHAPTER 1. THE POPULAR TRADITION

1. I shall use the proper noun Burma as the country name except in those cases when it is appropriate to use the current name, Myanmar.

2. In most cases Buddhist terms will be in their Pali form, the scriptural language of Theravāda Buddhism. When the context demands, Sanskrit or a vernacular term will be used.

3. See Max Weber, *The Religions of India*, trans. and ed. Hans H. Gerth and Don Martindale (New York: The Free Press, 1958), chaps. 6 and 7.

4. For example, see Melford E. Spiro, *Buddhism and Society: A Great Tradition and Its Burmese Vicissitudes*, 2d ed. (Berkeley: University of California Press, 1982).

5. See Winston L. King, *In the Hope of Nibbana. An Essay on Theravada Buddhist Ethics* (LaSalle, Ill.: Open Court, 1964). A recent critique of King's analysis is Damien Keown, *The Nature of Buddhist Ethics* (New York: St. Martin's Press, 1992), chap. 4.

6. For a discussion of this issue, see Steven Collins, *Selfless Persons. Imagery and Thought in Theravāda Buddhism* (Cambridge: Cambridge University Press, 1982), Part I.

7. Of the available films on Theravāda Buddhism in Southeast Asia, *The Smile* offers a sensitive interpretation of the seeming paradox between the highest ideals of Buddhism and its cultural expressions. The film reenacts a day in the life of a young Burmese novice who attends an elderly monk. The polarity is drawn between the old man who seems to symbolize the meditative attainments of equanimity and nonattachment and the young boy who obviously enjoys life as he encounters it: a water buffalo in a field, a leaf worm's handiwork, Burmese boxers, lovely girls bathing at a well, and a traveling puppet show. The film juxtaposes the nibbanic ideal with the actual experience of Buddhism within a particular culture. What is Buddhism: the elderly monk who seems removed from the world? Or the young boy who smiles at the water buffalo? Or is it both?

8. The *jātakas* purport to be stories of previous lives of the Buddha. Because they are folk traditions incorporated into a set form and tied together by the *bodhisatta* concept, they provide a rich source for the popular tradition of Indian Buddhism. In addition to the Pali *jātakas* there are extensive vernacular *jātaka* traditions, such as the *Pannasajātaka (Fifty Jātakas)* written in northern Thailand. The specific virtues represented by the last ten *jātaka* tales are patience, energy, determination, renunciation, wisdom, morality, truth, love, equanimity, and generosity.

9. The film, *Gautama the Buddha*, uses statues, reliefs, paintings, and architectural sites to recreate the story of the Buddha. However, the narration and soundtrack make it less than ideal for classroom instruction. The commercial film, *Little Buddha*, presents an appealing interpretation of the Buddha.

10. The film, *Being the Buddha in L.A.*, includes footage of a novitiate ordination of a Cambodian teenager at a Cambodian monastery in Los Angeles. *Buddhism. Be Ye Lamps Unto Yourselves* is structured around two ordination ceremonies, and it also includes scenes of a variety of monastic activities including meditation

and study. Its sequence on morning alms rounds has some exceptionally beautiful photography. It is also the only major film on Southeast Asian Buddhism to include a funeral ceremony. The narration not only explains the visual background but discusses the cardinal teachings of Thai Buddhism through interviews and quotations from Theravāda texts.

11. For purposes of simplicity I have glossed over the distinctions between *stūpa*, *cetiya* (Thai: *cedi*), *dhātugarbha* (Sinhalese: *dagoba*). See Chapter 2 for a discussion of the *stūpa*. The solid dome or pyramidal architectural structures to which these terms refer embody both a cosmic referent (*axis mundi*) and a Buddhist referent. The latter derives from the fact that they enshrine some sort of artifact—not always a relic—associated with the person and life of the Buddha or a Buddhist saint.

12. For a discussion of the supreme saintly ideal in Theravāda Buddhism, see George D. Bond, "The Arahant: Sainthood in Theravāda Buddhism," in *Sainthood. Its Manifestations in World Religions*, ed. Richard Kieckhefer and George D. Bond (Berkeley: University of California Press, 1988), pp. 140–171. See also Stanley J. Tambiah, "The Buddhist Arahant: Classical Paradigm and Modern Thai Manifestations," in *Saints and Virtues*, ed. John S. Hawley (Berkeley: University of California Press, 1987), pp. 111–126.

13. Margaret Cone and Richard Gombrich, *The Perfect Generosity of Prince Vessantara* (Oxford: Clarendon Press, 1977). Contemporary critics have subjected the Vessantara Jātaka to social, economic, and political criticism. For example, see Louis Gabaude, "Controverses modernes autour du Vessantara Jātaka," *Cahiers de l'Asie du Sud-Est*, nos. 29–30 (1991): 51–73.

14. Despite the differing theological contexts, there are structural parallels between the story of Abraham's sacrifice of Isaac in the Hebrew scriptures and Vessantara's sacrifice of his family.

15. Steven Collins, in *Selfless Persons*, provides a detailed analysis of the not-self doctrine in the Pali scriptures and its implications for Buddhist institutional life and practice.

16. See the section on Women and Buddhism in Chapter 3.

17. See Nancy Auer Falk, "Exemplary Donors of the Pali Tradition," in *Ethics, Wealth, and Salvation: A Study in Buddhist Social Ethics.*, ed. Russell Sizemore and Donald K. Swearer (Columbia: University of South Carolina Press, 1990), pp. 124–143.

18. Susan Murcott, *The First Buddhist Women* (Berkeley, Calif.: Parallax Press, 1991), pp. 50–51.

19. See S. J. Tambiah, *The Buddhist Saints of the Forest and the Cult of Amulets. A Study in Charisma, Hagiography, Sectarianism, and Millennial Buddhism.* (Cambridge: Cambridge University Press, 1984), Part II. For a discussion of sacred biography see, *The Biographical Process: Studies in the History of the Psychology of Religion*, ed. Frank E. Reynolds and Donald Capps (The Hague: Mouton, 1976).

See Chapter 3 for a discussion of Āchān Mun and the forest tradition. (I follow Tambiah's translation of the name Mun.)

20. Sanitsuda Ekachai, "Right Religion. Women Weighing Equality, Struggle, and Serenity," *Bangkok Post* 49, no. 42 (February 11, 1994), p. 23.

21. See Chapter 3 for a discussion of Buddhadāsa.

22. Ekachi, "Right Religion."

23. See the discussion of Devadatta in Edward J. Thomas, *The Life of the Buddha in Legend and History*, 3d ed. (London: Routledge and Kegan Paul, 1949), pp. 131ff.

24. Bonnie Pacala Brereton, *The Phra Malai Legend in Thai Buddhist Literature* (Tempe: Arizona State University Press, 1995).

25. See Robin Lovin and Frank E. Reynolds, *Cosmology and Ethical Order. New Studies in Comparative Ethics* (Chicago: University of Chicago Press, 1985), especially the Introduction and chapter 8. The cosmology of reward and punishment is suggested in the discussion of merit making in the films *Buddhism: Footprint of the Buddha*, and *Buddhism: Be Ye Lamps Unto Yourselves*. The first film appears in the popular series, *The Long Search*, produced by the BBC. The film takes the viewer on a journey in Sri Lanka in a search for the nature of Theravāda Buddhism as it is lived, practiced, and taught. We see Sri Lankan Buddhism through the eyes of Ronald Eyre, the observer-interlocutor, who begins his search at the impressive rock-hewn statutes of the Buddha at Polonnaruwa and then moves sequentially to the site of the Buddha's enlightenment at Bodhgayā in India, an ordination ceremony, monks on their morning alms rounds, a rains retreat ceremony on the May full moon sabbath day, and finally monks meditating at the Dambulla cave monastery north of Kandy, the last seat of the Sinhalese monarchy. These stops provide occasions for a discussion of Theravāda beliefs and practices including the moral precepts and the Noble Eightfold Path, the nature of the Buddha, astrology, supernatural powers, gift giving and merit, and the nature of Buddhist mindfulness. The film is structured around the poles of withdrawal-meditation and involvement-service, both of which figure in the Buddha's journey to a higher goal (*nibbāna*) achieved by one's own effort without reliance on an outside power or authority.

26. *Cariyāpiṭaka* [Basket of Conduct], trans. I. B. Horner in *Minor Anthologies of the Pali Canon, Part III*, Sacred Books of the Buddhists, vol. 26 (London: Routledge and Kegan Paul, 1975), pp. 22–23.

27. Spiro, *Buddhism and Society*, pp. 191–192.

28. Ibid., p. 192.

29. S. J. Tambiah, *The Buddhist Saints of the Forest and the Cult of Amulets*, Part III. Peter Brown's study of the cult of Christian saints, *The Cult of the Saints* (Chicago: University of Chicago Press, 1981), has played a major role in stimulating academic interest in religious saints and their cults.

30. For example, see Michael Ames, "Magical-Animism and Buddhism: A Structural Analysis of the Sinhalese Religious System," *Journal of Asian Studies* 23 (June 1964): 21–52.

31. Gananath Obeyesekere, "The Buddhist Pantheon in Ceylon and Its Extensions," in *Anthropological Studies in Theravāda Buddhism*, ed. Manning Nash (New Haven, Conn.: Yale University Southeast Asian Studies, 1966), pp. 1–27.

32. See Melford Spiro, *Burmese Supernaturalism* (Englewood Cliffs, N.J.: Prentice-Hall, 1967).

33. See S. J. Tambiah, *Buddhism and Spirit Cults in Northeast Thailand* (Cambridge: Cambridge University Press, 1970); Marcel Zago, *Rites et Ceremonies en Milieu Bouddhiste Lao* (Roma: Universita Gregoriana Editrice, 1972).

34. For a discussion of the historical formation and use of the *paritta* in Sri Lanka, see Lily de Silva, "The Paritta Ceremony of Sri Lanka: Its Antiquity and Symbolism"; and Hammalawa Saddhatissa, "The Significance of Paritta and Its Application in the Theravāda Tradition," in *Buddhist Thought and Ritual*, ed. David J. Kalupahana (New York: Paragon House, 1991).

35. *Petavatthu: Stories of the Departed*, trans. H. S. Gehman, in *The Minor Anthologies of the Pali Canon*, Part IV (London: Pali Text Society, 1974), p. 5.

36. Ibid., pp. 27–28.

37. It has been suggested that this basic pattern of reciprocity reflects the ancient Vedic notion of sacrificial efficacy. Brahman priests would make an offering on behalf of lay patrons or sponsors to secure for them a benefit or boon from a deity.

38. The reciprocal relationship between the monk and the laity is suggested in *Buddhism: Be Ye Lamps Unto Yourselves* and *Buddhism. Footprint of the Buddha* by their presentations of monks on alms rounds (*piṇḍapāta*). *Piṇḍapāta* is also observed in *Vejen*, a film focusing on a Burmese monk. This film attempts to have us be participants in Burmese Buddhism rather than merely observers. It focuses on the activities of a young boy who attends to the needs of a senior monk. We see ritual activities at the Shwe-dagon Pagoda in Yangon (Rangoon), an informal class at a monastery, monks on their food rounds, and finally, the boy's ordination as a novice monk (*shinbyu*). Against this background the narration discusses some of the essential teachings and ideals of the Theravāda tradition; e.g., *kamma, samsāra, nibbāna*. The film conveys simplicity and directness without sacrificing the variegated nature of Burmese Buddhism.

39. The literal meaning of *kaṭhina* is "frame." Originally monks would take the cloth received on this day, stretch it on a frame (much like a quilting frame) and work jointly to stitch the pieces together. In northern Thailand this custom sometimes is still observed.

40. Sukumar Dutt, *The Buddha and Five After-Centuries* (London: Luzac and Company, 1957).

41. Tambiah, *Buddhism and Spirit Cults*, p. 158.

42. Adapted from *A Manual of Buddhist Chants and Ordination Procedures* (Chicago: Wat Dhammarama Press, 1993), pp. 60–61.

43. Spiro, *Buddhism and Society*, p. 301.

44. For a more extensive description and analysis of the Buddha image consecration ceremony in northern Thailand, see my article, "Hypostasizing the Buddha. Buddha Image Consecration in Northern Thailand," *History of Religions* 34, no. 3 (Feb 1995): 263–280. See also my translation of the *Buddha Abhiseka* [Consecrating the Buddha Image] in *Buddhism in Practice*, ed. Donald S. Lopez, Jr. (Princeton, N.J.: Princeton University Press, 1995).

45. Richard F. Gombrich, "Consecration of a Buddha Image," *Journal of Asian Studies* 26, no. 1 (1966): 23–36.

46. For a broad, comparative study of the power of images, see David Freedberg, *The Power of Images* (Chicago: University of Chicago Press, 1989).

47. *The Book of Protection* [*Paritta*], trans. with an introduction by Piyadassi Thera (Kandy: Buddhist Publication Society, 1975), p. 5.

48. Ibid., p. 12.

49. Ibid., pp. 14–17. The chanting of *paritta* in the Theravāda tradition is similar to *mantra* chanting in Hinduism, Mahāyāna, and Tantrayāna Buddhism.

50. T. W. Rhys Davids, *Buddhist Birth Stories* (Varanasi and Delhi: Indological Book House, 1972), p. 187.

51. Shway Yoe (Sir James George Scott), *The Burman. His Life and Notions.* (New York: W. W. Norton, 1963), pp. 336–337.

52. Informants also interpret the three knowledges as the Buddha's omniscience; i.e., knowledge of the past, present, and future.

53. *The Dhammapāda*, trans. Narada Thera (London: J. Murray, 1954), p. 46.

54. A. K. Coomaraswamy, *Medieval Sinhalese Art*, 2d ed. (New York: Pantheon Books, 1956), p. 71.

55. Gombrich and Obeyesekere see the introduction of Buddhist *sacralia* into the Sri Lankan wedding ceremony as a sign of the "embourgeoisement" of this rite. See Richard F. Gombrich and Gananath Obeyesekere, *Buddhism Transformed: Religious Change in Sri Lanka* (Princeton, N.J.: Princeton University Press, 1988), pp. 255–273.

56. Tambiah, *Buddhism and Spirit Cults*, p. 160.

57. Scholars have argued that the consequentialist view of the efficacy of ritual action in Buddhism is a Brahmanical influence with roots in the intentionality of the Vedic ritual sacrifice, where ritual offerings obligate the deities to act on behalf of the sponsor of the sacrifice.

58. Phya Anuman Rajadhon, *Thet Maha Chat Ceremony* (Bangkok: Fine Arts Department, 1969); G. E. Gerini, *The Thet Maha Chat Ceremony* (Bangkok: Santhirakoses-Nagapradipa Foundation, 1976); Tambiah, *Buddhism and Spirit Cults*, pp. 160–168. My description also incorporates field notes from observations of the ceremony performed in 1976 and 1989.

59. Sanguan Chotisukharat, *Praphaenī Thai Pāk Nu'a* [Customs of Northern Thailand] (Bangkok: Odian, 1972), pp. 125 ff.

60. Tambiah, *Buddhism and Spirit Cults*, p. 153. For a discussion of Buddhist holidays in Laos see René de Berval, *Kingdom of Laos* (Saigon: France-Asie, 1959).

61. Shway Yoe, *The Burman*, pp. 350–351.

62. Spiro, *Buddhism and Society*, p. 200.

63. The story is taken from *Folk Tales and Legends of the Dai People*, trans. Ying Yi, ed. John Hoskin and Geoffrey Walton (Bangkok: DK Books, 1992), pp. 10–12.

64. Ibid., p. 10.

65. Ibid., p. 12.

66. The definitive study of the sand mountain in Laos and Thailand is Louis Gabaude's *Les ceitya de sable au Laos et en Thaïlande* (Paris: EEFO, 1979). In Thailand it is believed that the purpose of the sand mountain is to replenish the soil worn away during the preceeding year. Pious Thais fear appropriating even the smallest portion of monastic property (information provided by Geoff DeGraff/Thanissaro Bhikkhu).

67. Chotisukharat, *Praphenī Thai Phāk Nu'a*, p. 6.

68. Tambiah, *The Buddhist Saints of the Forest*, pp. 230–242.

69. The film, *Vesak*, provides an impressionistic view of the Visākhā Pūja celebration in Sri Lanka.

70. Adapted from Plaek Santhirak, *Latthi Prapenī lae Phithī Kamma* [Customs and Merit-Making Rituals] (Bangkok: Pannakhan, 1972), pp. 302 ff and quoted in Donald K. Swearer, *Wat Haripuñjaya. A Study of the Royal Temple of the Buddha's Relic, Lamphun, Thailand*, AAR Studies in Religion, No. 10 (Missoula, Mont.: Scholars Press, 1976), pp. 43–46. Bumphen Rawin, Professor of Thai at Chiang Mai University, has edited the Northern Thai version of the *Pathamasambodhi*, probably originally written in Chiang Mai in the fifteenth or sixteenth century: Bumphen Rawin, *Pathamasambodhi Samnuan Lānnā* [Lānnā Pathamasambodhi] (Bangkok: Odian Store, 1992). Two nineteenth century Thai versions are Kromsomdet Phra Paramānuchitchinōrot, *Pathamabodhikathā* (Bangkok: Mahāchulalongkorn Buddhist University, 1960) and Somdet Phrasangharāja Sā Pussadeva, *Pathamasambodhi* (Bangkok: Mahāmakuta Buddhist University, 1985). A comparison of these versions in the light of traditional Buddha biographies, e.g., *Nidāna Kathā, Lalitavistara, Buddhacarita*, would make a valuable contribution to our understanding of the development of Buddha biography.

71. Swearer, *Wat Haripuñjaya*, chap. 3.

72. The *Loi Krathong* celebration in northern Thailand is justly famous. Even though it has become overly commercialized in Chiang Mai, the northern capital, the quiet beauty of the lighted *krathongs* on the northern rivers and the community spirit experienced in the celebration make it a particularly delightful experience. The film *Chiang Mai, Northern Capital* has an appealing sequence on *Loi Krathong*.

73. Phya Anuman Rajadhon, *Essays on Thai Folklore* (Bangkok: Social Science Association Press, 1968), p. 39.

74. Kenneth E. Wells, *Thai Buddhism: Its Rites and Activities* (Bangkok: Suriyabun Publishers, 1975), p. 114. For a discussion of the cult of Upagutta (Sanskrit: Upagupta) in Southeast Asia, see John S. Strong, *The Legend and Cult of Upagupta* (Princeton, N.J.: Princeton University Press, 1992).

75. Singkha Wannasi, *Praphaenī Lae Ngan Nakkhatrik Haeng Lānnā Thai* [Customs and Astrological Celebrations of Lanna Thai]. Mimeograph, n.d., p. 1.

76. Wells, *Thai Buddhism*, p. 142.

77. See Charles F. Keyes, *The Golden Peninsula: Culture and Adaptation in Mainland Southeast Asia* (New York: Macmillan Publishing Co., 1977) for a discussion of the afterbirth ritual of lying by the fire.

78. Tambiah, *Buddhism and Spirit Cults in Northeast Thailand*, p. 192.

79. Although there was a *bhikkhunī* order in India and Sri Lanka that eventually died out and because there is no *bhikkhunī sangha* in Theravāda Southeast Asia, it would be misleading to consider entrance into the monastic order as being inclusive of both men and women. Consequently, the following discussion of ordination deals primarily with male initiation. Women renunciants will be discussed in Chapter 3 in conjunction with changing roles of monk and laity. The film, *Buddhism. Be Ye Lamps Unto Yourselves*, is structured around two ordination ceremonies.

80. Sukumar Dutt, *Buddhist Monks and Monasteries of India: Their History and Contribution to Indian Culture* (London: G. Allen and Unwin, 1962), p. 36. For a description of an ordination ritual, see Henry C. Warren, *Buddhism in Translations*. New York, Atheneum, 1963, pp. 393–401. For a description of Theravāda monastic life, see Mohan Wijayaratna, *Buddhist Monastic Life*, trans. Claude Grangier and Steven Collins (Cambridge: Cambridge University Press, 1990).

81. From the *bhikkhu vagga* chapter of the *Dhammapāda*.

82. Spiro, *Buddhism and Society*, p. 322.

83. Ibid., p. 338. Spiro's study of the motivational structure of monastic recruitment in Burma was not enthusiastically received in that country.

84. David K. Wyatt, "The Buddhist Monkhood as an Avenue of Social Mobility in Traditional Thai Society," in David K. Wyatt, *Studies in Thai History* (Bangkok: Silkworm Books, 1994), pp. 710–722.

85. This pattern also reflects the Hindu *brahmacari* stage of life.

86. See Charles F. Keyes, "Mother, Mistress, But Never a Monk: Buddhist Notions of Female Gender in Rural Thailand," *American Anthropologist* 11, no. 2 (May 1984): 223–241. See also *Gender and Religion: On the Complexity of Symbols*, ed. C. W. Bynum, S. Harrell, and P. Richman (Boston: Beacon Press, 1986).

87. Donald K. Swearer, "The Layman Extraordinaire in Northern Thai Buddhism," *Journal of the Siam Society* 64, no. 1 (January 1976): 151–168. Also Tambiah, *Buddhism and Spirit Cults in Northeast Thailand*.

88. Wells, *Thai Buddhism*, pp. 214–215.

89. For a description of a Theravāda ordination in Sri Lanka, see Henry C. Warren, *Buddhism in Translations* (New York: Atheneum Press, 1963), pp. 393–401. See also Vajirañāṇavarorasa, *Entrance to the Vinaya* (Bangkok: Mahāmākut University, 1960).

90. Alan Sponberg analyzes four types of attitudes toward women in the Buddhist tradition in his article, "Attitudes toward Women and the Feminine in Early Buddhism" in *Buddhism, Sexuality, and Gender*, ed. José Ignacio Cabezón (Albany: SUNY Press, 1992). See Chapter 3.

91. Ingrid Jordt, "Bhikkhuni, Thilashin, Mae-Chii: Women Who Renounce the World in Burma, Thailand and the Classical Buddhist Texts," *Crossroads: An Interdisciplinary Journal of Southeast Asian Studies* 4, no. 1 (Fall 1988): 31. Feminist studies have contributed to a growing literature on issues of women, sexuality, and gender in Buddhism. For example, see J. I. Cabezón, *Buddhism, Sexuality, and Gender*.

92. For a description of renunciant women's groups in Thailand see Chatsumarn Kabilsingh, *Women in Thai Buddhism* (Berkeley: Parallax Press, 1992).

93. Shway Yoe (Sir James George Scott), *The Burman*, p, 57.

94. Adapted from Piyadassi Thera, *The Book of Protection* (Kandy: Buddhist Publication Society, 1975), pp. 29–30. In the summer of 1991 I witnessed a remarkable Buddhist-Christian wedding in the Wellesley, Mass., Congregational Church. The groom was a Burmese Buddhist and the bride was the daughter of the pastors of the church. Burmese monks led the first half of the ceremony in which they chanted the *Mangala Sutta* in Pali.

95. Sanguan Chotisukharat, *Prapaenī Thai Phāk Nu'a* [Customs of Northern Thailand] (Bangkok: Odian Store, B.E. 2510/C.E. 1967), pp. 53–61; Mani Phayọmyong, *Prapaenī Sibsọng Du'an Lānnā Thai* [The Twelve Month Traditions and Customs of Lānnā Thai], vol. 1 (Chiang Mai: Chiang Mai University, B.E. 2529/C.E. 1986), pp. 89–101.

96. The number 108 represents cosmological completeness or totality—the sum total of the power valences of the four elements (earth, water, fire, air), or in mathematical terms the multiple of the square of 1, 2, and 3.

97. The film *Buddhism: Be Ye Lamps Unto Yourselves* includes a section on a funeral ceremony held at a monastery near Bangkok. Slides of a funeral are also included in *Buddhism in Southeast Asia and Ceylon*, produced by the American Academy of Religion.

98. For example see Shway Yoe, *The Burman. His Life and Notions*, chap. 64; S. J. Tambiah, *Buddhism and Spirit Cults in Northeast Thailand*, chap. 11.

99. I am particularly indebted to Konrad Kingshill, *Ku Daeng: The Red Tomb. A Village Study in Northern Thailand*, 3d ed. (Bangkok: Suriyaban, 1976), pp. 206–224.

100. Wells, *Thai Buddhism. Its Rites and Activities*, pp. 214–215.

101. Kingshill, *Ku Daeng: The Red Tomb*, p. 212.

102. Normally Thai people try to sleep with their heads to the east, the direction of life. Customarily, Buddhist temples also face the east.

103. Ibid.; Tambiah, *Buddhism and Spirit Cults in Northeast Thailand*, p. 180.

104. Kingshill, *Ku Daeng: The Red Tomb*, pp. 220–223.

CHAPTER 2. BUDDHISM AS CIVIL RELIGION

1. For example, see Bardwell L. Smith, ed., *Religion and Legitimation of Power in Sri Lanka* (Chambersburg, Pa.: Anima Books, 1978); Bardwell L. Smith, ed., *Religion and Legitimation of Power in Thailand, Laos, and Burma* (Chambersburg, Pa.: Anima Books, 1978); Manuel Sarkisyanz, *Buddhist Backgrounds of the Burmese Revolution* (The Hague: Martinus Nijhoff, 1965); S. J. Tambiah, *World Conqueror and World Renouncer: A Study of Buddhism and Polity in Thailand Against a Historical Background* (Cambridge: Cambridge University Press, 1976); Yoneo Ishii, *Sangha, State, and Society: Thai Buddhism in History*, trans. Peter Hawkes (Honolulu: University of Hawaii Press, 1986); Trevor Ling, *Buddhism, Imperialism and War: Burma and Thailand in Modern History* (London: George Allen and Unwin, 1979); Heinz Bechert, "Aspects of Theravāda Buddhism in Sri Lanka and Southeast Asia," in *The Buddhist Heritage*, ed. T. Skorupski (Trink, U.K.: Institute of Buddhist Studies, 1989); George Bond, *The Buddhist Revival in Sri Lanka: Religious Tradition, Reinterpretation and Response* (Columbia: University of South Carolina Press, 1988), chaps. 1–3.

The government of India has produced several films on some important Indian Buddhist sites. They include *Cave Temples of India—Buddhist* which focuses on Ajantā; *Immortal Stupa* (Sāñcī), *Nālandā*, and *Land of Enlightenment*, a brief survey of classical Buddhist sites in Bihār, such as Bodhgayā, Sārnāth. The BBC has produced a film on Sāñcī, *The Glory That Remains*. Borobudur has been the subject of two films, *Borobudur: The Cosmic Mountain* and *The Buddha: Temple Complex at Borobudur*. For Angkor Wat, *Angkor: The Ancient City*. (See Appendix II.)

With a few exceptions transliterations of Burmese and Thai place names and proper names follows generally accepted usage. For example, Sukhothai rather than Sukhōthai or Sukhōdaya.

2. Heinz Bechert, "Aspects of Theravāda Buddhism in Sri Lanka and Southeast Asia," pp. 20–21. As we shall see, the concept of the *devarāja* as the apotheosis of a human being is a matter of debate.

3. The Pali terms for the Ten Royal Virtues are *dāna, sīla, pariccaga, ajjava, maddava, tapa, akkodha, ahiṃsa, khanti, avirodhana*. See *Jātaka* V.378.

4. See John Irwin " 'Asokan' Pillars: A Reassessment of Evidence," *Burlington Magazine* 115, (November 1973): 706–722. Irwin argues that the so-called Asokan or Mauryan pillars, the earliest surviving stone monuments in India, are pre-

Mauryan in their architectural form. He contends that the pillars were fundamentally religious in nature rather than imperial or secular, and that the main symbolic function of the pillars was "to serve as an esoteric link between the Waters of Creation in the netherworld and the celestial sphere above" (p. 720). Irwin, therefore, speculates that the primordial meaning of the pillar, later appropriated by Asoka, was an Indian variant of an *axis mundi* cosmology. This theory links the archaic meaning of the pillar with the *stūpa* (see the following discussion of the Sāñcī *stūpa*).

5. John S. Strong discusses the Asokan legends, inscriptional evidence, and scholarly interpretations in *The Legend of King Aśoka: A Study and Translation of the Aśokāvadāna* (Princeton, N.J.: Princeton University Press, 1983), chap. 1.

6. Northern Thai chronicles (*tamnān*) often portray the Buddha and King Asoka as simultaneously present at the actual or predicted establishment of towns and sacred sites, e.g., *Tamnān Ang Salung* [The Chronicle of the Water Basin], trans. Donald K. Swearer and Phaitun Dokbuakaew (Chiang Mai: Chiang Mai University, 1995).

7. On the basis of Asoka's Bhabru rock edict Thanissaro Bhikkhu (Geoff DeGraff) proposes that Asoka recommends to all Buddhists, ordained or not, the following *suttas*: *Vinaya-samukase* (Mv.VI.40.1), *Aliya-vamsa* (A.IV.28), *Anaggata-bhayani* (A.V.77–80), *Muni Sutta* (Sn.I.12), *Cula-Rahulaovāda Sutta* (M.61). See Thanissaro Bhikkhu, *That the True Dhamma Might Last a Long Time* (Valley Center, Calif.: Metta Forest Monastery, n.d.).

8. Pillar Edict, No. 2. Quoted in T. W. Rhys Davids, *Buddhist India*, 8th ed. (Calcutta: Susil Gupta, 1959), p. 134.

9. See S. J. Tambiah's analysis of the structure of the *Aggañña Sutta* in *World Conqueror and World Renouncer*, chap. 2.

10. Bardwell L. Smith, "The Ideal Social Order as Portrayed in the Chronicles of Ceylon," in *The Two Wheels of Dhamma: Essays on the Theravāda Tradition in India and Ceylon*, ed. B. L. Smith, AAR Studies in Religion, No. 3 (Chambersburg, Pa.: American Academy of Religion, 1972), p. 40. In the same volume see Frank E. Reynolds, "The Two Wheels of Dhamma. A Study of Early Buddhism."

11. Also transliterated from the Pali as Aniruddha. I have elected to follow Paul Strachan's convention in *Pagan: Art and Architecture of Old Burma*.

12. Hsüan Tsang's diary testifies to the omnipresence of *stūpas* and their centrality to popular piety through his travels in India. See Hsüan-tsang, *Si-Yu-Ki: Buddhist Records of the Western World*, trans. Samuel Beal, reprint ed. (Delhi: Munshiram Manoharal, 1969).

13. *The Image of the Buddha*, ed. David Snellgrove (New York and Tokyo: Kodansha International/UNESCO, 1978), p. 404. The *stūpa* as pilgrimage site and the cult of Buddha relics has been one of the hallmarks of the relationship between kingship and Buddhism. In the *Mahāparinibbāna Sutta*, the eight world rulers

divide the relics of the Buddha after his death. Legend claims that King Asoka increased the number of relics to 84,000.

14. A recent detailed study of the *stūpa* in Buddhist Asia is by Adrian Snodgrass, *The Symbolism of the Stūpa* (Ithaca, N.Y.: Cornell University Southeast Asian Studies Program, 1985). Snodgrass is indebted to previous work on *stūpa* symbolism by Heinrich Zimmer, Mircea Eliade, and in particular, Paul Mus' monumental *Barabudur: Esquisse d'une histoire du bouddhisme fondee sur la critique archeologique des texts*, 2 vols. (Hanoi and Paris: École Française d'Extrême Orient, 1978). A collection of interpretative essays is *The Stūpa: Its Religious, Historical and Architectural Significance*, ed. Anna Libera Dallapiccola (Wiesbaden: Franz Steiner, 1980).

15. See Paul Mus, *Barabudur*; A. M. Hocart, "'The Origin of the Stūpa," *Ceylon Journal of Science* 1, no. 1 (1924).

16. John Irwin, "The Stūpa and the Cosmic Axis: The Archaeological Evidence," *South Asian Archaeology, 1977*, vol. 2, ed. Maurizio Taddei (Naples: Instituto Universitario Orientale, 1979), p. 842, quoted from W. Norman Brown, "The Creation Myth of the Rig-veda," *Journal of the American Oriental Society* 62: 85–98.

17. Irwin, ibid., p. 826.

18. Benjamin Rowland, Jr., *The Art and Architecture of India* (London: Penguin Books, 1953), p. 51. The number, 84,000, also refers to the totality of the Buddha's teaching, or, if you will, the sum total of reality. This cosmological reference underlies the mythic association of 84,000 with relics.

19. Sukumar Dutt, *The Buddha and Five After-Centuries* (London: Luzac and Company, 1957), p. 174.

20. Heinrich Zimmer, *The Art of Indian Asia* (New York: Pantheon Books, 1960), vol. 1, p. 233.

21. Dutt, *The Buddha and Five After-Centuries*, p. 178.

22. Zimmer, *The Art of Indian Asia*, p. 236.

23. Dutt, *The Buddha and Five After-Centuries*, p. 170. Dutt makes an even stronger, but unsubstantiated, identification with King Asoka.

24. Tambiah, *World Conqueror and World Renouncer*, p. 70.

25. Michael Aung-Thwin, *Pagan: The Origins of Modern Burma* (Honolulu: University of Hawaii Press, 1985), p. 47.

26. Robert von Heine-Geldern, *Conceptions of State and Kingship in Southeast Asia*, Southeast Asia Data Paper 18 (Ithaca, N.Y.: Cornell University, 1956). See also Tambiah, *World Conqueror and World Renouncer*, p. 109.

27. George Coedès, *Angkor: An Introduction*, trans. and ed. Emily Floyd Gardiner (London, New York and Hong Kong: Oxford University Press, 1963), quoting from Robert von Heine-Geldern, "Weltbild und Bauform in Sudostasien," *Wiener Beitrage zur Kunst und Kultur Asiens*, 1930.

28. I have greatly expanded the discussion of Angkor and Pagan from the first edition and have added Sukhothai. Because a major stele inscription attributed

to King Ram Khamhaeng and a cosmological treatise (*Traibhūmi Phraruang*) attributed to his grandson, King Lu'thai, have been important in recent scholarly debates on Thai national identity, our discussion of Sukhothai leads naturally into the final section of the chapter on Buddhism and modern Southeast Asian nationalisms.

The first edition of this book included a discussion of Borobudur, the magnificent ninth century *stūpa* built on the Kedu plain near modern Jogjakarta. I have eliminated Borobudur from this chapter of the second edition, but because of its inherent signficance and its connections with a cosmological-royal interpretation of the Buddhist *stūpa*, a revised and abbreviated description of this site is included as Appendix 3.

29. Charles Higham, *The Archaeology of Mainland Southeast Asia from 10,000 B.C. to the Fall of Angkor* (Cambridge and New York: Cambridge University Press, 1989), p. 254. Scholars who have interpreted the classical polities of Southeast Asia in terms of mandalic structure, galactic polity, and the categories of center-periphery include Oliver W. Wolters, *History, Culture and Region in Southeast Asian Perspective* (Singapore: Institute of Southeaast Asian Studies, 1982) and S. J. Tambiah, *World Conqueror and World Renouncer.*

30. See Paul Mus, "A Thousand-Armed Kannon: A Mystery or a Problem?" *Journal of Indian and Buddhist Studies* (Tokyo, 1964): 1–33.

31. Tambiah, *World Conqueror and World Renouncer*, p. 5.

32. Ibid., p. 109.

33. Ibid., pp. 108–111. Tambiah focuses his analysis on the Thai kingdom of Ayutthaya and its transformations into the Bangkok period.

34. Hermann Kulke, *The Devarāja*, Southeast Asia Program Data Paper 108 (Ithaca, N.Y.: Cornell University Press, 1978). Kulke challenges the interpretation of the *devarāja* concept in which the king is seen as an apotheosis of a divine being.

35. Coedès, *Angkor*, p. 31.

36. Lawrence P. Briggs, "The Syncretism of Religions in Southeast Asia, Especially in the Khmer Empire," *Journal of the American Oriental Society* 71, no. 4 (1950): 235.

37. von Heine-Geldern, *Conceptions of State and Kingship in Southeast Asia*, pp. 5–6.

38. See Jean Filliozat, "New Researches on the Relations Between India and Cambodia," *Indica* (Bombay), 3: 95–106; I. W. Mabbett, "Devarāja," *Journal of Southeast Asian History* 10 (September 1969): 202ff; Kulke, *The Devarāja.*

39. Kulke, ibid., p. 33.

40. Two illustrated studies of Angkor are Michael Freeman, *Angkor: The Hidden Glories* (Boston: Houghton Mifflin, 1990); and Joan L. Cohen and Bila Kalman, *Angkor: The Monuments of the God Kings* (London: Thames and Hudson, 1975). See also Bernard Groslier and Jacques Arthaud, *Angkor: Art and Civilization*, rev. ed. (New York: Frederick A. Praeger, 1966); and Coedès, *Angkor.*

41. A. K. Coomaraswamy, *History of Indian and Indonesian Art* (New York: Dover Publications, 1965), p. 204.

42. George Coedès, *The Making of Southeast Asia*, trans. H. M. Wright (Berkeley: University of California Press, 1966), p. 57.

43. H. G. Quartich Wales, *The Making of Greater India* (London: Bernard Quartich, 1961), p. 188.

44. Ibid., p. 195. H. G. Quartich Wales makes the strongest argument for influence of the cult of mountain deities on the construction of the religio-royal monumental structures in Southeast Asia. See his *The Mountain God: A Study in Early Religion and Kingship* (London: B. Quartich, 1953).

45. Zimmer, *The Art of Indian Asia*, p. 210.

46. See Coomaraswamy, *History of Indian and Indonesian Art*, pp. 192–194; Zimmer, ibid., pp. 209–212; Groslier and Arthaud, *Angkor*; Cohen and Kalman, *Angkor*.

47. See Coedès, *Angkor*, chap. 5. Mountains and oceans are fundamental components of mythic world construction.

48. Quoted in Coedès, *Angkor*, pp. 54–55.

49. Ibid., p. 64. See also Higham, *The Archaeology*, p. 335.

50. Coedès, ibid., p. 65, quoting Paul Mus, "Angkor in the Time of Jayavarman VII," *Indian Arts and Letters* (1937).

51. According to Burmese chronicle sources, Theravāda Buddhism was adopted by the Burmese from the Mon of central Burma. Theravāda Buddhism also was mediated to the Thais through the Mon state of Dvāravatī. The conventional view identifying Pali, Theravāda Buddhism with mainland Southeast Asia ignores the diversity of Buddhist influences in the area which more recent scholarship has demonstrated. In his study of the cult of Upagupta, for example, John S. Strong convincingly demonstrates the influence of Sanskritic Hīnayāna Buddhism in Burma, Thailand, and Laos. John S. Strong, *The Legend and Cult of Upagupta: Sanskrit Buddhism in North India and Southeast Asia* (Princeton, N.J.: Princeton University Press, 1992).

52. See *Religion and Legitimation of Power in Thailand, Laos, and Burma*, ed. Bardwell L. Smith (Chambersburg, Pa.: Anima Books, 1978).

53. Variously transliterated as Anōratha, Aniruddha, Anuruddha, Anawrahta. I am following Paul Strachan's transliterations in *Pagan: Art and Architecture of Old Burma*.

54. The doyen of Pagan studies is G. H. Luce. See G. H. Luce, *Old Burma–Early Pagan*, vols. 1–3 (Locust Valley, N.Y.: J. J. Augustin, 1969–1970). A recent, well-illustrated study of Pagan is Paul Strachan, *Pagan: Art and Architecture of Old Burma*. For an analysis of the Pagan conception of Buddhist kingship, see Michael Aung-Thwin, *Pagan*.

55. See Michael Mendelson, "Observations on a Tour in the Region of Mount Popa, Central Burma," *France-Asie* 179: 786–807.

56. See the *Glass Palace Chronicle of the Kings of Burma*, trans. Pe Maung Tin and G. H. Luce (London: Oxford University Press, 1923), pp. 86–89, for the building of the Shwe-zigon.

57. Strachan, *Pagan*, p. 14.

58. Coomaraswamy, *History of Indian and Indonesian Art*, p. 211. See also Aung Thaw, *Historical Sites in Burma* (Rangoon: Ministry of Culture, 1972), chap. 5; Reginald Le May, *The Culture of Southeast Asia* (London: George Allen and Unwin, 1956), chap. 3.

59. See Strachan, *Pagan*, pp. 65–71, for a description of the Ananda Temple.

60. Aung Thaw, *Historical Sites in Burma*, p. 58.

61. Charles F. Keyes, *The Golden Peninsula. Culture and Adaptation in Mainland Southeast Asia* (New York: Macmillan Publishing Co., 1977), p. 72.

62. Of particular interest for the study of Sukhothai history, art, religion, and kingship are Betty Gosling, *Sukhothai: Its History, Culture, and Art* (Oxford: Oxford University Press, 1991); A. B. Griswold, *Towards a History of Sukhodaya Art* (Bangkok: Fine Arts Department, 1967); Jean Boisselier, *The Heritage of Thai Sculpture* (New York and Tokyo: Weatherhill, 1975); *The Ram Khamhaeng Controversy: Collected Papers*, ed. James R. Chamberlain (Bangkok: The Siam Society, 1991); Frank E. Reynolds and Mani B. Reynolds, *Three Worlds According to King Ruang: A Thai Buddhist Cosmology* (Berkeley, Calif.: Asian Humanities Press, 1982), George Coedès, "The Traibhūmikathā: Buddhist Cosmology and Treatise on Ethics," *East and West* 7 (1957): 349–352. See also Tambiah, *World Conqueror and World Renouncer*, Part I.

63. Here I follow the interpretation of Betty Gosling, *Sukhothai*, chap. 4. Gosling disagrees with the usual identification of the Manaṅsīlāpātra with a stone platform or throne currently located in the Royal Palace, Bangkok. See Hiram W. Woodward, Jr., "Ram Khamhaeng's Inscription: The Search for Context," in *The Ram Khamhaeng Controversy*, ed. James R. Chamberlain, pp. 419–437. Gosling sees similarities between the stepped Kon Laeng altar or platform and Chinese altars to the gods of earth located at the southern periphery of the city.

64. Gosling, ibid., p. 43.

65. Reynolds and Reynolds, *The Three Worlds According to King Ruang*, p. 5. Considerable scholarship has been devoted to Lu'thai and the *Traibhūmikathā*. See George Coedès, "The Traibhūmikathā," pp. 349–352; Barbara Watson Andaya, "Statecraft in the Reign of Lü Tai of Sukhodaya (ca. 1347–1374)," in *Religion and Legitimation of Power in Thailand, Laos, and Burma*, ed. Smith, pp. 2–19. Recent scholarship has challenged Lu'thai's authorship of the *Traibhūmikathā*. See Michael Vickery, "On Traibhūmikathā," *Journal of the Siam Society* 79, part 2 (1991): 24–36, who argues the text was not authored by Lu'thai but was probably written as part of the restoration of the Thai monarchy by Rāma I in the aftermath of the Burmese sack of Ayutthaya. Vickery represents a trend among some historians who challenge traditionally ascribed authorship of classical texts or inscriptions, viz. the authorship

of the Ram Khamhaeng stele inscription. Debates about the *Traibhūmikathā* have had a particular currency regarding the issue of Thai identity. See Peter A. Jackson, "Thai-Buddhist Identity: Debates on the Traiphuum Phra Ruang," in *National Identity and Its Defenders: Thailand, 1939–1989*, ed. Craig J. Reynolds, Monash Papers on Southeast Asia, no. 25 (Victoria, Australia: Monash University, 1991).

66. Gosling, *Sukhothai*, p. 64.

67. Andaya, "Statecraft in the Reign of Lü Tai of Sukhodaya," p. 9.

68. For a discussion of the Phra Buddha Singha image see, S. J. Tambiah, *The Buddhist Saints of the Forest and the Cult of Amulets* (Cambridge: Cambridge University Press, 1984), chap. 16.

69. Andaya, "Statecraft in the Reign of Lü Tai of Sukhodaya," p. 9.

70. See *The Ram Khamhaeng Controversy*, ed. Chamberlain.

71. See Vickery, "On *Tribhūmikathā*." Vickery argues his position on linguistic rather than political grounds.

72. Peter A. Jackson, "Thai-Buddhist Identity: Debates on the *Traiphuum Phra Ruang*," p. 210. Jackson's analysis of the use of the *Tribhūmi* by liberal reformists relies primarily on Phra Dhammapitaka (formerly Phra Depvedi), who has emerged as the most articulate and highly respected interpreter of Buddhism in Thailand.

73. Coedès, *Angkor*, p. 50.

74. It is interesting to note that the Buddha's first discourse is called *Turning the Wheel of the Law* (*Dhammacakkappavattana Sutta*), and the Buddhist world ruler is called the *Wheel Turner* (*cakkavattin*).

75. A film of special interest in connection with this discussion is *In the Steps of the Buddha*, which uses the Kelaniya Temple Murals near Colombo to show in visual form the *Dīpavaṃsa's* record of the three visits of the Buddha to Sri Lanka to convert the aboriginals and enshrine Buddha relics, to bring peace to warring factions, and to visit Sumantakuta (Adam's Peak) and Kelaniya.

76. *The Glass Palace Chronicle of the Kings of Burma*, trans. Pe Maung Tin and Luce, pp. 6–7.

77. Ibid., p. xiii.

78. Ratanapañña Thera, *The Sheaf of Garlands of the Epochs of the Conqueror* (*Jinakālamālīpakaraṇaṁ*), trans. N. A. Jayawickrama, Pali Text Society Translation Series, 36 (London: Luzac and Co., 1968), pp. 107–108.

79. Ibid., p. 109.

80. This discussion of the image of the Emerald Buddha could be put within the framework of an art historical study of the Buddha image in Thailand or the Buddha image in Buddhist Asia. For the former, *Thai Images of the Buddha* is appropriate, especially when used in conjunction with the catalogue prepared for the exhibit, The Arts of Thailand. The broader context could be provided by the slide set, *The Evolution of the Buddha Image*, for which a catalogue was also printed. Numerous slides of Buddha images in various traditions and contexts are also are included in the Image Bank, Audio-Visual Resources for the Teaching of Asian Religions. See Appendix 2.

81. Adapted from Frank E. Reynolds, "The Holy Emerald Jewel," in *Religion and Legitimation of Power in Thailand, Laos, and Burma*, ed. Bardwell L. Smith (Chambersburg, Pa.: Anima Books, 1978), p. 176.

82. Ibid., pp. 183–184. The extensive "travels" of the Emerald Buddha in northern Thailand and the several temples named after it suggest the possibility that the image may have functioned not only as a palladium of a particular Tai city state, but also as a means of linking or enforcing political alliances among various Tai states.

83. See Tambiah, *World Conqueror and World Renouncer*, chap. 2.

84. Government of the Union of Burma Land Nationalization Act, 1948, p. 29, para 9, quoted in Manuel Sarkisyanz, *Buddhist Backgrounds to the Burmese Revolution* (The Hague: Martinus Nijhoff, 1965), p. 215. The film *Buddhism, Burma, and Neutralism* represents a 1950s American political slant on U Nu's interpretation of Buddhism supporting Burma's neutrality in the arena of international political conflict (See Appendix 2).

85. Donald K. Swearer, *Buddhism in Transition* (Philadelphia: Westminster Press, 1970), pp. 38ff.

86. *The Nation* (October 1958). Quoted in Richard Butwell, *U Nu of Burma* (Palo Alto, Calif.: Stanford University Press, 1963), p. 62.

87. Donald E. Smith, *Religion and Politics in Burma* (Princeton, N.J.: Princeton University Press, 1965), pp. 318–319.

88. Tin Maung Maung Than, "Sangha and Sasana in Socialist Burma," *Sojourn: Social Issues in Southeast Asia* 3, no. 1 (February 1989): 27.

89. See Aung San Suu Kyi, *Freedom From Fear* (New York: Penguin Books, 1991). See Bruce Matthews, "Buddhism Under a Military Regime," *Asian Survey* 33, no. 4 (1993): 408–423. For a historical and political study of contemporary Burma, see Robert H. Taylor, *The State in Burma* (London: C. Hurst and Company, 1987); and David J. Steinberg, *The Future of Burma. Crises and Choice in Myanmar* (Lanham, Md.: University Presses of America, 1990). In the latter volume Steinberg argues that political power is calculated primarily in personal terms, hence the dominance of a strong man like General Ne Win or the SLORC leader Lt. Gen. Khin Nyunt. Aung San Suu Kyi, the daughter of the assassinated leader of the Burmese nationalist movement against British colonialism, therefore, is a particularly potent figure given the personalized basis of political power.

90. Tin Maung Maung Than, "Sangha and Sasana in Socialist Burma," p. 41. See also by the same author, "Sangha Reforms and Renewal of Sasana in Myanmar: Historical Trends and Contemporary Practice," in *Buddhist Trends in Southeast Asia*, ed. Trevor Ling (Singapore: Institute of Southeast Asian Studies, 1993), pp. 6–63.

91. Sao Htun Hmat Win, "The Unique Solidarity of the Sangha Order," *The Light of the Dhamma* [Rangoon] 1, no. 1 (August 1981): 28.

92. Heinz Bechert, "S. W. R. D. Bandaranaike and the Legitimation of Power Through Buddhist Ideals," in Bardwell L. Smith (ed.), *Religion and Legitimation of Power in Sri Lanka* (Chambersburg, Pa.: Anima Books, 1978), p. 204.

93. S. W. R. D. Bandaranaike, *Speeches and Writings* (Columbo: Dept. of Broadcasting and Information, 1963), p. 308.

94. On the Anagārika Dharmapāla, see B. G. Gokhale, "Anagārika Dharmapāla: Toward Modernity Through Tradition in Ceylon," in *Tradition and Change in Theravāda Buddhism*, ed. Bardwell L. Smith, Contributions to Asian Studies, vol. 4 (Leiden: E. J. Brill, 1973), pp. 30–39.

95. Several major studies of the Tamil-Sinhalese conflict have appeared since the mid-1980s. For example, see S. J. Tambiah, *Sri Lanka: Ethnic Fratricide and the Dismantling of Democracy* (Chicago: University of Chicago Press, 1986). For a study of the conflict through the interpretative lens of fundamentalism, see Donald K. Swearer, "Fundamentalistic Movements in Theravāda Buddhism," in *Fundamentalisms Observed*, Martin Marty and R. Scott Appleby, ed. (Chicago: University of Chicago Press, 1989), pp. 628–690. For a recent study of religious nationalisms that puts the Sri Lankan case within a broad comparative context, see Mark Juergensmeyer, *The New Cold War. Religious Nationalism Confronts the Secular State* (Berkeley: University of California Press, 1993). A recent bibliography on the subject of religion and violence is Christopher Candland, *The Spirit of Violence: An Interdisciplinary Bibliography of Religion and Violence*, Occasional Papers of the Harry Frank Guggenheim Foundation, No. 6. (New York: Guggenheim Foundation, 1992).

96. See Juergensmeyer.

97. See Yoneo Ishii, *Sangha, State, and Society: Thai Buddhism in History*, trans. Peter Hawkes (Honolulu: University of Hawaii Press, 1986); Somboon Suksamran, *Political Buddhism in Southeast Asia: The Role of the Sangha in the Modernization of Thailand* (New York: St. Martin's Press, 1976) and his more recent *Buddhism and Political Legitimacy* (Bangkok: Chulalongkorn University, 1993); Charles F. Keyes, "Buddhism and National Integration in Thailand," *Journal of Asian Studies* 33, no. 3 (May 1971): 551–567 and "Buddhist Politics and Their Revolutionary Origins in Thailand," *International Political Science Review* 10, no. 2 (1989): 121–142.

98. See Ishii, *Sangha, State, and Society*, chap. 4.

99. See Peter A. Jackson, *Buddhism, Legitimation, and Conflict. The Political Functions of Urban Thai Buddhism* (Singapore: Institute of Southeast Asian Studies, 1989); Keyes, "Buddhist Politics and Their Revolutionary Origins in Thailand," pp. 121–142.

CHAPTER 3. MODERNIZATION

1. A detailed historical survey of Southeast Asia from the eighteenth century through the Vietnam War is *In Search of Southeast Asia: A Modern History*, rev. ed., ed. David J. Steinberg, et al. (Honolulu: University of Hawaii Press, 1987).

2. David P. Chandler, *The Tragedy of Cambodian History, Politics, War and Revolution Since 1945* (New Haven, Conn.: Yale University Press, 1991), p. 236.

3. For discussions of Buddhism in specific cultural areas, see *The World of Buddhism*, ed. Heinz Bechert and Richard Gombrich (London: Thames and Hudson, 1991). Dated but still useful is Heinrich Dumoulin and John C. Maraldo (eds.), *The Cultural, Political, and Religious Significance of Buddhism in the Modern World* (New York: Collier Books, 1976).

Films on this topic are limited. The challenge modernization poses to the *sangha* is suggested at the end of *Buddhism: Be Ye Lamps Unto Yourselves*. In a sequence depicting a monk leaving a monastery to meet with what appears to be a group of civil servants, *Temple of the Twenty Pagodas* hints at some of the changes taking place in the Thai *sangha*. *Thailand*, one of public television's *Views of Asia* series, includes one of the longest sequences dealing specifically with the monastic order's response to the challenges of today. Some slides in *Buddhism in Southeast Asia and Ceylon* (Nos. 139–148), produced for the American Academy of Religion, pertain to issues of modernization discussed in this chapter. See also the Image Bank for Teaching World Religions.

4. I am indebted to Thanissaro Bhikkhu (Geoff DeGraff) for suggesting the basic content of this paragraph. In general, Buddhist social ethics tends to emphasize the importance of the attitude or intention underlying action rather than a strict adherence to a set of rules. This emphasis on intentionality is seen, for example, in the Buddhist attitude toward the acquisition and use of wealth. See *Ethics, Wealth, and Salvation: A Study in Buddhist Social Ethics*, ed. Russell F. Sizemore and Donald K. Swearer (Columbia: University of South Carolina Press, 1990).

5. The Vietnamese Zen monk Thich Nhat Hanh analyzes the Vietnam war from a Buddhist perspective in *Lotus in a Sea of Fire* (London: SCM Press, 1961). Nhat Hanh has become one of the outstanding spokespersons for an activist social involvement which he has referred to as "Engaged Buddhism."

6. Western scholarly interest in the political involvement of the Buddhist Sangha in Sri Lanka and Southeast Asia peaked in the 1960s and 1970s. The role of Buddhism in the postcolonial–early nationalist period and the Buddhist protest against the Diem regime during the Vietnam war contributed to this interest. Jerrold Schechter's *The New Face of Buddha* (Tokyo: John Weatherhill, 1967) typifies a popular, journalistic approach to this issue. Two substantial collections of scholarly articles on the subject in both historical and modern contexts were edited by Bardwell L. Smith: *Religion and Legitimation of Power in Sri Lanka* (1978) and *Religion and Legitimation of Power in Thailand, Laos, and Burma* (1978).

7. I discuss this issue in Donald K. Swearer, "Community Development and Thai Buddhism. The Dynamics of Tradition and Change," *Visākhā Pūja 2516* (Bangkok: Buddhist Association of Thailand, 1973), pp. 35–47.

8. *The Buddhist* 38, no. 2 (July 1967): 47.

9. For a discussion of the Phra Phimontham case, see Peter A. Jackson, *Buddhism, Legitimation and Conflict: The Political Functions of Urban Thai Buddhism* (Singapore: Institute of Southeast Asian Studies, 1989), chap. 5; also Somboon Suksamran, *Buddhism and Politics in Thailand* (Singapore: Institute of Southeast Asian Studies, 1982), chap. 3. The Phra Phimontham case also involved sectarian rivalry within the Thai *sangha*.

10. Charles F. Keyes, "Political Crisis and Militant Buddhism in Contemporary Thailand," in Smith (ed.), *Religion and Legitimation of Power in Thailand, Laos, and Burma*; Suksamran, *Buddhism and Politics in Thailand*, chap. 5. I cite this case at some length as an illustration of one type of politicization of the *sangha*. In 1994 Kitthiwuttho's proposed Buddhist retirement center involved the monk in yet another controversy.

11. Kitthiwuttho, *Sing Thī Kuan Kham Nu'ng* (Bangkok: Abhidhamma Foundation, 1971), p. 8.

12. Ibid., p. 48.

13. Keyes, "Political Crisis and Militant Buddhism in Contemporary Thailand," p. 153.

14. Ibid.

15. Kitthiwuttho, *Khā Communist Mai Pāpa* [Killing Communists Is Not Demeritorious], (Bangkok: Abhidhamma Foundation, 1976), pp. 49–52.

16. Ibid., p. 48.

17. See Jackson, *Buddhism. Legitimation, and Conflict*, chap. 8; Edwin Zehner, "Reform Symbolism of a Thai Middle-Class Sect: The Growth and Appeal of the Thammakai Movement," *Journal of Southeast Asian Studies*, 21, no. 2 (September 1990): 402–425; Suwanna Satha-Anand, "Religious Movements in Contemporary Thailand: Buddhist Struggles for Modern Relevance," *Asian Survey* 30, no. 4 (April 1990): 395–408; J. L. Taylor, "New Buddhist Movements in Thailand: An 'Individualistic Revolution,' Reform and Political Dissonance," *Journal of Southeast Asian Studies* 21, no. 1 (March 1990): 135–154; Donald K. Swearer, "Fundamentalistic Movements in Theravāda Buddhism," in *Fundamentalisms Observed*, ed. Martin E. Marty and R. Scott Appleby (Chicago and London: University of Chicago Press, 1990), pp. 628–690.

18. Satha-Anand, "Religious Movements in Contemporary Thailand," p. 402.

19. See Paisal Sricharatchanya and Ian Buruma, "Praise the Buddha and Pass the Baht," *Far Eastern Economic Review* (June 18, 1987): 53–55.

20. Thanissaro Bhikkhu (Geoff DeGraff) has suggested that the following typology might be applied to monks actively involved in reformist movements and national development projects in Thailand: (1) those, possibly influenced by Western Christian models, who believe that monks should be directly involved in the economic uplift of the poor, e.g., Phra Khrū Sakorn; (2) those who draw on the traditional alliance between the *sangha* and the state, e.g., the Dhammakāya movement; (3) those who seek inspiration from the forest tradition, the original roots of the tradition, e.g., Buddhadāsa, Bodhiraksa's Santi Asok movement.

21. In a sequence from the film *Thailand*, an abbot exhorts his followers to work hard for modernization, and monks attend classes to acquaint themselves with government and private social welfare institutions. A few slides in *Buddhism in Southeast Asia and Ceylon* show monks graduating from a development training program in Chonburi, Thailand. A set of slides on Thai monks working in various community development projects is available through the International Network of Engaged Buddhists, 127 Soi Santipap, Nares Rd., Bangkok 10500, Thailand.

22. F. Bruce Morgan, "Vocation of Monk and Layman: Signs of Change in Thai Buddhist Ethics," in *Tradition and Change in Theravāda Buddhism*, Contributions to Asian Studies, vol. 4, ed. Bardwell L. Smith (Leiden: E. J. Brill, 1973), p. 71.

23. E. Michael Mendelson, *Sangha and State in Burma: A Study of Monastic Sectarianism and Leadership*, ed. John P. Ferguson (Ithaca, N.Y.: Cornell University Press, 1975), pp. 306ff.

24. Donald K. Swearer, *Buddhism in Transition*, pp. 46ff.

25. See George D. Bond, *The Buddhist Revival in Sri Lanka: Religious Tradition, Reinterpretation and Response* (Columbia: University of South Carolina Press, 1988), chap. 7.

26. Ibid., p. 241.

27. Phra Mahāchai Aphakaro, "Kān Praprung Botbat Khong Phra Sangha" [Reforming the Role of the Sangha], *Kalpa Phrksa* 1, no. 1 (1972): 1. Note the contrast between the interpretations of the Western scholar Bruce Morgan and Phra Mahāchai.

28. Ibid., pp. 14–23. As is true for many of the young monks involved in development programs during this period, Phra Mahāchai has left the monastic order. Mahāchai, however, remains actively concerned as a lay person in issues of social transformation.

29. Somboon Suksamran, "A Buddhist Approach to Development: The Case of 'Development Monks' in Thailand," in *Reflections on Development in Southeast Asia*, ed. Teck Ghee (Singapore: Institute of Southeast Asian Studies, 1988), p. 26. See also Somboon Suksamran, *Political Buddhism in Southeast Asia: The Role of the Sangha in the Modernization of Thailand* (New York: St. Martin's Press, 1977).

30. Ibid, pp. 26–27.

31. Most studies of Thai monks involved in social and economic development issues have focused on its political aspects, e.g., Suksamran, *Political Buddhism in Southeast Asia*, chap. 4. For a descriptive account of the work of individual monks, see Seri Phongphit, *Religion in a Changing Society: Buddhism, Reform and the Role of Monks in Community Development in Thailand* (Hong Kong: Arena Press, 1988). For work on development and forest conservation monks, see the work of Susan M. Darlington: "Monks and Environmental Conservation: A Case Study in Nan Province," *Seeds of Peace* 9, no. 1: 7–10; "Putting the Dhamma

into Social Practice: Monks and Environmental Action in Thailand," *Buddhist Forum* (forthcoming); and "Buddhism, Morality, and Change: The Local Response to Development in Thailand." Ph.D. dissertation, Ann Arbor, Mich.: University Microfilm, 1990.

32. Phongphit, ibid., p. 45.

33. Ibid., p. 49.

34. Ibid, p. 51.

35. Ibid. p. 52.

36. Ibid., p. 57.

37. The Foundation for Children in Bangkok claims there were 2.5 million prostitutes in Thailand in 1994 with an increasing number of child prostitutes, both male and female. Other NGOs project a figure of 1 million. Government estimates are much lower. Prostitution has greatly abetted the spread of AIDS in Thailand, a problem largely ignored until 1990. Today both the government and NGOs are actively seeking ways to stop the spread of the HIV virus. The Thai *sangha* is responding somewhat more slowly although several monasteries have established AIDS treatment centers.

38. For a brief biography of Phra Thepkavī and a description of the work of FEDRA in both Thai and English, see *Thī Ra Lu'k 71 Pī Phra Thepkavī* [In Honor of Phra Thepkavī's 71st Birthday] (Chiangmai: Foundation for Rural Development, B.E. 2532/C.E. 1992.

39. Adapted from *Wisdom of Ven. Phra Thepkavī*, trans. S. Chandra Ngarm (Chiang Mai, 1988).

40. See Susan M. Darlington, "The Embodiment of Buddhist Ecology," Unpublished manuscript.

41. Suchira Payulpitack, "Buddhadāsa's Movement: An Analysis of Its Origins, Development, and Social Impact." Doctoral dissertation, University of Bielefeld (Germany), 1991, chap, 7. I visited Āchān Pongsak at Wat Phālād in 1990 and his current center at Doi Tham Tu Pū, Chọm Thong, in 1994. The wat has considerable information about his conservation work, although this discussion focuses largely on Suchira Payulpitack's dissertation. Payulpitack is professor at Payap University in Chiang Mai and lives at Wat Phālād. She analyzes Āchān Pongsak as an example of an activist monk-follower of Buddhadāsa Bhikkhu.

42. Ibid., p. 226, with minor adaptations.

43. See Kitsiri Malalgoda, *Buddhism in Sinhalese Society 1750–1900* (Berkeley: University of California Press, 1976).

44. E. Michael Mendelson, *Sangha and State in Burma: A Study of Monastic Sectarianism and Leadership*, ed. John P. Ferguson (Ithaca, N.Y.: Cornell University Press, 1975), pp. 93ff. See also John P. Ferguson's article, "The Quest for Legitimation by Burmese Monks and Kings: The Case of the Shwegyin Sect (19th–20th Centuries)," in *Religion and the Legitimation of Power in Thailand, Laos, and Burma*, pp. 66–86. S. J. Tambiah's subsequent study of forest monks

in Thailand (*The Buddhist Saints of the Forest and the Cult of Amulets*) develops Ferguson's theme—the relationship between king/politicans and monk—more fully.

45. Mendelson, *Sangha and State*, p. 88.

46. For the rules of the Shwegyin sect, see Than Tun, *Essays on the History and Buddhism of Burma* (Whiting Bay, Scotland: Kiscadale Publications, 1988), pp. 167–173.

47. See Michael Carrithers detailed discussion of the nineteenth and early twentieth century revival of the forest tradition in *The Forest Monks of Sri Lanka* (Delhi: Oxford University Press, 1983).

48. George D. Bond argues this point in *The Buddhist Revival in Sri Lanka*, chaps. 4–6. Bond provides the most complete available description of the nature and role of meditation in the revival of Buddhism in Sri Lanka.

49. S. J. Tambiah, *World Conqueror and World Renouncer: A Study of Buddhism and Polity in Thailand Against a Historical Background* (Cambridge: Cambridge University Press, 1976), pp. 208–212.

50. Charles F. Keyes, "Buddhist Politics and Their Revolutionary Origins in Thailand," *International Political Science Review* 10, no. 2 (1989): 124.

51. Tambiah, *World Conqueror and World Renouncer*, pp. 208–218. Thanissaro Bhikkhu has suggested that a more accurate characterization would be a strict scripturalism with regard to the Vinaya, a more critical rationalism with regard the Dhamma, and a critical-historical approach to the commentaries (personal communication).

52. Charles F. Keyes, "Buddhism and National Integration in Thailand," *Journal of Asian Studies* 33, no. 3 (May 1971): 551–567.

53. Also transliterated as Ăchān Man. Here I follow the usage of S. J. Tambiah.

54. Tambiah, *The Buddhist Saints of the Forest and the Cult of Amulets*, chap. 6.

55. See Jack Kornfeld, *Living Buddhist Masters* (Santa Cruz, Calif.: Unity Press, 1977) for selections from the writings of several modern Theravāda meditation teachers, including Buddhadāsa.

56. The slide set *Buddhism in Southeast Asia and Ceylon* includes pictures of Buddhadāsa and his center in southern Thailand. The main building is called a Spiritual Theater. It contains a collection of paintings and murals selected from different religious traditions depicting the themes of attachment and nonattachment. A video film on Buddhadāsa, *Life and Work of Buddhadāsa*, is available for purchase through the International Network of Engaged Buddhists, 127 Soi Santipap, Nares Rd., Bangkok 10500, Thailand.

57. Buddhadāsa Bhikkhu, *Ten Years in Suan Moke* (Bangkok: Pacharayasarn Editorial Board, 1984), pp. 15–16. Quoted in Suwanna Satha-Anand, "Religious Movements in Contemporary Thailand," *Asian Survey* 30, no. 4 (April 1990): 397.

58. Buddhadāsa has been the subject of several doctoral dissertations in the USA, France, Germany, and Australia. One is Peter A. Jackson, *Buddhadāsa. A Buddhist Thinker for the Modern World* (Bangkok: Siam Society, 1988). However, the most

thorough treatment is Louis Gabaude, *Une Hermeneutique Bouddhique Contemporaine de Thailand: Buddhadāsa Bhikkhu* (Paris: École Française d'Extrême-Orient, 1988). A collection of Buddhadāsa's essays is available in *Me and Mine: Selected Essays of Bhikkhu Buddhadasa*, ed. Donald K. Swearer (Albany: SUNY Press, 1989). Suchira Payulpitack's doctoral dissertation, "Buddhadāsa's Movement: An Analysis of Its Origins, Development and Social Impact" (University of Bielefeld, 1991) is as yet unpublished.

59. Buddhadāsa's interpretation of Buddhism has been influenced by many sources: reformist Buddhist voices from Asia and the West, Western thought including Christianity and, in particular, Zen Buddhism. Some critics of Buddhadāsa accuse him of being a crypto-Mahāyānist because of his emphasis on emptiness. Buddhadāsa's major themes, especially his critical stance toward any kind of essentialism, are consistent with several contemporary interpreters of Theravāda and early Buddhism. For example, see David J. Kalupahana, *A History of Buddhist Philosophy: Continuities and Discontinuities* (Honolulu: University of Hawaii Press, 1992) for a sophisticated, text-based interpretation of Buddhism as an antiessentialist, antifoundationalist position. Kalupahana develops this theme in many of his books including his study of Nāgārjuna and his interpretation of the *Dhammapāda*, as well as his forthcoming University of Hawaii Press monograph on Buddhist ethics.

60. Buddhadāsa Bhikkhu, *Buddhasāsanik Kap Kānanurak Thamachāt* [Buddhists and the Conservation of Nature] (Bangkok: Komol Khemthong Foundation, 1990).

61. Interview with the author, November 10, 1976.

62. Buddhadāsa, *Kān Tham Ngān Duae Cit Wāng* [Working with a Liberated Mind] (Bangkok: Society for the Propagation of Buddhism, 1975), p. 13.

63. Ibid., pp. 14–15.

64. Buddhadāsa's philosophy of interdependence is a basic theme in contemporary reformist Buddhism, especially socially engaged Buddhism. See Thich Nhat Hanh, *Interbeing: Commentaries on the Tiep Hien Precepts* (Berkeley, Calif.: Parallax Press, 1987).

65. Payulpitack, "Buddhadasa's Movement," p. 178.

66. Jackson, *Buddhism, Legitimation, and Conflict*, p. 120.

67. During the first few months of 1994 both Thai and English language newspapers carried almost daily coverage of the Phra Yantra case. The most serious charge brought against the monk was that he committed the *pārājika* offense of sexual intercourse, which calls for explusion from the monastic order. The Department of Religious Affairs and the Supreme Sangha Council reviewed the case and found insufficient evidence to substantiate the charges. A group of forty-three professors from Chiang Mai University requested that the SSC review the case. Phra Payom has used the occasion to call into question the adulation afforded popular, charismatic monks, which, he contends, is more appropriate for movie stars than renunciants. Phra Dhammapiṭaka, makes made a similar point, seeing

the Phra Yantra case as a symptom of a chronic problem in Thai society, where consumerism has become the new religion and monks are treated as just one more commodity. In an earlier day, Dhammapiṭaka contends, the laity gave to the monastic order to get rid of selfishness and elevate one's state of mind. Now, however, people do not "give" but "buy" what they believe will help them grow richer. (Taken from Sanitsuda Ekachai, "Why Wisdom Is Better Than Magic," *Bangkok Post* 49, no. 76, [March 17, 1994]: 25).

Gender, sexuality and sexual behavior have become major religious issues today, especially in relationship to celibate monastic traditions. The Phra Yantra case is similar to widely publicized incidents in both Roman Catholicism and Protestantism in America, such as the tele-evangelist Jimmy Swaggert. Sexuality has become an occasion for heated debate and discussion in Thailand. One monk phrased the dilemma of celibacy in modern Thai consumerist society as follows: "There seems to be no more room for monks in this society. . . . If we look [straight] ahead we are criticised as not being *riap-roi* [polite]. If we lower our eyes, we cannot see the cluttered way [in front of us]. If we look up, there it is—the advertisement for women's underpants" (Quoted in "Buddhism at Odds with Sexuality" *Bangkok Post* 49, no. 63 [March 4, 1994]).

68. Sulak Sivaraksa and Chatsumarn Kabilsingh are discussed in the following section. Dr. Praves Wasi, former rector of Mahidol University and recipient of the Magsaysay Award for his outstanding contribution to medical research, advises several Buddhistically grounded NGOs and has written extensively on issues of Buddhism and the problems of contemporary Thai society.

69. In addition to Bodhirak, several popular contemporary Buddhist teachers became monks from secular backgrounds, e.g., the founders of the Dhammakāya movement. Buddhadāsa, himself, broke away from a more traditional monastic career when he established Suan Mokkhabalārāma. Although Bodhirak had been an admirer of Buddhadāsa, he later became a severe critic.

70. Phra Bodhirak, *Sacca Haeng Chīwit* [My Life Story] (Bangkok: Dhammasanti Foundation, 1982), p. 186. Quoted in Donald K. Swearer, "Fundamentalistic Movements in Theravada Buddhism," in *Fundamentalisms Observed* (Chicago and London: University of Chicago Press, 1990), p. 669.

For the purposes of this monograph I am interpreting Santi Asok as a particular transformation or expression of the forest tradition rather in term of categories I have used previously, i.e., a fundamentalistic or neotraditional type movement. (See my essays previously cited, "Fundamentalistic Movements in Theravāda Buddhism," [1990] and "Sulak Sivaraksa's Buddhist Vision for Renewing Society" [1991].)

71. See J. L. Taylor, "New Buddhist Movements in Thailand: An 'Individualistic Revolution,' Reform and Dissonance," *Journal of Southeast Asia Studies* 21, no. 1 (1990): 145–150; Duncan J. McCargo, "The Three Paths of Major-General Chamlong Srimuang," *Southeast Asia Research* 1, no. 1 (March 1993): 43–46.

This article is based on McCargo's Ph.D. dissertation, "The Political Leadership of Major-General Chamlong Srimuang" (University of London, 1993).

72. McCargo, "The Political Leadership of Major-General Chamlong Srimuang," p. 128.

73. This issue will also be discussed under the rubric "Buddhism and the West," which concludes this chapter.

74. Phra Rājavaramunī, *Pačhanānukrom Phutthasāt Chapap Pramuan Tham* [Dictionary of Buddhism. Dhamma] (Bangkok: Mahāchulālongkorn University, B.E. 2528/C.E. 1983); Phra Debvedi, *Pačhanānukrom Phutthasāt Chapap Pramuan Sap* [Dictionary of Buddhism. Vocabulary] (Bangkok: Mahāchulālongkorn University, B.E 2531/C.E. 1986). The first edition of *Buddhadhamma*, trans. Grant A. Olson, will be published by SUNY Press (forthcoming).

75. Bhikkhu P. A. Payutto (Phra Dhammapiṭaka), *A Buddhist Solution for the Twenty-first Century* (Chiang Mai: The Buddhist Association, 1993), p. 7.

76. See Phra Debvedi, *Helping Yourself to Help Others*, trans. Puriso Bhikkhu (Bangkok: Buddhadhamma Foundation, 1990) for an approach to the self-other ethical polarity.

77. The film *I Am a Monk* (Hartley Productions) focuses on meditation and illustrates the nature of mindfulness training in Theravāda Buddhism.

78. See Winston L. King, "Contemporary Burmese Buddhism," in *The Cultural, Political, and Religious Significance of Buddhism in the Modern World*, ed. Heinrich Dumoulin and John C. Maraldo. New York: Collier Books, 1976, pp. 95–96.

79. For example, see Mahasi Sayadaw, *The Progress of Insight* (Kandy: Buddhist Publication Society, 1965); *Practical Insight Meditation* (Kandy: Buddhist Publication Society, 1971).

80. Winston L. King, *A Thousand Lives Away* (Cambridge, Mass.: Harvard University Press, 1974), p. 227.

81. Ibid., p. 226–227.

82. Ibid., p. 227.

83. Bond, *The Buddhist Revival*, pp. 212ff. Bond places a major emphasis on meditation movements in the revival of Buddhism in Sri Lanka.

84. *Dhammadāna Khong Khun Mae Dr. Siri Krinchai* [Mother Dr. Siri Krinchai's Gift of Dhamma], 5th printing, (Bangkok: Horatanachaikan Press, B.E. 2536/C.E. 1993), pp. 48–52. Published in honor of Dr. Siri Krinchai's seventy-second birthday, this volume includes a biography, an essay on her philosophy of meditation, and testimonials by her followers. Her workshops are very demanding. Participants spend most of the day in meditation. I am grateful to Sukhon Polpatipicharn, one of her followers and an associate at the United States Information Service in Bangkok, for her generous gift of this book.

85. *Prawat Wat Rampung* [History of Wat Rampung] (Chiang Mai: Chang Pu'ak Press, n.d.), p. 9.

86. This practice focuses on the rising and falling of the abdomen. In Thailand it is usually referred to simply as the "rising and falling" (*phǫng-nǫ/up-nǫ*) insight (*vipassanā*) method. Although several different types of meditation practice are current in Thailand, practioners often ask if you practice the *vipassanā* method of *phǫng-nǫ/up-nǫ*, i.e., the Mahasi Sayadaw method, or the concentration (*samatha*) method of *Phuto. . .Phuto* (focusing on the name of the Buddha) associated with Āchān Mun.

87. The Thai term *chī* is derived from the Pali *pabbajitā* (one who has gone forth, a renunciant).

88. This method is presented in a booklet available at the monastery, *Khumu' Kānpatipat Vipassanākammaṭṭhāna* [Handbook for Meditation Practice] (Chiang Mai, 1993).

89. Tipawadee Amawattana et al. "The Use of Vipassana Meditation as a Strategy for Developing Qualitative Counseling Service." A paper delivered at the Fifth International Conference on Thai Studies, School of Oriental and African Studies, London University, July 8, 1993. Several *wats* throughout the country are also developing meditation based AIDS and addictive drug treatment centers. Especially noteworthy is Wat Doi Kung in Mae Hong Sǫn Province.

90. Ibid., pp. 7–8.

91. This observation corresponds to Robert Bellah's characterization of the individualistic character of the "modern" stage of religious development. See, "Religious Evolution," in Robert Bellah, *Beyond Belief* (New York: Harper and Row, 1970). See also J. L. Taylor, "New Buddhist Movements in Thailand," for a similar point made from a different analytical perspective.

92. *The Buddhist* 37, no. 1 (June 1966): 7.

93. Discussed in Donald K. Swearer, "Lay Buddhism and the Buddhist Revival in Ceylon," *Journal of the American Academy of Religion* 38, no. 3 (September 1970): 266ff.

94. Nyanaponika's best known book in the West is *The Heart of Buddhist Meditation* (London: Rider, 1962); however, his articles and translations cover a wide range of subjects, in particular the Abhidhamma. Nyanaponika, himself, was a student of the German monk, Nyanatiloka, who founded the Island Hermitage monastery near Colombo. Particularly noteworthy scholarly work published by the society include translations by the British monk-scholars Soma Thera and Nyanamoli Thera and the American monk Bhikkhu Bodhi.

95. Studies of Ariyaratne and the Sarvodaya movement include, Joanna Rogers Macy, *Dharma and Development: Relgion as Resource in the Sarvodaya Self Help Movement* (West Hardford, Conn.: Kumarian Press, 1983); George D. Bond, *The Buddhist Revival in Sri Lanka: Religious Tradition, Reinterpretation and Response* (Columbia: University of South Carolina Press, 1988), chap. 7; Richard Gombrich and Gananath Obeyesekere, *Buddhism Transformed: Religious Change in Sri Lanka*

(Princeton, N.J.: Princeton University Press, 1988), chap. 7; Denis Goulet, *Survival with Integrity* (Colombo: Marga Institute, 1981); Detlef Kantowsky, *Sarvodaya: The Other Development* (Delhi: Vikas, 1980). Gombrich and Obeyesekere offer the most critical interpretation of the movement as an expression of "protestant Buddhism." They see much of what has been written about Sarvodaya as good-hearted but naive reflections of their authors' "own utopian fantasies of a benevolent social order" (p. 243). Bond's more descriptive view contrasts Sarvodayan "engaged Buddhism" with the chauvinistic, militant civil religion Buddhism attacked by S. J. Tambiah in *Buddhism Betrayed? Religion, Politics and Violence in Sri Lanka.* (Chicago: University of Chicago Press, 1992). George D. Bond, "Political Buddhism and the Sarvodaya Shramadāna Movement: Interpreting Buddhism for Identity and Peace." Unpublished lecture, University of Hawaii, November 24, 1993.

96. Joanna Rogers Macy, "Dependent Co-arising: The Distinctiveness of Buddhist Ethics," *Journal of Religious Ethics* 7, no. 1 (Spring 1979): 49.

97. Ariyaratne, lecture, University of Hawaii, September 17, 1993.

98. Macy, "Dependent Co-arising," p. 50.

99. Bond, "Political Buddhism and the Sarvodaya Shramadāna Movement."

100. Sulak has written extensively in both Thai and English. His 1984 autobiography, *Chuang Haeng Chīwit* [Phases of My Life] (Bangkok: Thianwan Press), lists eighty-four of his Thai book titles. The list continues to grow rapidly. The following discussion about Sulak Sivaraksa is based on my article, "Sulak Sivaraksa's Buddhist Vision for Renewing Society," *Crossroads* 7, no. 1 (January 1991), and also as the Afterword to the Thai edition of a collection of Sulak's essays, *Seeds of Peace: A Buddhist Vision for Renewing Society* (Berkeley, Calif.: Parallax Press/International Network of Engaged Buddhists, 1992), pp. 132–190. A revision of this essay is included in *Engaged Buddhism: Buddhist Liberation Movements in Asia*, ed. Sallie B. King and Christopher S. Queen (Albany: SUNY Press, 1995).

101. Sulak Sivaraksa, *Siamese Resurgence* (Bangkok: Asian Forum on Development, 1985), p. 316.

102. A group that Sulak was instrumental in initiating, the Committee on Religion and Development, publishes the journal *Sekhiyadhamma*. Its stated purpose is the exchange of ideas and experiences regarding ways to make Buddhism both personally and socially relevant to the problems of contemporary Thailand. The committee sponsors monthly meetings of monks actively committed to social transformation.

103. Swearer, "Sulak Sivaraksa's Buddhist Vision for Renewing Society," pp. 46–47.

104. Sanitsuda Ekachai, "Buddhism at Odds with Sexuality," *Bangkok Post* 49, no. 63 (March 4, 1994): 29.

105. *Anguttara Nikāya*. II.82.3. [Ānanda Asks the Buddha], "Pray, lord, what is the reason, what is the cause why women neither sit in a court of justice, nor

embark on business, nor reach the heart of any matter?" To which Gotama replied, "Women are uncontrolled, Ānanda, Women are envious, Ānanda. Women are greedy, Ānanda. Women are weak in wisdom, Ānanda. This is the reason why women do not sit in a court of justice, do not embark on business, do not reach the heart of the matter."

106. Alan Sponberg, "Attitudes Toward Women and the Feminine in Early Buddhism," in José Ignacio Cabezón, *Buddhism, Sexuality, and Gender* (Albany: SUNY Press, 1992), p. 8.

107. Academic studies of women and Buddhism have prompted a wide range of feminist and gender related issues as well. See the several essays in Cabezón, ibid.

108. Thomas Kirsch, "Buddhism, Sex Roles and the Thai Economy," in *Women of Southeast Asia*. ed. Penny Van Esterick. Center for Southeast Asia Studies, Occasional Paper No. 9 (DeKalb: Northern Illinois University, 1982), pp. 16–41.

109. See Khin Thitsa (Khin-Thi-Da Lwin), *Providence and Prostitution: Image and Reality for Women in Buddhist Thailand* (London: Change International Reports [Women and Society], 1980).

110. Charles F. Keyes, "Mother or Mistress but Never a Monk: Buddhist Notions of Female Gender in Rural Thailand," *American Ethnologist* 11, no. 2 (May 1984): 223–241.

111. See Chatsumarn Kabilsingh, "Buddhist Nuns in Other Countries," in *Thai Women in Buddhism* (Berkeley, Calif.: Parallax Press, 1991), pp. 89–91; Ingrid Jordt, "Bhikkhuni, Thilashin Mae-chii: Women Who Renounce the World in Burma, Thailand and the Classical Pali Buddhist Texts," *Crossroads* 4, no. 1 (Fall 1988). On women renunciants in Sri Lanka, see Tessa Bartholomeusz, "The Female Mendicant in Buddhist Sri Lanka," in *Buddhism, Sexuality, and Gender*, pp. 37–61, also her *Women Under the Bo Tree* (Cambridge: Cambridge University Press, 1994); Gombrich and Obeyesekere, *Buddhism Transformed*, chap. 8.

112. Sulak Sivaraksa couples consumerism and the preoccupation with sexuality-sexuality in Thai society today. He proposes three general solutions: admit women into the *sangha*, decrease the prominence of consumerist values, and create more favorable conditions for practising the *dhamma* by men and women, renunciants and laity. "Buddhism at Odds with Sexuality," p. 29.

113. The story of Voramai Kabilsingh is taken from "Two Bhikkhunī Movements in Thailand," Chatsumarn Kabilsingh, *Thai Women in Buddhism*, pp. 45–54.

114. Among American Buddhist women, Rita M. Gross, professor of comparative studies in religion, University of Wisconsin, Eau Claire, and president, Society for Buddhist-Christian Studies, plays a major role in the international Buddhist women's movement. Currently she is treasurer of Sakyadhītā. For Gross's interpretation of Buddhism and women see, Rita M. Gross, *Buddhism After Patriarchy* (Albany: SUNY Press, 1992).

115. See Guy Richard Welbon, *Buddhist Nirvāṇa and Its Western Interpreters* (Chicago: University of Chicago Press, 1968).

116. For example, see David J. Kalupahana, *Buddhist Philosophy: A Historical Analysis* (Honolulu: University of Hawaii Press, 1976); *A History of Buddhist Philosophy*; Padmasiri de Silva, *An Introduction to Buddhist Psychology*, 2d ed. (London and New York: Macmillan Publishing Company, 1992); *Twin Peaks: Compassion and Insight. Emotions and the "self" in Buddhist and Western Thought* (Singapore: Buddhist Research Society, 1991).

117. Nolan P. Jacobson, *Buddhism: The Religion of Analysis* (London: George Allen and Unwin, 1966).

118. In addition to Kalupahana's two surveys of Buddhist philosophy he has written interpretations of the *Dhammapāda* (*A Path of Righteousness* [Lanham, Md.: University Press of America, 1987]), the *Abhidhamma* (*The Principles of Buddhist Psychology* [Albany: SUNY Press, 1987]), and Nāgārjuna (*Nāgārjuna* [Albany: SUNY Press, 1987]). He argues that the middle way philosophy of early Buddhism was fashioned as a counter to essentialism, on the one hand, and nihilism, on the other. He contends, furthermore, that the history of Buddhist philosophy—ethics, epistemology, psychology, logic—has been a struggle to maintain that middle way.

119. David Kalupahana and Indrani Kalupahana, *The Way of Siddhartha: A Life of the Buddha* (Lanham, Md.: University Press of America, 1987).

120. See Rick Fields, *How the Swans Came to the Lake* (Boulder: Shambala Press, 1981) and Charles Prebish, *American Buddhism* (North Scituate, Mass.: Duxbury Press, 1979), for a description of Buddhism in America.

121. For example, see Haing Ngor, *A Cambodian Odyssey* (New York: Macmillan Publishing Co., 1987). For visual images of the war in Cambodia see the commercial film *The Killing Fields*. The PBS Series, *Vietnam: A Television History*, chronicles the devastating consequences of America's blindness to the historical and cultural realities of Vietnam, Cambodia, and Laos. For a personal, culturally sensitive narrative of an American conscientious objector who served in Vietnam, read John Balaban, *Remembering Heaven's Face: A Moral Witness in Vietnam* (New York: Poseidon, 1991), especially chap. 18, "Heaven, Humankind, Earth." For a descriptive account of Lao Buddhism in North America, see Penny Van Esterick, *Taking Refuge: Lao Buddhists in North America* (North York, Ont.: York Lanes Press, 1993). An excellent film on the problems faced by Lao Buddhists in America is *Blue Collar and Buddha* (See Appendix 2).

122. See Rājavaramunī, *Thai Buddhism in the Buddhist World* (Bangkok: Unity Progress Press, 1984).

123. The Religious Pluralism Project at Harvard University under the direction of Diana Eck is collaborating with WGBH Boston in the production of a series of films on religion in America. The pilot film on Buddhism in America (*Being the Buddha in L.A.*) was produced in 1993.

APPENDIX 1. SIGĀLAKA SUTTA

1. Adapted from Vajirañāṇavarorasa, *Navakovāda* [Instructions to the Newly Ordained] (Bangkok: Mahāmakuta, 1971), pp. 86-94.

APPENDIX 3. BOROBUDUR

1. Two films on Borobudur, *Borobudur: The Cosmic Mountain* and *The Buddha: Temple Complex at Borobudur*, differ dramatically. The latter reduces the Borobudur bas-reliefs to presentations of episodes from the life of the Buddha. The former connects this great monument with the past, present, and future of Indonesia, explores the structure and meaning of Borobudur and puts the site within a broader cultural context (see Appendix 2).

2. Recent contributions to the study of Borobudur include John Miksic, *Barabudur: Golden Tales of Buddhas* (Boston: Shambala Press, 1990), R. Soekmono, J. G. De Casparis et al., *Borobudur: Prayer in Stone* (London: Thames and Hudson, 1990), and *Barabudur: History and Significance of a Buddhist Monument*, ed. Luis O. Gomez and Hiram W. Woodward, Jr. (Berkeley: Asian Humanities Press, 1981). See also H. G. Quartich Wales, *The Making of Greater India* (London: Bernard Quartich, 1961); George Coedès, *The Indianized States of Southeast Asia*, ed. W. F. Vella (Honolulu: University of Hawaii Press, 1968); Heinrich Zimmer, *The Art of Indian Asia*, 2d ed., vol. 1. Bollingen Series 39 (New York: Pantheon Books, 1960), pp. 298–317; A. K. Coomaraswamy, *History of Indian and Indonesian Art* (New York: Dover Publications, 1965), pp. 203–216.

3. J. G. de Casparis, "Introduction," in *Borobudur: Prayer in Stone*, p. 14.

4. Miksic, *Borobudur*, p. 47.

5. See ibid., 49, for a discussion of the distinction between the terms *stūpa* and *cetiya*.

6. The symbolism of the *stūpa* has been translated into a variety of forms and idioms including levels of spiritual development in yogic and meditative states of consciousness. These particular idioms are not the primary concern of this appendix. They are, however, explored in several monographs including Mircea Eliade, *Yoga: Freedom and Immortality* (New York: Pantheon Books, 1958), Lama Anagarika Govinda, *Psycho-Cosmic Symbolism of the Buddhist Stupa* (Emeryville, Calif: Dharma Publications, 1976), Roderick S. Bucknell and Martin Stuart-Fox, *The Twilight of Language* (New York: St. Martin's Press, 1986).

7. Reginald Le May, *The Culture of Southeast Asia* (London: George Allen and Unwin, 1954), p. 98.

8. Paul Mus, *Barabudur: Esquisse d'une histoire du bouddhisme foundee la critique archeologique des textes* (Hanoi: École Française d'Extrême-Orient, 1932).

9. Wales, *The Making of Greater India*, p. 123, referring to J. G. De Casparis, *Prasati Indonesia*, vol. 1, 1950.

10. Soekmono, *Borobudur: Prayer in Stone*, p. 32.

11. The collection of essays on Borobudur in Luis O. Gomez and Hiram W. Woodward, Jr. *Barabudur* provides an overview of various interpretations of the monument.

Glossary

Abhidhamma Literally the "higher (*abhi*) teaching (*dhamma*)." Refers to the third division (*piṭaka*) of the Pali language scriptures of Theravāda Buddhism. Contains a diverse body of texts but many of them represent more technical or scholastic interpretations of the dialogue (*sutta*) texts.

Abhiseka Literally "to pour water." To consecrate as in royal consecration (*rāja-abhiseka*) or the consecration of Buddha images (*buddha-abhiseka*).

Ādi Buddha Literally "the beginning or original Buddha." In Mahāyāna and Vajrayāna Buddhism often identified as the central Buddha of the five *dhyāni* Buddhas; usually the Buddha Vairocana.

Aggañña Sutta One of the *suttas* in the Long Discourses (*Dīgha Nikāya*), which deals with the origin of the world and the reason for the selection of a righteous ruler.

Ānanda In the Pali *sutta* texts of Theravāda Buddhism Ānanda appears as one of the most important disciples of the Buddha. From a literary point of view Ānanda acts as a foil to the Buddha in the famous *Maha-parinibbāna Sutta*.

Anāthapiṇḍika A banker of Sāvatthī. A paradigm of lay support of the Buddha's almspersons (*dāyaka*). Visākhā is his female counterpart.

Anawrahta (Aniruddha) (1040-1077 C.E.). Considered to be the founder of the unified Burmese kingdom with the capital at Pagan.

Angulimāla A robber who became a follower of the Buddha and later attained arahantship. A story in the *Middle Length Discourses* (Majjhima Nikāya 11.103–104) tells how he eased a woman's labor pains by an act of truth (*saccakiriya*) that came to be regarded as a *paritta* to ward off dangers.

Anattā Literally "not (*an-*) self (*atta*)." One of the seminal concepts in the teachings of the Buddha. Often misinterpreted as a world-denying term.

Anicca Impermanence, not-enduring. One of the three characteristics of existence together with suffering and not-self.

209

Arahant   Literally, one who is worthy, deserving. A Pali term applied to one who has attained *nibbāna*.

Āsāḷaha Pūjā   A celebration remembering the Buddha's first discourse, "Setting the Wheel of the Law in Motion" (*Dhammacakkappavattana Sutta*) delivered at the Deer Park in Vārāṇasī (Benares). It occurs on the full moon sabbath of the eighth lunar month (*āsāḷāha*).

Āsava   An outflowing, canker. The four *asavas* to be overcome to gain freedom are sensuality (*kāma*), desire for rebirth (*bhava*), attachment to views (*diṭṭhi*), and ignorance (*avijjā*).

Bhikkhu/Bhikkhunī   The term used to designate monastic followers of the Buddha. Literally, "almsperson," the word refers to the fact that Theravāda monks depend upon the generosity of the laity for their material well-being. The Theravāda monastic order is referred to as the *bhikkhu-sangha/bhikkhunī-sangha*, the order of male and female almspersons.

Bimbisāra   King of Magadha and patron of the Buddha.

Bodhisattva (Pali, *Bodhisatta*)   Literally, a "wisdom (*bodhi*) being (*sattva*)." In the Theravāda tradition the term usually refers to the Buddha in his various earthly rebirths. In the Mahāyāna tradition the term comes to be applied to all beings seeking enlightenment or those who will be future Buddhas.

Brahmaloka   Literally, the "world (*loka*) of Brahma," one of the abodes of the gods in the Theravāda cosmology.

Cakkavatti(n)   Literally, a "wheel turner." The term refers to the Buddhist monarch whose power in the secular realm parallels the power of the Buddha in the sacred realm.

Cakkavatti Sīhanāda Sutta   A *sutta* in the Long Discourses (*Dīgha Nikāya*), which is an important source of information about the traditional understanding of the *cakkavatti*(n) concept.

Cariyāpiṭaka   One of the fifteen books of the *Khuddaka Nikāya* (Collection of Gradual Sayings). Sets forth the Buddha's ten moral perfections (*pāramī*) by which he attained enlightenment.

Cetiya (Thai, *cedi*)   A tumulus, a reliquary monument embodying cosmological and cosmogonic symbolism, especially the world axis or *axis mundi*.

Čhao   A Thai term with several different possible meanings: spirit, deity, lord.

Chiang Mai   The major city of northern Thailand. The dominant power among various principalities in northern Thailand from the end of the thirteenth century to the present.

Dāna   The virtue of generosity, one of the principal Theravāda moral perfections (*pāramī*).

Devadatta Son of the Buddha's maternal uncle, became one of the Buddha's almspersons but later tried to kill the Buddha and split the order.

Devarāja Literally, "god-king." Thought to have been a notion of divine kingship that developed in the Khmer kingdom in the ninth century and played an important role in the monarchial traditions of the classical states of Southeast Asia.

Dhamma (Sanskrit, *dharma*) A central concept of Theravāda thought. It can mean the basic constituents of reality, the truth, the teachings of the Buddha. The Buddha's first discourse is entitled "Setting the Wheel of the Truth (or Law) in Motion" (*Dhammacakkapavattana Sutta*).

Dhammayut(ika) Nikāya Nineteenth century Buddhist sect founded by King Mongkut of Thailand.

Dhātu-gabbha The Pali form of the Sinhalese term *dāgoba*, referring to a reliquary mound; that is, a *cetiya*.

Dhyāni Buddha Literally, "meditation Buddha." In Vajrayāna Buddhism the five Buddhas of the center and four cardinal directions, such as the Buddha Amitābha of the West.

Dīpavaṃsa The *Island Chronicle*, one of the three major chronicles of Sinhalese Buddhism.

Divyāvadāna A Mahāyāna Buddhist text that contains a legendary account of the life of the Buddha.

Dukkha Suffering. The unsatisfactory nature of existence limited to the sensory or the mundane world.

Duṭṭhagāmaṇi Ruler of Sri Lanka (101–77 B.C.E.) noted for defeating the Tamils and reuniting the country under Sinhalese rule.

Gaṇḍavyūha A Mahāyāna text concerned with the enlightenment quest of Sudhana. Sometimes referred to as a Mahāyāna *Pilgrim's Progress*.

Haripuñjaya The pre-Thai Mon-Lawa center of culture and political power in northern Thailand. It was conquered by the Tai led by King Mengrai in the thirteenth century. Now known as Lamphun.

Indra A Hindu deity of the greatest importance in Vedic times. In Buddhism Indra is known as Sakka, the ruler of the gods.

Jātaka The tenth book of the *Khuddaka Nikāya* (Collection of Gradual Sayings) containing 547 legendary stories framed as the former lives of the Buddha.

Jātakamālā A "Garland of Birth Stories." A Sanskrit rendering of thirty-four *jātakas* ascribed to Ārya Sūra who may have lived in the first century C.E.

Jhāna States of consciousness attained through meditation. Divided into several stages, such as the four material and immaterial absorptions (D. III. 222).

Kamma (Sanskrit *karma*) Together with *dhamma* one of the central concepts in Theravāda Buddhist doctrine. In general parlance *kamma* means act or action; however, technically it refers to the Law of Kamma, that is, that good acts will bring good consequences and vice versa.

Kapilavattu An important city in northern India during the lifetime of the Buddha.

Karaṇīyamettā Sūtta [Metta Sutta] One of the central *paritta* texts excerpted from the *Saṃyutta Nikāya* (Collected Discourses).

Karuṇā The moral perfection of compassion.

Kaṭhina The robes presented to Buddhist monks at the end of the three-month rains retreat period of confinement. *Kaṭhina* celebrations usually take place during the month of November.

Khwan A Thai term meaning "spirit." In Thai Buddhism every individual possesses thirty-two *khwan* or spirits.

Kyanzittha The grandson of the founder of the Pagan dynasty in Burma and one of its most powerful rulers. He became king in 1084 C.E.

Lalitavistara A proto-Mahāyāna biography of the Buddha associated with the Sarvāstivāda tradition.

Liṅga A phallic symbol of the Hindu god Śiva. Taken by some scholars to be a symbol of the god-king (*devarāja*).

Loi Krathong The festival of the floating (*loi*) boats (*krathong*) celebrated in Thailand during the month of November and thought to be Brahmanical in origin.

Lokeśvara/Avalokiteśvāra A *bodhisattva* in diety form whose face dominates the Bayon, the central temple of the ancient Khmer capital of Angkor Thom; thought to be identified with the king, Jayavarman VII.

Lokiya Literally, "mundane" or "of the world."

Lokuttara Literally, "transmundane."

Mahākassapa One of the principal disciples of the Buddha.

Mahāparinibbāna Sutta The "Discourse of the Great Decease," which recounts the last days of the Buddha.

Mahāsammata A ruler of great justice. A term applied to the first monarch chosen to establish order in a chaotic world (see *Aggañña Sutta*).

Mahāvaṃsa "The Great Chronicle," probably the most celebrated chronicle of Sinhalese Buddhism. A product of the Mahāvihāra monastic lineage.

Mahāvihāra A great monastery of the Sinhalese Buddhist capital, Anurādhapura. Became the center of Thervāda Buddhism and repository of the Sinhalese commentaries. Buddhaghosa compiled his Pali commentaries there. Restored by Parakkama Bāhu I (twelfth century). Source of the spread of Theravāda in mainland Southeast Asia.

Mākha Pūjā   The celebration that marks the miraculous gathering of 1,250 disciples of the Buddha at Veluvanna Mahāvihāra in Rājagaha, north India.

Maṇḍala   A diagram usually in the form of a squared circle which in various ways symbolizes the unity of the individual, society and the cosmos. In Southeast Asia's ancient capitals, royal and religious buildings were constructed in the form of a *maṇḍala*.

Mantra   A word or chant thought to have special power or potency.

Māra   In the Theravāda tradition the equivalent of Satan. Māra tested the Buddha at his departure from Kapilavatthu and at his enlightenment under the Bodhi tree.

Mettā   Loving-kindness. The first of the Divine Abodes (*brahmavihāra*) or unlimited states of consciousness (*appamaññā*).

Moggalāna   One of the Buddha's chief disciples. In Buddhist iconography often depicted paying respects to the Buddha.

Mudra   A hand position of a Buddha image or a practioner. Buddha images are often known by their *mudras*.

Nat   A Burmese term for a powerful guardian spirit.

Nibbāna (Sanskrit, *Nirvāṇa*)   The soteriological goal in Theravāda Buddhism, meaning to have the passions extinguished, to have gained knowledge of the true nature of things.

Pabbajjā   Leaving the world, adopting an ascetic life, ordination as a novice.

Pacceka Buddha   One who becomes a Buddha by his or her own efforts but who does not share the fruits of enlightenment with others.

Pali   The canonical language of Theravāda Buddhism.

Pāpa   Evil, wicked, demeritorious action (*pāpakamma*).

Pāramī[ta]   Literally, "perfection." In Theravāda Buddhism the term often refers to the ten moral perfections personified in the last ten *jātaka* stories in the Pali canon, such as generosity, compassion.

Paritta   Literally, "protection, safeguard." Came to be applied to a group of Pali texts collated in Sri Lanka to be chanted at auspicious occasions.

Pathamasambodhi   A text thought to have been written in northern Thailand in the sixteenth century that recounts the life of the Buddha.

Paṭicca-samuppāda   Literally, "dependent coarising." The term refers to the basic teaching of canonical Theravāda Buddhism which appears in a classical twelvefold formula.

Pātimokkha   Refers to the 227 rules to which fully ordained monks subscribe in a confessional ceremony held fortnightly.

Pegu   An early Mon cultural, political and religious locale in central Burma.

Petaloka   The *petas* (Sanskrit, *preta*) are "hungry ghosts." The *petaloka* refers to one of the hells or places of punishment in the Theravāda cosmology.

Petavatthu   The seventh book of the *Khuddaka Nikāya* (Collection of Gradual Sayings). Stories of those reborn in the realm of the hungry ghosts because of their misdeeds.

Phī   A Thai term for spirits thought to have malicious or mischievous powers.

Phra Malai   A Thai Buddhist text about a saintly monk who visited those punished in hell for breaking the Buddhist precepts and those rewarded in heaven for keeping them. He then taught others the consequences of good and bad actions.

Pūjā   To make an offering, to worship, to hold a celebration.

Puñña   Meritorious acts which cause or influence good consequences.

Sāma   One of the final ten *jātaka* stories in the Theravāda canon. Sāma personifies the virtue of loving-kindness.

Samādhi   Concentration, intent state of mind. One of the constituents of the noble eightfold path.

Saṁsāra   Literally, "to come again and again," "revolve," hence, rebirth or transmigration.

Sangha   An assemblage. Usually refers to the assembly of monks (*bhikkhu*) and/or nuns (*bhikkhunī*).

Sariputta   One of the principal disciples of the Buddha often depicted with Moggalāna paying respects to the Buddha.

Sarvodaya Shramadāna   An organization dedicated to social service and rural uplift based on Buddhist principles. Founded by A. T. Ariyaratne in Sri Lanka.

Sigālaka Sutta   One of the discourses in the *Dīgha Nikāya* (Long Discourses) that prescribes the "ethic of the householder."

Sīla   Moral virtue. Often thought of in terms of the basic Buddhist precepts; that is, not to kill, steal, lie, and so on.

Sīmā   The boundary stones that set off monastic precincts or an ordination hall.

Śiva   One of the principal Hindu gods who plays varying roles in different Theravāda cultural traditions.

Stūpa   A Sanskrit term designating a sepulchral mound or monument, such as the Sāñcī Stūpa. (See *cetiya*.)

Suddhodana   The father of the Buddha.

Sumeru, Mt.   In Indian cosmology the central axis or mountain of the universe.

Suññatā   Literally, "emptiness." The term generally connotes: (1) all dhammas are empty of self, and (2) dependent coarising (paṭicca-samuppāda).

Sutta Literally, "thread." Represents the threads of discourse or dialogue texts in the Pali canon of Theravāda Buddhism. There are four sections or collections of *suttas*: long (*dīgha*), middle (*majjhima*), collected (*samyutta*), and gradual (*anguttara*).

Tathāgata A title for the Buddha. Refers to his "crossing over" to *nibbāna*, that is, his enlightenment. Literally, "thus come."

Tāvatimsa The second of the six *deva* or divine/heavenly realms in Theravāda cosmology. The Buddha is reputed to have preached the *Adhidhamma* there to his mother.

Theragātha/Therīgāthā Eighth and ninth books of the *Khuddaka Nikāya* (Collection of Gradual Sayings). Poems attributed to the male and female renunciant followers of the Buddha. Many are biographical in nature.

Tilokarāja (1442–1487 C.E.) Ruler of Chiang Mai, the dominant Tai state in northern Thailand.

Tusita The fourth of the six *deva* or divine-heavenly realms in Theravāda cosmology.

Upagutta (Sanskrit, Upagupta) An enlightened Buddhist saint to whom is ascribed protective powers because of his legendary victory over Māra. Prominent in legendary literature (*avadāna*) associated with the Sarvāstivāda tradition.

Upasampadā Higher ordination; the rite of entrance into the Buddhist monkhood.

Upekkhā Equanimity. One of the sublime states of consciousness.

Uposatha The Buddhist sabbath days that are calculated according to the four phases of the moon.

Uruvelā An important town in northern India during the lifetime of the Buddha.

Vassa The period of the monsoon rains retreat observed by Buddhist monks, usually between July and October.

Vessantara The last incarnation of the Buddha prior to his rebirth as Siddhattha Gotama. The last of the 547 Pali canonical *jātaka* stories; a personification of the virtue of generosity.

Vihāra Literally, "an abode or dwelling place." Also refers to a place where monks gather for services of chanting.

Vimānavatthu The sixth book of the *Khuddaka Nikaya* (Collection of Gradual Sayings). Stories describing the splendors of the celestial abodes belonging to different deities obtained as a reward in previous lives.

Vinaya The monk's discipline. The *Vinaya Piṭaka* refers to those texts which deal with the monastic order and the discipline.

Viññāna Consciousness. A mental quality constituent of individuality.

Vipassanā   Insight meditation as opposed to trance (*samatha*) meditation.

Visākhā   Daughter of a wealthy merchant. A supporter and patron of the Buddha's almspersons. Visākhā's male counterpart is Anāthapiṇḍika.

Visākhā Pūjā   An occasion celebrating the birth, enlightenment and death of the Buddha. Usually occurs in May.

Viṣṇu   One of the principal Hindu deities. Appears in various guises in different Theravāda cultures.

Yasodhara   Prince Siddhattha's wife.

Bibliography

Ames, Michael. "Magical-Animism and Buddhism: A Structural Analysis of the Sinhalese Religious System." *Journal of Asian Studies* 23 (June 1964): 21–52.

Andaya, Barbara Watson. "Statecraft in the Reign of Lü Tai of Sukhodaya (ca. 1347–1374)." In *Religion and Legitimation of Power in Thailand, Laos and Burma*, ed. Bardwell L. Smith, 2–19. Chambersburg, Pa: Anima Books, 1978.

Anuman Rajadhon, Phya. *Essays on Thai Folklore*. Bangkok: Social Science Association Press, 1968.

————. *Thet Maha Chat Ceremony*. Bangkok: Fine Arts Department, 1969.

Aphakaro, Phra Mahāchai. "Kān Praprung Botbat Khong Phra Sangha" [Reforming the Role of the Sangha]. *Kalpa Phrksa* 1:1 (1972): 1–5.

Aung San Suu Kyi. *Freedom From Fear*. New York: Penguin Books, 1991.

Aung Thaw. *Historical Sites in Burma*. Rangoon: Ministry of Culture, 1972.

Aung-Thwin, Michael. *Pagan: The Origins of Modern Burma*. Honolulu: University of Hawaii Press, 1985.

Balaban, John. *Remembering Heaven's Face. A Moral Witness in Vietnam*. New York: Poseidon, 1991.

Bandaranaike, S. W. R. D. *Speeches and Writings*. Colombo, Sri Lanka: Department of Broadcasting and Information, 1963.

Bartholomeusz, Tessa. "The Female Mendicant in Buddhist Sri Lanka." In *Buddhism, Sexuality and Gender*, ed. José Ignacio Cabezón. Albany, N.Y.: SUNY Press, 1989.

Bechert, Heinz. "Aspects of Theravāda Buddhism in Sri Lanka and Southeast Asia." In *The Buddhist Heritage*, ed. T. Skorupski. Trink, U.K.: Institute of Buddhist Studies, 1989.

————. "S. W. R. D. Bandaranaike and the Legitimation of Power Through Buddhist Ideals." In *Religion and Legitimation of Power in Sri Lanka*, ed. Bardwell L. Smith. Chambersburg, Pa: Anima Books, 1978.

————, and Richard Gombrich, ed. *The World of Buddhism*. London: Thames and Hudson, 1991.

217

Bellah, Robert N. "Religious Evolution." In *Beyond Belief*. New York: Harper and Row, 1970.

Berval, Rene de. *Kingdom of Laos: The Land of the Million Elephants and of the White Parasols*. trans. Teissier du Cros, et al. Saigon: France-Asie, 1959.

Bodhirak, Phra. *Sacca Haeng Chīwit*. [My Life Story]. Bangkok: Dhammasanti, 1982.

Boisselier, Jean. *The Heritage of Thai Sculpture*. New York and Tokyo: Weatherhill, 1975.

Bond, George D. *The Buddhist Revival in Sri Lanka: Religious Tradition, Reinterpretation and Response*. Columbia: University of South Carolina Press, 1988.

———. "Political Buddhism and the Sarvodaya Shramadāna Movement: Interpreting Buddhism for Identity and Peace." Unpublished lecture at the University of Hawaii, Honolulu on 24 November 1993.

Brereton, Bonnie Pacala. *The Phra Malai Legend in Thai Buddhist Literature*. Tempe: Arizona State University Press, 1994.

Briggs, Lawrence P. "The Syncretism of Religions in Southeast Asia, Especially in the Khmer Empire." *Journal of the American Oriental Society* 71, no. 4 (October–December 1951): 230–249.

Brown, W. Norman. "The Creation Myth of the Rig-veda." *Journal of the American Oriental Society* 62 (1942): 85–98.

Brown, Peter. *The Cult of Saints*. Chicago: University of Chicago Press, 1981.

Bucknell, Roberick S., and Martin Stuart-Fox. *The Twilight of Language*. New York: St. Martin's Press, 1986.

Buddhadāsa Bhikkhu. *Buddhasāsanik Kap Kānanurak Thamachāt*. [Buddhists and the Conservation of Nature]. Bangkok: Komol Khemthong Foundation, 1990.

———. *Kān Tham Ngān Duœ Cit Wāng*. [Working with a Liberated Mind]. Bangkok: Society for the Propagation of Buddhism, 1975.

———. *Me and Mine. Selected Essays of Bhikkhu Buddhadāsa*, ed. Donald K. Swearer. Albany, N.Y.: SUNY Press, 1989.

———. *Ten Years in Suan Moke*, trans. Mongkol Dejnakarintra. Bangkok: Pacharayasarn Editorial Board, 1984.

Bynum, C. W., S. Harrell, and P. Richman, ed. *Gender and Religion. On the Complexity of Symbols*. Boston: Beacon Press, 1986.

Cabezón, José Ignacio, ed. *Buddhism, Sexuality, and Gender*. Albany, N.Y.: SUNY Press, 1992.

Candland Christopher. *The Spirit of Violence: An Interdisciplinary Bibliography of Religion and Violence*, Occasional Papers of the Harry Frank Guggenheim Foundation, no. 6. New York: Guggenheim Foundation, 1992.

Carrithers, Michael. *The Forest Monks of Sri Lanka*. Delhi: Oxford University Press, 1983.

Chamberlain, James R., ed. *The Ram Khamhaeng Controversy: Collected Papers.* Bangkok: The Siam Society, 1991.

Chandler, David P. *The Tragedy of Cambodian History, Politics, War and Revolution Since 1945.* New Haven, Conn.: Yale University Press, 1991.

Chotisukharat, Sanguan. *Prapaenī Thai Phāk Nu'a.* [Customs of Northern Thailand]. Bangkok: Odian Store, B.E. 2510 [C.E. 1967].

Coedès, George. *Angkor: An Introduction.* trans. and ed. Emily F. Gardiner. Hong Kong, New York and London: Oxford University Press, 1963.

––––––. *The Indianized States of Southeast Asia.* ed. W. F. Vella. Honolulu: University of Hawaii Press, 1968.

––––––. *The Making of Southeast Asia.* trans. H. M. Wright. Berkeley: University of California Press, 1966.

––––––. "The Traibhūmikathā Buddhist Cosmology and Treatise on Ethics." *East and West* 7 (1957): 349–352.

Cohen, Joan L., and Bila Kalman. *Angkor: The Monuments of the God Kings.* London: Thames and Hudson, 1975.

Collins, Steven. *Selfless Persons. Imagery and Thought in Theravada Buddhism.* Cambridge: Cambridge University Press, 1982.

Cone, Margaret, and Richard Gombrich. *The Perfect Generosity of Prince Vessantara.* Oxford: The Clarendon Press, 1977.

Coomaraswamy, A. K. *History of Indian and Indonesian Art.* New York: Dover Publications, 1965.

––––––. *Medieval Sinhalese Art,* 2d ed. New York: Pantheon Books, 1956.

Dallapiccola, Anna Libera, ed. *The Stūpa: Its Religious, Historical and Architectural Significance.* Wiesbaden: Franz Steiner, 1980.

Darlington, Susan M. "Buddhism, Morality and Change: The Local Response to Development in Thailand." Ann Arbor, Mich.: University Microfilm, 1990.

––––––. "Monks and Environmental Conservation: A Case Study in Nan Province." *Seeds of Peace* 9, no. 1: 7–10.

––––––. "Putting the Dhamma into Social Practice: Monks and Environmental Action in Thailand." *Buddhist Forum.* Trink, U.K.: Buddhist Studies Institute, forthcoming.

Davids, T. W. Rhys. *Buddhist Birth Stories.* Varanasi: Indological Book House, 1972.

––––––. *Buddhist India,* 8th ed. Calcutta: Susil Gupta, 1959.

Debvedi, Phra. [See Dhammapiṭaka, Payutto, Rājavaramuni]. *Helping Yourself to Help Others,* trans. Puriso Bhikkhu. Bangkok: Buddhadhamma Foundation, 1990.

de Silva, Lily. "The Paritta Ceremony of Sri Lanka: Its Antiquity and Symbolism." In *Buddhist Thought and Ritual,* ed. David J. Kalupahana, 139–150. New York: Paragon House, 1991.

de Silva, Padmasiri. *An Introduction to Buddhist Psychology*, 2d ed. London and New York: Macmillan Publishing Company, 1992.

————. *Twin Peaks: Compassion and Insight. Emotions and the "self" in Buddhist and Western Thought*. Singapore: Buddhist Research Society, 1991.

————. *Pačhanānukrom Phutthasāt Chapap Pramuan Sap* [Dictionary of Buddhism: Vocabulary]. Bangkok: Mahāchulālongkorn University, B.E. 2531 [C.E. 1986].

Dhammadāna Khong Khun Mae Dr. Siri Krinchai [Mother Dr. Siri Krinchai's Gift of Dhamma]. Bangkok: Horatanachaikan Press, B.E. 2536 [C.E. 1993].

Dhammapiṭaka, Phra. *Buddhadhamma*, trans. Grant A. Olson. Albany, N.Y.: SUNY Press, forthcoming.

Dumoulin, Heinrich, and John C. Maraldo, eds. *The Cultural, Political, and Religious Significance of Buddhism in the Modern World*. New York: Collier Books, 1976.

Dutt, Sukumar. *The Buddha and Five After-Centuries*. London: Luzac and Company, 1957.

————. *Buddhist Monks and Monasteries of India: Their History and Contribution to Indian Culture*. London: G. Allen and Unwin, 1962.

Ekachai, Sanitsuda. "Buddhism At Odds With Sexuality." *Bangkok Post*, March 4, 1994.

————. "Right Religion. Women Weighing Equality, Struggle, and Serenity." *Bangkok Post*, February 11, 1994.

————. "Why Wisdom is Better than Magic." *Bangkok Post*, March 17, 1994.

Eliade, Mircea, ed. *The Encyclopedia of Religion*, vol. 2. New York: Macmillan Publishing Company, 1986. s.v. "Buddhism in Southeast Asia," by Donald K. Swearer.

————. *Yoga: Freedom and Immortality*. New York: Pantheon Books, 1958.

Falk, Nancy Auer. "Exemplary Donors of the Pāli Tradition." In *Ethics, Wealth, and Salvation*, eds. Russell F. Sizemore and Donald K. Swearer, 124–143. Columbia: University of South Carolina Press, 1990.

Ferguson, John P. "The Quest for Legitimation by Burmese Monks and Kings: The Case of the Shwegyin Sect 19th–20th Centuries." In *Religion and the Legitimation of Power in Thailand, Laos, and Burma*, ed. Bardwell L. Smith, 66–86. Chambersburg, Pa: Anima Books, 1978.

Fields, Rick. *How the Swans Came to the Lake*. Boulder, Colo.: Shambala Press, 1981.

Fililozat, Jean. "New Researches on the Relations Between India and Cambodia." *Indica* 3 (Bombay): 95–106.

Freedberg, David. *The Power of Images*. Chicago: University of Chicago Press, 1989.

Freeman, Michael. *Angkor: The Hidden Glories*. Boston: Houghton Mifflin and Co. 1990.

Gabaude, Louis. "Controverses modernes autour du Vessantara Jataka," *Cahiers de l'Asie du Sud-Est*, Nos. 29–30 (1991): 51–73.

————. *Les ceitya de sable au Laos et en Thaïlande*. Paris: École Francaise d'Extrême-Orient, 1979.

————. *Une Herméneutique Bouddhique Contemporaine de Thaïlande: Buddhadasa Bhikkhu*. Paris: École Française d'Extrême-Orient, 1988.

Geertz, Clifford. "Ethos, World View, and the Analysis of Sacred Symbols." In *The Interpretation of Cultures*. New York: Basic Books, 1973.

Gerini, G. E. *The Thet Maha Chat Ceremony*. Bangkok: Santhirakoses-Nagapradipa Foundation, 1976.

Gokhale, B. G. "Anakarika Dharmapala: Toward Modernity Through Tradition in Ceylon." In *Tradition and Change in Theravāda Buddhism*. ed. Bardwell L. Smith, vol. 4, Contributions to Asian Studies, 30–39. Leiden: E. J. Brill, 1973.

Gombrich, Richard F. "Consecration of a Buddha Image." *Journal of Asian Studies*, 26, no. 1 (1966): 23–36.

————. *Theravada Buddhism: A Social History from ancient Benares to modern Colombo*. London and New York: Routledge and Kegan Paul, 1988.

————, and Gananath Obeyesekere. *Buddhism Transformed: Religious Change in Sri Lanka*. Princeton, N.J.: Princeton University Press, 1988.

Gomez, Louis O., and Hiram W. Woodward, Jr. eds. *Barabudur. History and Significance of a Buddhist Monument*. Berkeley: Asian Humanities Press, 1981.

Gosling, Betty. *Sukothai. Its History, Culture and Art*. Oxford: Oxford University Press, 1991.

Govinda, Lama Anagarika. *Psycho-cosmic Symbolism of the Buddhist Stupa*. Emeryville, Calif.: Dharma Publications, 1976.

Griswold, A. B. *Towards a History of Sukhodaya Art*. Bangkok: Fine Arts Department, 1967.

Groslier, Bernard, and Jacques Arthaud. *Angkor: Art and Civilization*, rev. ed. New York: Frederick A. Praeger, 1966.

Gross, Rita M. *Buddhism After Patriarchy*. Albany, N.Y.: SUNY Press, 1992.

Hanh, Thich Nhat. *Interbeing: Commentaries on the Tiep Hien Precepts*. Berkeley, Calif.: Parallax Press, 1987.

————. *Lotus in a Sea of Fire*. London: SCM Press, 1961.

Hawley, John S., ed. *Saints and Virtues*. Berkeley: University of California Press, 1987.

Heine-Geldern, Robert von. *Conceptions of State and Kingship in Southeast Asia*, Southeast Asia Program Data Paper 18. Ithaca, N.Y.: Cornell University, 1956.

Higham, Charles. *The Archaeology of Mainland Southeast Asia from 10,000 B.C. to the Fall of Angkor*. Cambridge and New York: Cambridge University Press, 1989.

Hocart, A. M. "The Origin of the Stūpa." *Ceylon Journal of Science* 1, no. 1 (1924).

Horner, I. B., trans. *Minor Anthologies of the Pali Canon, Part III.* Chronicle of the Buddhas (Buddhavaṁsa) and Basket of Conduct (Cariyapiṭaka). Sacred Books of the Buddhists, vol. 26. London: Pali Text Society, 1975.

———. *Minor Anthologies of the Pali Canon, Part IV.* Stories of the Departed (Petavatthu) and Stories of the Mansions (Vimānavatthu). Sacred Books of the Buddhists, vol. 25. London: Pali Text Society, 1974.

Hoskin, John and Geoffrey Walton, eds. *Folk Tales and Legends of the Dai People,* trans. Ying Yi. Bangkok: DD Books, 1992.

Hsüan-tsang. *Si-Yu-Ki: Buddhist Records of the Western World,* trans. by Samuel Beal. Reprint Edition. Delhi: Munshiram Manoharal, 1969.

Htun Hmat Win, Sao. "The Unique Solidarity of the Sangha Order." *The Light of the Dhamma* [Rangoon] 1, no. 1 (August 1981): 28–31.

Irwin, John. "Asokan Pillars: A Reassessment of Evidence." *Burlington Magazine,* 115 (November 1973): 706–722.

———. "The Stūpa and the Cosmic Axis: The Archaeological Evidence," *South Asian Archaeology* 2, ed. Maurizio Taddei. Naples: Instituto Universitario Orientale, 1979.

Ishii, Yoneo. *Sangha, State, and Society. Thai Buddhism in History,* trans. Peter Hawkes. Honolulu: University of Hawaii Press, 1986.

Jackson, Peter A. *Buddhadāsa: A Buddhist Thinker for the Modern World.* Bangkok: The Siam Society, 1988.

———. *Buddhism, Legitimation and Conflict: The Political Functions of Urban Thai Buddhism.* Singapore: Institute of Southeast Asian Studies, 1989.

———. "Thai-Buddhist Identity: Debates on the Traiphuum Phra Ruang." In *National Identity and Its Defenders. Thailand 1939–1989,* ed. Craig J. Reynolds, Monash Papers on Southeast Asia, No. 25. Victoria, Australia: Monash University, 1991.

Jacobson, Nolan Pliny. *Buddhism: The Religion of Analysis.* London: Allen and Unwin, 1966.

Jordt, Ingrid. "Bhikkhuni, Thilashin, Mae-Chii: Women who Renounce the World in Burma, Thailand and the Classical Pali Buddhist Texts." *Crossroads: An Interdisciplinary Journal of Southeast Asian Studies* 4, no. 1 (Fall 1988): 31.

Juergensmeyer, Mark. *The New Cold War. Religious Nationalism Confronts the Secular State.* Berkeley: University of California Press, 1993.

Kabilsingh, Chatsumarn. "Buddhist Nuns in Other Countries." In *Thai Women in Buddhism,* 89–91. Berkeley, Calif.: Parallax Press, 1991.

———. *Thai Women in Buddhism.* Berkeley, Calif.: Parallax Press, 1991.

———. "Two Bhikkuni Movements in Thailand." In *Thai Women in Buddhism.* Berkeley, Calif.: Parallax Press, 1991.

Kalupahana, David J. *Buddhist Philosophy: A Historical Analysis.* Honolulu: University of Hawaii Press, 1976.

———. ed. *Buddhist Thought and Ritual.* New York: Paragon House, 1991.

———. *A History of Buddhist Philosophy: Continuities and Discontinuities.* Honolulu: University of Hawaii Press, 1992.

———, and Indrani Kalupahana. *The Way of Siddhartha. A Life of the Buddha.* Lanham, Md.: University Press of America, 1987.

Keown, Damien. *The Nature of Buddhist Ethics.* New York: St. Martin's Press, 1992.

Keyes, Charles F. "Buddhism and National Integration in Thailand." *Journal of Asian Studies* 33, no. 3 (May 1971): 551–567.

———. "Buddhist Politics and Their Revolutionary Origins in Thailand." *International Political Science Review* 10, no. 2 (1989): 121–142.

———. *The Golden Peninsula: Culture and Adaption in Mainland Southeast Asia.* New York: Macmillan Publishing Company, 1977.

———. "Mother, Mistress, But Never a Monk: Buddhist Notions of Female Gender in Rural Thailand." *American Ethnologist* 11, no. 2 (May 1984): 223–241.

———. "Political Crisis and Militant Buddhism in Contemporary Thailand." In *Religion and Legitimation of Power in Thailand, Laos, Burma,* ed. Bardwell L. Smith, 147–164. Chambersburg, Pa.: Anima Books, 1978.

Khin Thitsa (Khin-Thi-Da Lwin). *Providence and Prostitution: Image and Reality for Women in Buddhist Thailand.* London: Change International Reports [Women and Society], 1980.

Khumu' Kānpatipat Vipassanākammaṭṭhāna. [Handbook for Meditation Practice]. Wat Rampung: Chiang Mai, Thailand, 1991.

Kieckhefer, Richard, and George D. Bond, ed. *Sainthood. Its Manifestations in World Religions.* Berkeley: University of California Press, 1988.

King, Winston L. "Contemporary Burmese Buddhism." In *The Cultural, Political, and Religious Significance of Buddhism in the Modern World,* eds. Heinrich Dumoulin and John C. Maraldo, 95–106. New York: Collier Books, 1976.

———. *In the Hope of Nibbana: An Essay on Theravada Buddhist Ethics.* LaSalle, Ill.: Open Court, 1964.

———. *A Thousand Lives Away.* Cambridge, Mass.: Harvard University Press, 1974.

Kingshill, Konrad. *Ku Daeng: The Red Tomb. A Village Study in Northern Thailand,* 3d ed. Bangkok: Suriyaban, 1976.

Kirsch, Thomas. "Buddhism, Sex Roles and the Thai Economy." In *Women of Southeast Asia,* ed. Penny Van Esterick. Center for Southeast Asia Studies, Occasional Paper No. 9, 16–41. DeKalb: Northern Illinois University, 1982.

Kitagawa, Joseph M. and Mark D. Cummings, eds. *Buddhism and Asian History.* New York: Macmillan Publishing Company, 1989.

————. *The Religious Traditions of Asia*. New York: Macmillan Publishing Company, 1989.

Kittiwuttho, *Khā Communist Mai Pen Pāp* [Killing Communists is not Demeritorious]. Bangkok: Abhidhamma Foundation, 1976.

————. *Sing Thī Kuan Kham Nu'ng*. [Things We Should Reflect On]. Bangkok: Abhidhamma Foundation, 1971.

Kornfeld, Jack. *Living Buddhist Masters*. Santa Cruz, Calif.: Unity Press, 1977.

Kulke, Hermann. *The Devarāja*. Southeast Asia Program Data Paper 108. Ithaca, N.Y.: Cornell University, 1978.

Le May, Reginald. *The Culture of Southeast Asia*. London: George Allen and Unwin, 1956.

Ling, Trevor. *Buddhism, Imperialism and War. Burma and Thailand in Modern History*. London: George Allen and Unwin, 1979.

Lovin, Robin, and Frank E. Reynolds. *Cosmology and Ethical Order. New Studies in Comparative Ethics*. Chicago: University of Chicago Press, 1985.

Luce, G. H. *Old Burma-Early Pagan*. 3 vols. Locust Valley, NY: J. J. Augustin, 1969-1970.

Mabbett, I. W. "Devarāja." *Journal of Southeast Asian History* 10 (September 1969): 202–223.

Macy, Joanna Rogers. "Dependent Co-arising: The Distinctiveness of Buddhist Ethics." *Journal of Religious Ethics* 7, no. 1 (Spring 1979): 38–53.

————. *Dharma and Development: Religion as Resource in the Sarvodaya Self Help Movement*. West Hartford, Conn.: Kumarian Press, 1983.

Malalgoda, Kitsiri. *Buddhism in Sinhalese Society 1750–1900*. Berkeley: University of California Press, 1976.

A Manual of Buddhist Chants and Ordination Procedures. Chicago: Wat Dhammarama Press, 1993.

Matthews, Bruce. "Buddhism Under a Military Regime." *Asian Survey* 33, no. 4 (1993): 408–423.

McCargo, Duncan J. "The Political Leadership of Major-General Chamlong Srimuang." Ph.D. diss., University of London, 1993.

————. "The Three Paths of Major-General Chamlong Srimuang." *Southeast Asia Research* 1, no. 1 (March 1993): 43–56.

McDermott, Robert A., ed. *Focus on Buddhism*. Chambersburg, Pa: Anima Books, 1981.

Mendelson, E. Michael. "Observations on a Tour in the Region of Mount Popa, Central Burma." *France-Asie* 179: 786–807.

————. *Sangha and State in Burma. A Study of Monastic Sectarianism and Leadership*, ed. John P. Ferguson. Ithaca, N.Y.: Cornell University Press, 1975.

Miksic, John. *Borobudur: Golden Tales of Buddhas*. Boston: Shambala Press, 1990.

Morgan, F. Bruce. "Vocation of Monk and Layman: Signs of Change in Thai Buddhist Ethics." In *Tradition and Change in Theravāda Buddhism*. ed. Bardwell L. Smith, vol. 4, Contributions to Asian Studies, 68–77. Leiden: E. J. Brill, 1973.

Murcott, Susan. *The First Buddhist Women*. Berkeley, Calif.: Parallax Press, 1991.

Mus, Paul. "Angkor in the Time of Jayavarman VII." *Indian Arts and Letters*, 1937.

————. *Barabudur. Esquisse d'une histoire du boddhisme fondee sur la critique archeologique des texts*. 2 vols. Hanoi and Paris: École Française d'Extrême-Orient, 1932; reprint, 1978.

————. "A Thousand-Armed Kannon: A Mystery or a Problem?" *Journal of Indian and Buddhist Studies* (1964): 1–33.

Narada Thera, trans. *The Dhammapāda*. London: J. Murray, 1954.

Ngor, Haing. *A Cambodian Odyssey*. New York: Macmillan Publishing Company, 1987.

Norman, K. R. *Pali Literature*. Wiesbaden: Otto Harrassowitz, 1983.

Nyanamoli Thera, trans. *A Treasury of the Buddha's Words. Discourses from the Middle Collection* [Majjhima Nikāya] 3 vols., ed. Phra Khantipalo. Bangkok: Mahāmakuta Rājavidyālaya Press, 1992.

Nyanaponika Thera. *The Heart of Buddhist Meditation*. London: Rider, 1962.

Obeyesekere, Gananath. "The Buddhist Pantheon in Ceylon and Its Extensions." In *Anthropological Studies in Theravāda Buddhism*, ed. Manning Nash, 1–27. New Haven, Conn.: Yale University Southeast Asian Studies, (1966).

Paramānuchitchinōrot, Kromsomdet Phra. *Pathamabōdhikathā* [The Buddha's First Enlightment]. Bangkok: Mahāchulālongkorn Buddhist University, 1960.

Payulpitack, Suchira. "Buddhadasa's Movement: An Analysis of Its Origins, Development, and Social Impact." Ph.D. diss. for the Faculty of Sociology, University of Bielefeld, Germany, 1991.

Payutto, Bhikkhu P.A. [See Debvedi, Dhammapiṭaka, Rājavaramunī]. *A Buddhist Solution to the Twenty-first Century*. Chiang Mai: The Buddhist Association, 1993.

————. *Toward Sustainable Science: A Buddhist Look at Trends in Scientific Development*, trans. B. G. Evans. Bangkok: Buddhadhamma Foundation, 1993.

Pe Maung Tin and G. H. Luce, trans. *The Glass Palace Chronicle of the Kings of Burma*. London: Oxford University Press, 1923. Reprint. Rangoon: Rangoon University, 1960.

Phayọmyong, Manī. *Prapaenī Sibsọng Du'an Lānnā Thai* [The Twelve Month Traditions and Customs of Lanna Thai]. 2 vols. Chiang Mai, Thailand: Chiang Mai University, B.E. 2529 [C.E. 1986].

Phongphit, Seri. *Religion in a Changing Society: Buddhism, Reform and the Role of Monks in Community Development in Thailand*. Hong Kong: Arena Press, 1988.

Piyadassi Thera, trans. *The Book of Protection* [Paritta]. Kandy: Buddhist Publication Society, 1975.

Prawat Wat Rampung [History of Wat Rampung]. Chiang Mai, Thailand: Chang Pu'ak Press, n.d.

Prebish, Charles. *American Buddhism*. North Scituate, Mass.: Duxbury Press, 1979.

Rājavaramunī, [See Debvedi, Dhammapiṭaka, Payutto]. *Looking to America to Solve Thailand's Problems*, trans. Grant A. Olson. Bangkok: Sathirakoses-Nagapradipa Foundation, 1987.

————. *Pačhanānukrom Phutthasāt Chapap Pramuan Tham* [Dictionary of Buddhism: Dhamma]. Bangkok: Mahāchulālongkorn University, B.E. 2528 [C.E. 1983].

————. *Thai Buddhism in the Buddhist World*. Bangkok: Unity Progress Press, 1984.

Ratanapañña Thera. *The Sheaf of Garlands of the Epochs of the Conqueror* [Jinakālamālīpakaraṇaṁ], trans. N. A. Jayawickrama, Pali Text Society Translation Series 36. London: Luzac and Company, 1968.

Rawin, Bumphen. *Pathamasambōdhi Samnuan Lānnā* [The Northern Thai Version of the Buddha's First Enlightenment]. Bangkok: Odian Store, 1992.

Reynolds, Frank E. "The Holy Emerald Jewel." In *Religion and Legitimation of Power in Thailand, Laos, and Burma*. ed. Bardwell L. Smith, 175–193. Chambersburg, Pa.: Anima Books, 1978.

————. "The Two Wheels of Dhamma. A Study of Early Buddhism." In *The Two Wheels of Dhamma. Essays on the Theravāda Tradition in India and Ceylon*, AAR Studies in Religion, ed. B. L. Smith, no. 3, 6–30. Chambersburg, Pa.: American Academy of Religion, 1972.

————, and Donald Capps, eds. *The Biographical Process. Studies in the History of the Psychology of Religion*. The Hague: Mouton, 1976.

————, and Mani B. Reynolds. *Three Worlds According to King Ruang: A Thai Buddhist Cosmology*. Berkeley, Calif.: Asian Humanities Press, 1982.

Rowland, Benjamin, Jr. *The Art and Architecture of India*. London: Penguin Books, 1953.

Saddhatissa, Hammalawa. "The Significance of Paritta and Its Application in the Theravāda Tradition." In *Buddhist Thought and Ritual*, ed. David J. Kalupahana, 125–138. New York: Paragon House, 1991.

Santhirak, Plaek. *Latthi Prapeni lae Phithī Kam* [Customs and Merit-Making Rituals]. Bangkok: Pannakhan, 1972.

Sarkisyanz, Manuel. *Buddhist Backgrounds of the Burmese Revloution*. The Hague: Martinus Nijhoff, 1965.

Satha-Anand, Suwanna. "Religious Movements in Contemporary Thailand. Buddhist Struggles for Modern Relevance." *Asian Survey*, 30, no. 4 (April 1990): 395–408.

Sayadaw, Mahasi. *Practical Insight Meditation*. Kandy: Buddhist Publication Society, 1971.

——. *The Progress of Insight*. Kandy: Buddhist Publication Society, 1965.

Schechter, Jerrold. *The New Face of Buddha*. Tokyo: John Weatherhill, Inc., 1967.

Shway Yoe [Sir James George Scott]. *The Burman. His Life and Notions*. New York: W. W. Norton, 1963.

Sivaraksa, Sulak. *A Buddhist Vision for Renewing Society*, third printing with addenda. Bangkok: Thai Inter-Religious Commission for Development, 1994.

——. *Seeds of Peace. A Buddhist Vision for Renewing Society*. Berkeley, Calif.: Parallax Press/International Network of Engaged Buddhists, 1992.

——. *Siamese Resurgence*. Bangkok: Asian Forum on Development, 1985.

——. *A Socially Engaged Buddhism*. Bangkok: Thai Inter-Religious Commission for Development, 1983.

Sizemore, Russell F., and Donald K. Swearer, eds. *Ethics, Wealth, and Salvation. A Study in Buddhist Social Ethics*. Columbia: University of South Carolina Press, 1990.

Smith, Bardwell L. "The Ideal Social Order as Portrayed in the Chronicles of Ceylon." In *The Two Wheels of Dhamma: Essays on the Theravāda Tradition in India and Ceylon*. AAR Studies in Religion, ed. B. L. Smith, no. 3. Chambersburg, Pa.: America Academy of Religion, 1972.

——. ed. *Religion and Legitimation of Power in Sri Lanka*. Chambersburg, Pa.: Anima Books, 1978.

——. ed. *Religion and Legitimation of Power in Thailand, Laos and Burma*. Chambersburg, Pa.: Anima Books, 1978.

Smith, Donald E. *Religion and Politics in Burma*. Princeton, N.J.: Princeton University Press, 1965.

Smith, Wilfred Cantwell. "The Study of Religion and the Study of the Bible." *Journal of the American Academy of Religion* 29: no. 2 (June 1971): 131–140.

Snellgrove, David, ed. *The Image of the Buddha*. New York and Tokyo: Kodansha International and UNESCO, 1978.

Snodgrass, Adrian. *The Symbolism of the Stūpa*. Ithaca, NY: Cornell University Southeast Asian Studies Program, 1985.

Soekmono, R., J. G. De Casparis et al. *Borobudur. Prayer in Stone*. London: Thames and Hudson, 1990.

Spiro, Melford E. *Buddhism and Society. A Great Tradition and Its Burmese Vicissitudes*, 2d ed. Berkeley: University of California Press, 1982.

——. *Burmese Supernaturalism*. Englewood Cliffs, N.J.: Prentice-Hall, 1967.

Sponberg, Alan. "Attitudes Toward Women and the Feminine in Early Buddhism." In *Buddhism, Sexuality and Gender*, ed. José Ignacio Cabezón, 3–36. Albany, N.Y.: SUNY Press, 1992.

Sricharatchanya, Paisal, and Ian Buruma. "Praise the Buddha and Pass the Baht." *Far Eastern Economic Review*, (June 18, 1987): 53–55.

Steinberg, David Joel. *The Future of Burma. Crises and Choice in Myanmar.* Lanham, Md.: University Presses of America, 1990.
———, ed. *In Search of Southeast Asia. A Modern History.* rev. ed. Honolulu: University of Hawaii Press, 1987.
Strachan, Paul. *Pagan. Art and Architecture of Old Burma.* Whiting Bay, Scotland: Kiscadale Publications, 1989.
Stratton, Carol, and Miriam McNair Scott. *The Art of Sukhodaya. Thailand's Golden Age.* Oxford and Kuala Lumpur: Oxford University Press, 1981.
Strong, John S. *The Legend of King Aśoka: A Study and Translation of the Aśokavadāna.* Princeton, N.J.: Princeton University Press, 1983.
———. *The Legend and Cult of Upagupta: Sanskrit Buddhism in North India and Southeast Asia.* Princeton, N.J.: Princeton University Press, 1992.
Suksamran, Somboon. *Buddhism and Political Legitimacy.* Bangkok: Chulalongkorn University, 1993.
———. "A Buddhist Approach to Development: The Case of 'Development Monks' in Thailand." In *Reflections on Development in Southeast Asia,* ed. Teck Ghee. Singapore: Institute of Southeast Asian Studies, 1988.
———. *Buddhism and Politics in Thailand. A Study of Socio-Political Change and Political Activism of the Thai Sangha.* Singapore: Institute of Southeast Asian Studies, 1982.
———. *Political Buddhism in Southeast Asia. The Role of the Sangha in the Modernization of Thailand.* New York: St. Martin's Press, 1976.
Swearer, Donald K. "Buddha Abhiseka" [Consecrating the Buddha Image]. In *Buddhism in Practice,* ed. Donald S. Lopez, Jr. Princeton, N.J.: Princeton University Press, 1995.
———. "Buddhism in Southeast Asia." In the *Encyclopedia of Religion,* ed. Mircea Eliade, vol. 2, 385–400. New York: Macmillan Publishing Company, 1987.
———. *Buddhism in Transition.* Philadelphia, Pa.: Westminster Press, 1970.
———. "Community Development and Thai Buddhism. The Dynamics of Tradition and Change." *Visakha Puja 2516.* Bangkok: Buddhist Association of Thailand, 1973.
———, and Patrick Henry. *For the Sake of the World: The Spirit of Buddhist and Christian Monasticism.* Minneapolis: Augsburg-Fortress Press and Collegeville, Minn.: Liturgical Press, 1989.
———. "Fundamentalistic Movements in Theravāda Buddhism." In *Fundamentalisms Observed,* eds. Martin E. Marty and R. Scott Appleby, 628–690. Chicago and London: University of Chicago Press, 1990.
———. "Hypostasizing the Buddha. Buddha Image Consecration in Northern Thailand." *History of Religions* 34, no. 3 (February 1995).
———. "Lay Buddhism and the Buddhist Revival in Ceylon." *Journal of the American Academy of Religion* 38, no. 3 (September 1970): 255–275.

———— "The Layman Extraordinaire in Northern Thai Buddhism." *Journal of the Siam Society* 64, no. 1 (January 1976): 151–168.

————. ed. *Me and Mine. Selected Essays of Bhikkhu Buddhadāsa.* Albany, N.Y.: SUNY Press, 1989.

————. *Secrets of the Lotus: Studies in Buddhist Meditation.* New York: Macmillan Publishing Company, 1971.

————. "Sulak Sivaraksa's Buddhist Vision for Renewing Society." *Crossroads. An Interdisciplinary Journal of Southeast Asian Studies.* (January 1991): 17–57.

————. *Wat Haripuñjaya: A Study of the Royal Temple of the Buddha's Relic, Lamphun, Thailand.* AAR Studies in Religion. no. 10. Missoula, Mont.: Scholars Press, 1976.

Tambiah, S. J. *Buddhism Betrayed? Religion, Politics and Violence in Sri Lanka.* Chicago: University of Chicago Press, 1992.

————. *Buddhism and Spirit Cults in Northeast Thailand.* Cambridge: Cambridge University Press, 1970.

————. *The Buddhist Saints of the Forest and the Cult of Amulets. A Study in Charisma, Hagiography, Sectarianism, and Millennial Buddhism.* Cambridge: Cambridge University Press, 1984.

————. *Sri Lanka: Ethnic Fratricide and the Dismantling of Democracy.* Chicago: University of Chicago Press, 1986.

————. *World Conqueror and World Renouncer. A Study of Buddhism and Polity in Thailand Against A Historical Background.* Cambridge: Cambridge University Press, 1976.

Taylor, J. L. "New Buddhist Movements in Thailand: An 'Individualistic Revolution,' Reform and Dissonance." *Journal of Southeast Asian Studies* 21, no. 1 (March 1990): 135–154.

Taylor, Robert H. *The State in Burma.* London: C. Hurst and Company, 1987.

Than Tun. *Essays on the History and Buddhism of Burma.* Whiting Bay, Scotland: Kiscadale Publications, 1988.

Thanissaro Bhikkhu [Geoff DeGraff]. *That the True Dhamma Might Last a Long Time.* Valley Center, Calif.: Metta Forest Monastery, n.d.

Thepkavī, Phra. *Wisdom of Ven. Phra Thepkavi*, trans. S. Chandra Ngram. Chiang Mai, Thailand, n.d.

Thī Ra Lu'k 71 Phra Thepkavī [In Honor of Phra Thepkavī's 71st Birthday]. Chiang Mai, Thailand: Foundation for Rural Development, B.E. 2532 [C.E. 1992]

Thomas, Edward J. *The Life of the Buddha in Legend and History,* 3d ed. London: Routledge and Kegan Paul, 1949.

Tin Maung Maung Than. "Sangha Reforms and Renewal of Sasana in Myanmar: Historical Trends and Contemporary Practice." *Buddhist Trends in Southeast Asia*, ed. Trevor Ling, 6–63. Singapore: Institute of Southeast Asian Studies, 1993.

————. "Sangha and Sasana in Socialist Burma." *Sojourn. Social Issues in Southeast Asia.* 3, no. 1 (February 1989): 26–61.

Tipawadee Amawattana, et al. "The Use of Vipassana Meditation as a Strategy for Developing [a] Qualitative Counseling Service." A paper delivered at the Fifth International Conference of Thai Studies held at the School of Oriental and African Studies at London University, July 8, 1993.

Van Der Leeuw, G. *Religion in Essence and Manifestation*. New York: Harper and Row, 1963.

Van Esterick, Penny. *Taking Refuge: Lao Buddhists in North America*. North York, Ont.: York Lanes Press, 1993.

Varjirañāṇvarorasa. *Entrance to the Vinaya*. Bangkok: Mahāmakut University, 1960.

———. *Navakovāda* [Instructions to the Newly Ordained]. Bangkok: Mahāmakuta University, 1971.

Vickery, Michael. "On Traibhūmikathā." *The Journal of the Siam Society* 79, Part 2 (1991): 24–36.

Wales, H. G. Quaritch. *The Making of Greater India*. London: Bernard Quartich, 1961.

———. *The Mountain God: A Study in Early Religion and Kingship*. London: Bernard Quartich, 1953.

Walshe, Maurice, trans. *Thus I Have Heard. The Long Discourses of the Buddha* [Dīgha Nikāya]. London: Wisdom Publications, 1987.

Wannasai, Singkha. *Praphaenī Lae Ngān Nakkhatriksa Haeng Lānnā Thai* [Customs and Astrological Celebrations of Lānnā Thai]. Mimeograph, n.d.

Warren, Henry C. *Buddhism in Translations*. New York: Atheneum Press, 1963.

Weber, Max. *The Religions of India*, trans. and ed. Hans H. Gerth and Don Martindale. New York: The Free Press, 1958.

Welbon, Guy R. *Buddhist Nirvāṇa and Its Western Interpreters*. Chicago: University of Chicago Press, 1968.

Wells, Kenneth E. *Thai Buddhism. Its Rites and Activities*. Bangkok: Suriyabun Publishers, 1975.

Wijayaratna, Mohan. *Buddhist Monastic Life*, trans. Claude Grangier and Steven Collins. Cambridge: Cambridge University, 1990.

Wolters, Oliver W. *History, Culture, and Region in Southeast Asian Perspective*. Singapore: Institute of Southeast Asian Studies, 1982.

Woodward, Hiram W. Jr. "Ram Khamhaeng's Inscription: The Search for Context." In *The Ram Khamhaeng Controversy*, ed. James R. Chamberlain. Bangkok: The Siam Society, 1991.

Wyatt, David K. *Studies in Thai History*. Bangkok: Silkworm Books, 1994.

Zago, Marcel. *Rites et Ceremonies en Milieu Bouddhiste Lao*. Roma: Universita Gregoriana Editrice, 1972.

Zehner, Edwin. "Reform Symbolism of a Thai Middle-Class Sect: The Growth and Appeal of the Thammakai Movement." *Journal of Southeast Asian Studies* 21, no. 2 (September 1990): 402–425.

Zimmer, Heinrich. *The Art of Indian Asia*, 2 vols. 2d ed., Bollingen Series 39. New York: Pantheon Books, 1960.

Index of Authors

231

Index of Subjects

abhidhamma
the Buddha on, 42
chanted at funerals, 57
Kalupahana's interpretation, 205n.118
Nyanaponika on, 129
aging ceremonies (Thai. *su'bchatā*), 32,
53, 55–56, 184n.95
Aggañña Sutta
on kingship, 66
Tambiah's analysis, 186n.9
See also Pali texts
alms. *See piṇḍapāta*
almsperson, 47
See also bhikkhu, bhikkhunī, female
renunciant, *mae chī*, monk, nun,
thilashin
amulets, 18, 21, 179n.29
See also relics
anagārika
defined, 128
See also Dharmapāla, Anagārika
Ānanda
See Buddha, disciples of
Ananda Temple
See Pagan
Anāthapiṇḍika, 12, 153
anattā (not-self)
and the Buddha, 8, 12
Buddhadāsa on, 133
central Theravāda doctrine of, 6, 61,
133
Anawrahta
builder of monuments, 94

builder of Shwe-zigon, 83–84
and Pagan, 67, 82–84
voitive and *jātaka* plaques, 90
See also Burma-kings
Angkor
Angkor Thom, 77, 80, 82 Figure 2.6
Bayon, 77, 79–81, 80 Figure 2.5, 82
Figure 2.6
described, 77–81, 78 Figure 2.4,
188n.40–41, 188n.46–50
devarāja concept, 76–77, 188n.35
and mimesis, 74
Sukhothai as model for, 86
See also mimesis
Aṅgulimāla Paritta
for difficult childbirth, 27
See also paritta
Aṅguttara Nikāya, 108
Buddha on women, 203–204n.105
See also Pali texts
Anantasounthne, the Venerable, 112
See also Buddhism-Laos
anicca (impermanence), 8
Buddhadāsa on, 133
subject preached at funerals, 57
Aniruddha, 189n.53
See also Anawrahta, Burma-kings of,
Pagan
animism, 19, 32, 40, 44–45, 49–50,
53–56, 73, 83
and aging ceremonies, 32, 53, 55–56
and Buddhist ritual, 32
čhao, 19, 180n.33

4 602